How to USE and UPGRADE to GM Gen III LS-Series Powertrain Control Systems

Mike Noonan

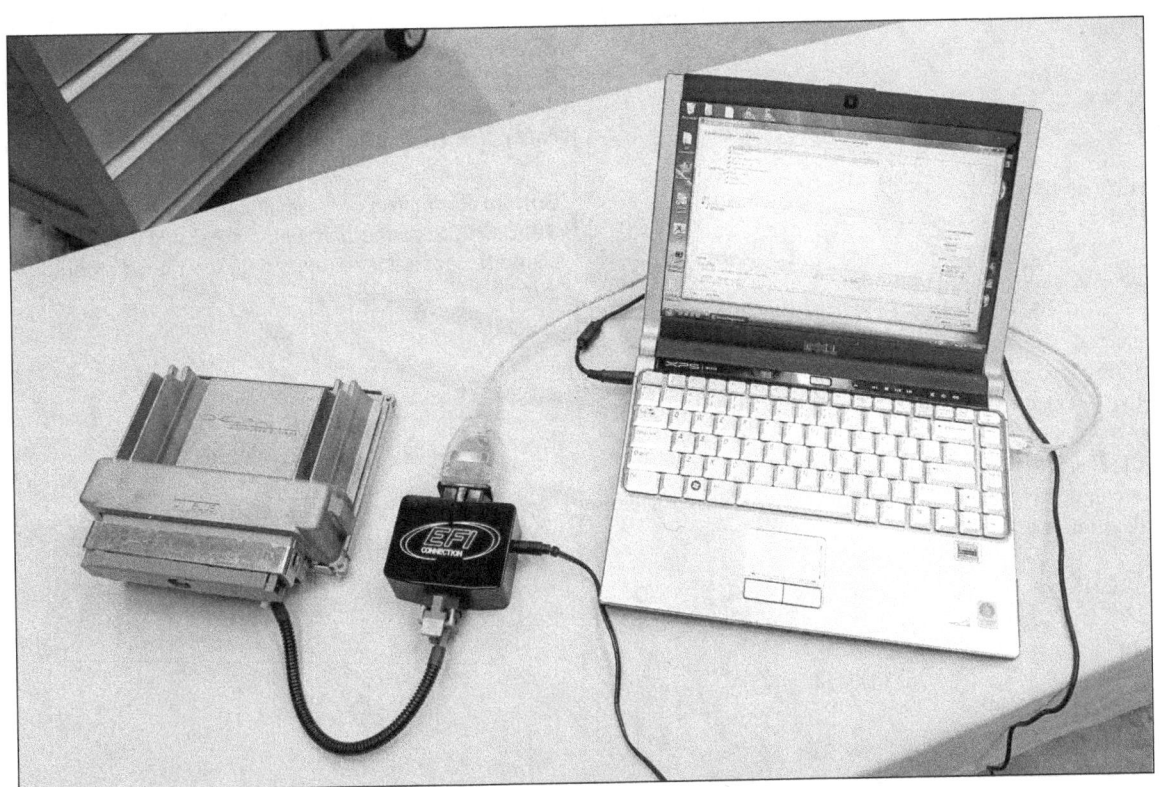

CarTech®

CarTech®

CarTech®, Inc.
6118 Main Street
North Branch, MN 55056
Phone: 651-277-1200 or 800-551-4754
Fax: 651-277-1203
www.cartechbooks.com

© 2013 by Mike Noonan

All rights reserved. No part of this publication may be reproduced or utilized in any form or by any means, electronic or mechanical, including photocopying, recording, or by any information storage and retrieval system, without prior permission from the Publisher. All text, photographs, and artwork are the property of the Author unless otherwise noted or credited.

The information in this work is true and complete to the best of our knowledge. However, all information is presented without any guarantee on the part of the Author or Publisher, who also disclaim any liability incurred in connection with the use of the information and any implied warranties of merchantability or fitness for a particular purpose. Readers are responsible for taking suitable and appropriate safety measures when performing any of the operations or activities described in this work.

All trademarks, trade names, model names and numbers, and other product designations referred to herein are the property of their respective owners and are used solely for identification purposes. This work is a publication of CarTech, Inc., and has not been licensed, approved, sponsored, or endorsed by any other person or entity. The publisher is not associated with any product, service, or vendor mentioned in this book, and does not endorse the products or services of any vendor mentioned in this book.

Edit by Bob Wilson
Layout by Monica Seiberlich

ISBN 978-1-61325-840-8
Item No. SA255P

Library of Congress Cataloging-in-Publication Data

Noonan, Mike.
  How to use and upgrade to GM GEN III LS-series powertrain control systems / by Mike Noonan.
    pages cm
  ISBN 978-1-61325-055-6
1. Automotive computers. 2. Automotive sensors. 3. General Motors automobiles--Power trains. I. Title.

TL272.53.N66 2013
629.2'72--dc23

2013004474

Written, edited, designed and printed in the U.S.A.

Title Page: GM repair technicians use a web-based subscription service to access on-board control module calibrations. When an on-board module is replaced during service, the technician will use TIS2Web for service programming. Occasionally a vehicle may receive a calibration update due to performance behavior undesirable by similar vehicle owners.

Back Cover Photos

Top Left: The 1997 LS1 engine was a redesign of the traditional small-block Chevy engine. Its intake manifold and cylinder head design are unlike the early GM engines. This LS-series engine was assembled with a 5.3L truck long block, LS2 GTO intake manifold, and LS2 Corvette front accessories.

Top Right: Due to the crankshaft seal area of the GM LT1 timing cover, a crankshaft reluctor and double-row timing set cannot be used. TPIS manufactures several anodized billet-aluminum timing cover solutions for use with EFI Connection's 24x small-block/LT1 crankshaft reluctor.

Middle Left: This Gen III PCM calibration table represents the main spark advance values when no detonation is present. The PCM switches to an equivalent low-octane spark table when knock is present. The PCM determines which values to use based on engine RPM and calculated airflow. The actual spark advance is based on other spark tables and parameters that take into consideration engine operating conditions such as coolant temperature and intake air temperature.

Middle Right: GM vehicles equipped with an LS-series PCM and electric fans operate both fans in low-speed and high-speed mode only. This requires two PCM outputs and three relays. By using the two PCM outputs and only two relays, two electric fans can be controlled independently.

Bottom Left: Because this car has been previously tuned, we pull the calibration file out of the LT1 PCM using the C.A.T.S. OBD-II tuner. The calibration will be used later as a reference while making a starter calibration file for the LS1 PCM using EFILive software.

Bottom Right: The early small-cap HEI distributor is replaced with a 1996–2002 Vortec distributor assembly. Hold on to the distributor clamp because it is required with the new distributor.

CONTENTS

Acknowledgments 4
About the Author 5
Introduction 5

Chapter 1: Understanding the Small-Block Generations ... 9
Generation I, with Multi-Port Fuel Injection 9
Generation II, 1992–1997 LT1 and 1996–1997 LT4 12
Generation III, 1997–2007 LS Series 12
Generation IV, LS Series 12

Chapter 2: Comparing Gen III Controllers ... 13
Tuned Port Injection ECMs 13
Generation III Powertrain Control Modules 14
Throttle Actuator Control Modules 17

Chapter 3: Crankshaft and Camshaft Signals and Ignition Systems ... 19
High-Resolution Crankshaft Signal 19
Low-Resolution Crankshaft Signal 22

Chapter 4: Tuning Software and Equipment ... 24
GM Tuning 24
Custom Tuning and Data Acquisition 25
Handheld Tuners 29
Tuning Equipment 30

Chapter 5: Sensors and Inputs ... 33
Throttle Position Sensor 33
Idle Air Control Valve 35
Engine Coolant Temperature Sensor 36
Air Temperature Sensor 37
Mass Airflow Sensor 38
Manifold Absolute Pressure Sensor 40
Knock Sensor 41
Oxygen Sensor 43
Oil Pressure Sensor 44
Vehicle Speed Sensor 44
Camshaft Position Sensor 45
Crankshaft Position Sensor 46
Accelerator Pedal Position Sensor 49
Park/Neutral Indicator 49
Gear Select Switch 49
Brake Switch 50
Clutch Pedal Position Switch 50
Fuel Enable Control 51

Chapter 6: PCM Signal Outputs ... 55
Engine Control Output 55
Fuel Pump Relay Control 57
Malfunction Indicator Lamp Control 57
Tachometer Output 59
Vehicle Speed Output 59
Electric Fan Control 59
Air Conditioning Control 59
Generator Control 60
Emissions Control 62
Skip Shift Solenoid Control 64
Reverse-Inhibit Solenoid Control 64
Transmission Control 64
Serial Data Output 65

Chapter 7: Changing the Firing Order ... 66
Injectors and Ignition Coils 66
Modifying Calibration 68

Chapter 8: Electronic Throttle Equipment ... 71
1997–2004 Corvette 71
2004–2005 Cadillac CTS-V 74
GM Truck 75
EFI Connection 24x Throttle Body Assemblies 80

Chapter 9: Electric Fan Operation ... 82
Air Conditioning Considerations 82
PCM Calibration 82
Camaro, Firebird and Corvette 83
Trucks 84
PCM Operation 84

Chapter 10: Transmission ... 85
Automatic Transmissions 85
Manual Transmissions 89

Chapter 11: Air Conditioning ... 91
Base Calibration 91
Operation Overview 91
PCM Conversion Recommendations 96

Chapter 12: Cruise Control ... 97
Cable Throttle Systems 97
Electronic Throttle Systems 102

Chapter 13: Wire Harness Selection ... 103
Used Wire Harnesses 103
New Wire Harnesses 105

Chapter 14: On-Board Diagnostics and Troubleshooting ... 107
Assembly Line Diagnostic Link 107
OBD-I System 108
OBD-1.5 System 109
OBD-II System 109
Troubleshooting Diagnostic Trouble Codes 111

Chapter 15: Gen III LS PCM Conversions ... 112
Project 1: 24x Small-Block Chevy in a 1933 Willys 112
Project 2: Twin-Turbo Small-Block Chevy in a 1998 GMC Truck 118
Project 3: Turbo 4.3L V-6 3x Conversion 122
Project 4: 24x LT1 Conversion to Eliminate Optispark in an F-Body 126
Project 5: Big-Block Ram Jet 502 24x Conversion 136

Glossary 142
Source Guide 144

ACKNOWLEDGMENTS

I am a work in progress. The knowledge I've obtained and the experiences I've been afforded have been the result of the efforts, patience, and generosities of many great people. My journey through the field of electronic fuel injection has led me through many challenges and several victories. My sincerest appreciation goes to those who have helped me along the way.

I first want to thank my dad, whose intentions for his son to build his first daily driver led to much greater things. Your attention to detail and perfection in all that you do has been an example to me that sets the bar high for the work that I do. You've freely given so much of your time and talent to see that I succeed in my passions. You make me want to do exceedingly more than I ever thought possible. You, along with Mom, surely didn't know what would become of that 5.7L Tuned Port Injection swap into the S10 pickup. Now a concerned parent, I agree it was a bad idea for a teenager, but it sure turned into a good thing!

Bill and Troy, I remember when we first met in my dad's pole barn to discuss Tuned Port Injection. We established an unexpected friendship that I will continue to cherish. You've jumped into the unknown with me, helped turn an idea into a final product, and continue to support my far-fetched ideas.

The guys of Tuned Port Induction Specialties—Myron, Jim, Dan, Clay, and Bob—your professionalism, experience, and quality have had a positive impact on what I do. Years ago I admired the products in your catalog; I never would have dreamed that you would be designing and manufacturing products for me. Myron, for the successful business you started so many years ago, "Well done!"

To all EFI Connection customers, your passion for your projects have shaped a simple side business into a full-time company that is dedicated to making quality products that you can rely on. Without your support, this book would not be possible. This book is ultimately for you.

The journey into LS-series fuel management for small-block Chevy and LT1/LT4 engines began with this group of guys. Mark Noonan (standing) was determined to eliminate the dreaded LT1 Optispark distributor and designed a camshaft signal solution that installs cleanly at the timing cover. Mike Noonan (left) is the owner of EFI Connection. Troy Adam (middle) helps with installations and PCM tuning. Bill Adam (right) is a skilled machinist who has assisted with the development of every machined part related to EFI Connection's 24x conversions. We had just completed a 24x small-block conversion for a 1989 Trans Am featured in GM High Tech Performance *magazine.*

ABOUT THE AUTHOR

Mike Noonan's professional background began with a Bachelor's degree in Management Information Systems (Penn State University) and then a seven-year career in software development. His introduction to automobiles began in high school with a father-and-son S10 pickup project that gave the experience of a frame-up vehicle restoration. His passion for fuel injection began with a 5.7L Tuned Port Injection engine swap into the pickup truck.

Through the requirement of custom tuning the TPI fuel injection system in the S10 pickup, he was exposed to aftermarket tuning and data logging equipment. This led to the curiosities of several different engine control unit (ECU) changes that required wire harness integration. These experiences gave an understanding of GM's first multi-port injection systems. After working with several LS1 swap projects, he was driven to bring LS-series fuel management to the early GM engines. Those efforts resulted in EFI Connection's 24x line of products.

Mike currently serves fuel injection enthusiasts, full-time, as the owner of EFI Connection, LLC. His day-to-day efforts involve assisting owners with their LS-series conversions and designing/manufacturing new products related to LS-series fuel management.

Author Mike Noonan, owner of EFI Connection, LLC.

INTRODUCTION

Let me first set the context for this book. The mere mention of LS-series electronics may lead to assumptions about do-it-yourself wire harness work or custom tuning. However, this book has a focus on the Gen III powertrain control module (PCM) and components it can be used with. Let's leave the used wire harness rework for the wire diagrams found in GM service manuals and the broad discussion of custom tuning to other books that cover this information in great detail. There is enough ground to cover related to the Gen III PCM to fill the pages of this book. The following content is relevant to LS-series as well as every other GM V-8 engine.

I've spoken with many enthusiasts who have purchased an LS-series engine assembly and have questions about transmission selection, throttle control, sensor compatibility, air conditioning support, and so on. Maybe you have an LS-series engine tucked away in the corner of your garage for that next project. Considering the many electronic components that were used in GM production vehicles since the introduction of the LS1 in 1997, you may wonder what options you have. I will bring clarity to your

INTRODUCTION

project and go as far as showing you that LS-series electronics and components can easily be used with the earliest GM electronic fuel-injected engines.

To get you started I review the popular GM V-8 electronic fuel injection (EFI) engines of the 1980s, 1990s, early 2000s, and today. You see the inefficiencies of these early ignition systems and the advances in Gen III ignition. A brief discussion of the early engine control modules (ECMs) sets the stage for the introduction of the Gen III PCMs and the improvements they offer.

Some think that because General Motors released the 5.7L Tuned Port Injection engine with a basic, PROM-based ECM that the engine cannot be used without it. This thinking is not unique to TPI conversions alone. In fact, many dismiss the LT1 series of engines because of a misunderstanding that the front-mount Optispark distributor, which has a reputation for unreliability and failure, is required for engine operation. I break down these engines to their basics to show you why the Gen III PCM has no trouble with ignition and fuel management for these early engines.

My first engine swap included a 5.7L TPI engine and 700R4 transmission. I was a teenager at the top of my game with a powerful and attractive EFI engine and popular transmission. My all-wheel-drive S10 pickup could nearly do full-throttle starts in the rain without wheel spin. I had all the acceleration I desired and loved it! After I destroyed the transmission, I used the downtime to install heads, cam, and intake manifold for even more power. I also purchased a replacement transmission built for more performance. I quickly ironed out the PROM tuning to address the upgraded engine and then noticed new shifting behavior that was an annoyance.

During a college car club Friday night cruise, I pulled up next to a friend's Mustang at a stoplight. We revved engines at the light and put the pedal to the floor when the light turned green! I had no trouble off the line with a powerful V-8 and all-wheel-drive on my side. I advanced on the Mustang until second gear, but second gear never came! Why didn't my transmission shift into second gear? Why did I have to back off the throttle for the 700R4 transmission to shift into second gear? When asked, my transmission builder said something about governor weights and that mechanical adjustments were required to "dial in" my transmission.

My pride and joy collected dust as my interests moved on to a 2000 Pontiac Firehawk restoration. This car had an LS1 engine and 4L60-E transmission that ran much better than the TPI and 700R4 in my S10 pickup. The Firehawk pulled smooth and the transmission performance was impressive. Why didn't my S10 pickup run this well? A look at the LS1 PCM's transmission calibration with EFILive tuning software instantly revealed to me why the 4L60-E worked so much better than the 700R4: The PCM controls the shifting!

Ten years later, my S10 pickup runs as smooth as any of today's new vehicles from the GM dealership. The TPI ECM was replaced with an LS1 PCM, the mechanical throttle for an electronic throttle, and the 700R4 for a 4L60-E transmission. Cruise control no longer has a noticeable vacuum lag. The truck is smooth, responsive, tame, and powerful. It's a joy to drive and, unless you get into the throttle, you would never know how aggressive it can be.

Over the years, I've sorted through just about all the components that have been used with GM V-8 electronic fuel management. I've assisted many enthusiasts to make good choices for their projects. The intimidation ends here as I guide you through the complexities of LS-series fuel management components and selection of parts for your next project. My goal is to keep the discussion in the following pages straightforward and easy to understand.

Benefits of the GM Gen III LS-Series PCM

General Motors has used many different ECMs and PCMs with its V-8 (and V-6) engines. The trend is that the later PCMs have more features, popular aftermarket tuning support, and better diagnostics than the early ECMs. Choosing the right ECM or PCM for your project depends largely on your budget and the features that must be supported.

Vehicle Integration and Component Selection

There are many things to consider when working with a fuel-injected engine: engine controller, compatibility with gauges, transmission type, electric fans, air conditioning, and so on. Whether you have an LS-series or an early small-block engine, an engine controller choice must be made in light of the other components in your vehicle. Chances are you are swapping a newer GM engine into an older GM vehicle. Fortunately, General Motors has done well regarding instrumentation standardization.

INTRODUCTION

As an example, GM vehicles in the 1980s began using an electronic speedometer that requires an input from the ECM of 4,000 pulses per mile. While these early ECMs are limited to a 4,000-pulse output (2,000 for cruise control), the Gen III controllers allow for a configurable pulse count output for speedometer use. Other functions such as the malfunction indicator lamp (MIL), fuel pump relay, and electric fan relay have remained the same. Even cruise control switches of the 1980s are functionally the same as used through some 2007 model vehicles. Where some aftermarket engine controllers lack vehicle compatibility, the Gen III PCMs integrate well into early vehicles.

Enthusiasts have many vehicle component choices: electronic transmissions, electric fans, cruise control, air conditioning, and so on. Choosing modern solutions for a restoration project requires methods of control. As you progress through this book, you see how well the Gen III PCMs provide all-in-one solutions, saving you the extra expense and headache of finding workarounds.

Swapping May Not Be Cheaper

I've experienced many apples-to-oranges comparisons as enthusiasts consider swapping a salvaged $750 LS-series engine into a vehicle powered by an early small-block engine. The budget often gets out of hand as the different front accessory drive causes unexpected expenses, the exhaust system is overhauled, oil pan clearance issues arise, and the old transmission does not bolt directly to the new engine. This book shows you that you can keep your current 4.3L V-6, small-block, LT1, or big-block engine and upgrade to Gen III fuel management.

Eliminate the LT1 Optispark Distributor

The 1992 LT1 engine was a step forward in the design of the popular small-block engine: reverse-flow cooling resulting in lower levels of detonation, a new short runner intake manifold for high-RPM performance, and a new ignition system.

Although the LT1 Optispark distributor was an advance over the traditional small-block distributor, common (and expensive) failures continue to leave many enthusiasts looking for other alternatives. This book goes into detail to present a Gen III PCM solution, with one-coil-per-cylinder ignition, which puts the Optispark distributor in the trash can.

Stick to Your Budget

A Gen III PCM is directly compatible with LS-series engines (1997-newer equipped with a 24x crankshaft reluctor) and 4.3L V-6, 5.0L V-8, 5.7L V-8, and 7.4L V-8 engines (1996-newer). Without question, the Gen III PCM is the most inexpensive choice for engine and transmission control. With the entry price of popular aftermarket ECU packages (ECU and universal wire harness) at about $2,000, a GM Gen III PCM solution deserves a little attention. It requires sourcing a PCM (used PCMs run about $100; new are about $175) and a custom-built wire harness (quality harnesses cost about $650).

Regardless of ECU choice (aftermarket or GM), final tuning should be completed with the use of a chassis dynamometer. Whether you bring an aftermarket ECU or GM PCM to the tuning session, you will likely pay the same price for the tuning services. With this in mind, you can choose to purchase popular OBD-II scanning/tuning software for a Gen III PCM for about $500. The $750 left in your pocket just might buy the power adder you've been wanting.

Who Can Tune My Car?

Early OBD-I GM ECMs contain the engine calibration in the memory storage of a programmable read-only memory (PROM) chip. To gain access to the PROM, the ECM must be removed from behind the vehicle's dash and then disassembled. The PROM is permanently soldered to a carrier called a MEMCAL and is intended to be a read-only chip. Although some PROMs can be erased (for reprogramming) using an ultra-violet lamp, others cannot be erased or reprogrammed. Enthusiasts have worked around this issue by installing an adapter that bypasses the original PROM with an erasable PROM (EPROM). With tuning software and an EPROM programming device, tuners can modify these OBD-I systems for upgraded engine applications.

Times have changed. Tuning facilities that agree to touch an OBD-I system are becoming more and more difficult to find, leaving enthusiasts to consider purchasing their own tuning equipment (minus the chassis dynamometer) or "just throw on a carburetor." With the popularity of OBD-II systems, OBD-I tuning is becoming a hobbyist's solution.

Those who don't want to climb the tuning learning curve often opt for mail-order tuning services. In this case, you provide engine details (engine size, heads, camshaft, etc.) and someone with OBD-I tuning equipment attempts to create accurate spark and fuel maps and parameters. The changes being made are a

INTRODUCTION

best guess based on the tuner's previous experience with (hopefully) a similar engine combination. The result may lead to another mail-order tuner who may finally get it right.

OBD-II Diagnostics

To the uninformed, OBD-II represents emissions, limitations, OEM proprietary controls, and so on. To the informed (the tuner, the repair technician, and anyone with a scan tool in hand) OBD-II is a wealth of information that reveals real-time data about engine operation and performance. More than that, the standardization of OBD-II protocols allows for universal, inexpensive, scan tool equipment that is easily obtained through many auto parts stores around the world. This book goes into great detail about the benefits of the OBD-II diagnostic protocol of the Gen III PCM.

What Will This Book Do For Me?

Here are a couple common situations, just *made* for this book:

Example 1:

You have a 2003 LQ9 (6.0L LS-series) engine from a salvaged Escalade. It has electronic throttle, but you're looking for reasons to either keep the electronic throttle control or install a cable throttle body. You're old school, so you have in mind to install a TH350 or 700R4 transmission, but know the engine was originally used with a 4L60-E transmission. You just opened a can of worms.

This book explains:

- Which LS-series PCM can be used with this throttle body
- Which throttle actuator control (TAC) module is required for this throttle body
- Which electronic pedal assemblies are available for this application (sometimes the truck pedal is just too big for a conversion)
- The benefits of electronic throttle
- A cable throttle alternative
- Which PCMs can be used if changing to cable throttle
- A cruise-control solution for cable throttle
- Reasons to use an electronic (4L60-E or 4L80-E) transmission

The book also discusses:

- Electric fans
- Air conditioning
- Wire harnesses
- Transmissions
- The OBD-II benefits of using an LS-series PCM rather than "upgrading" to a F.A.S.T., Motec, Holley, or Big Stuff 3 engine controller

You also get a view into the PCM calibration by seeing many EFILive software screen shots of how tables and parameters are presented. This may take the intimidation out of the tuning process and you may purchase tuning software.

Example 2:

If you're an early small-block or LT1 owner, this book goes even further to show how to equip these engines with 24x crank and 1x cam signals to make all of the information above relevant.

All these (and more) questions are answered:

- Is the throttle position sensor on the TPI throttle body compatible with the LS PCM, or do I have to retrofit the LS TPS to my throttle body?
- Which sensors are required?
- The LS engines have a different firing order. Doesn't this mean I have to purchase a custom camshaft to fix the firing order?
- Will the LS PCM control my gauges?
- Will my 1985–1992 TPI MAF sensor work with the LS PCM?
- I'm on a budget, so I'm planning to buy a hand held tuner. Will that work?
- What's the difference between the 1997–1998 LS PCM and the 1999-newer LS PCMs?
- I know the LS1 engines use a 4L60-E transmission, but I want to upgrade to a 4L80-E transmission. Will I have to buy an aftermarket transmission controller?

CHAPTER 1

UNDERSTANDING THE SMALL-BLOCK GENERATIONS

The identification of a GM engine is commonly referred to by its RPO code. A Regular Production Option (RPO) is made up of three alphanumeric characters to uniquely identify a vehicle option. In 1985, General Motors introduced the 5.7L multi-port injection engine as RPO "L98." However, while the RPO "LS1" is specific to the 5.7L engine in the 1997–2003 Corvette and 1998–2002 Camaro and Firebird, there are variations among these engines. Throttle type (cable or electronic), intake manifold, and oil pan are only a few examples of different equipment on these engines. The content of this book is relevant for the most popular GM V-8 fuel-injected engines; the L98, LT1, LS1, and LS-series truck engines.

Generation I, with Multi-Port Fuel Injection

The first GM 5.7L V-8 engine with electronic multi-port fuel injection was introduced with the 1985 Corvette as RPO L98. A smaller, 5.0L V-8 engine with electronic multi-port fuel injection was introduced with the 1985 Camaro and Firebird as RPO LB9. Both engines are commonly referred to as tuned port injection (TPI) because of the shared, long-tube runner, intake manifold design. With the exception of the distributor assembly, mass airflow sensor, and knock sensor, the sensors on these engines are fully compatible with Gen III PCMs.

The next 5.7L and 5.0L multi-port fuel-injected engines were installed in many 1996–2000 light-duty Chevrolet/GMC trucks, SUVs, and full-size vans. The Express Van continued to use these engines through 2002. The 1996–2002 5.7L and 5.0L engines are also known as Vortec 5700 (RPO L31) and Vortec 5000 (RPO L30), respectively.

The fuel injector arrangement inside the intake manifold has made these engines undesirable for conversions. The unique Vortec engine intake manifold bolt arrangement and raised intake runners on the cylinder heads limit intake manifold selection. A cast-iron marine engine manifold, however, with conventional injector and fuel rail configuration makes for

The 1985 L98 engine was a hit among modern enthusiasts. These TPI engines were a big leap forward in fuel management technology and remain popular today.

John Schaefer 383 LT1 Optispark vs. LS1 24X Ignition

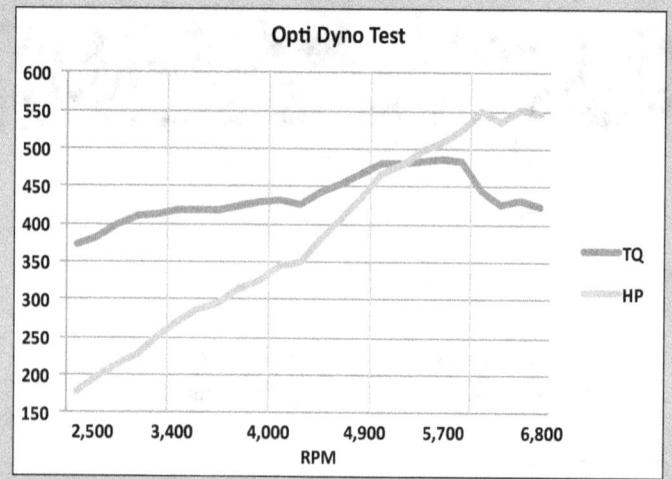

RPM	TQ	HP	RPM	TQ	HP	RPM	TQ	HP	RPM	TQ	HP
2,500	372.7	177.4	4,700	454.0	406.2	2,500	406.0	193.3	4,700	480.3	429.8
2,600	377.1	186.7	4,800	461.3	421.6	2,600	406.7	201.3	4,800	480.0	438.7
2,700	383.5	197.2	4,900	467.2	435.9	2,700	413.9	212.8	4,900	489.4	456.6
2,800	398.8	212.6	5,000	479.6	456.6	2,800	421.3	224.6	5,000	496.7	472.9
2,900	410.9	226.9	5,100	482.1	468.2	2,900	424.0	234.1	5,100	493.1	478.8
3,000	413.4	236.1	5,200	482.4	477.6	3,000	424.5	242.5	5,200	503.2	498.2
3,100	410.7	242.4	5,300	483.9	488.3	3,100	424.6	250.6	5,300	**506.7**	511.3
3,200	412.2	251.2	5,400	482.6	496.1	3,200	426.3	259.7	5,400	502.6	516.8
3,300	413.1	259.6	5,500	485.6	508.5	3,300	430.7	270.6	5,500	502.1	525.8
3,400	417.6	270.4	5,600	**486.6**	518.8	3,400	428.5	277.4	5,600	499.2	532.3
3,500	419.0	279.2	5,700	483.5	524.7	3,500	430.0	286.5	5,700	496.4	538.7
3,600	418.4	286.8	5,800	473.6	523.0	3,600	437.4	299.8	5,800	494.3	545.9
3,700	418.6	294.9	5,900	467.9	525.6	3,700	441.1	310.8	5,900	494.9	555.9
3,800	424.8	307.4	6,000	462.5	528.4	3,800	445.8	322.5	6,000	489.4	559.1
3,900	423.6	314.6	6,100	462.8	537.5	3,900	446.0	331.2	6,100	480.3	557.9
4,000	428.6	326.4	6,200	454.2	536.2	4,000	447.8	341.1	6,200	475.6	561.5
4,100	424.8	331.6	6,300	456.3	547.4	4,100	442.9	345.7	6,300	466.1	559.1
4,200	431.0	344.7	6,400	450.4	548.9	4,200	441.9	353.4	6,400	459.3	559.7
4,300	426.9	349.5	6,500	444.3	549.9	4,300	454.5	372.1	6,500	454.2	562.1
4,400	425.6	356.6	6,600	425.9	535.2	4,400	456.4	382.4	6,600	450.6	**566.3**
4,500	442.7	379.3	6,700	432.9	**552.2**	4,500	461.4	395.3	6,700	443.5	565.7
4,600	451.5	395.5	6,800	422.7	547.2	4,600	467.7	409.6	6,800	432.1	559.4

UNDERSTANDING THE SMALL-BLOCK GENERATIONS

OBD-I LT1 PCM

Displacement	383 ci
Block	Stock with splayed caps
Pistons	Diamond, .030 over
Camshaft	TPIS 242 solid roller
Intake/Exhaust (degrees)	242/242
Lift (inches)	.050
Intake/Exhaust Valve Lift (inches)	.558/.558
Centerline (degrees)	112
Rods	Callies Compstar, 6 inch
Heads	AFR 210-cc Comp Port
Oil Pan	Canton road race
Throttle Body	TPIS Monoblade
Crankshaft	Callies
Timing Chain	Cloyes
Intake	MiniRam LT
Ignition	GM Optispark with MSD 6AL
Compression Ratio	11.2:1
Ignition	Delphi 5 Wire MAF, 90-mm, 36-pound injectors at 60 psi, EFI connection

24X

Displacement	383 ci
Block	Stock with splayed caps
Pistons	Diamond, .030 over
Camshaft	TPIS 242 solid roller
Rods	Callies Compstar, 6 inch
Heads	AFR 210-cc competition port
Oil Pan	Canton road race
Throttle Body	Monoblade
Crankshaft	Callies
Timing Chain	Cloyes
Intake	MiniRam LT
Ignition	24X
Compression Ratio	11.2:1
Ignition	Delphi 5 Wire MAF, 90-mm, 36-pound injectors at 60 psi, EFI Connection 24X system

This is a back-to-back comparison of two different ignition systems. The first is a factory Optispark ignition with an MSD 6AL box and a TPIS coil. This MSD-enhanced factory ignition is how we've run the LT1/LT4 engines we've built for years. It was better than the factory produced it, but still had some long-term durability and misfire issues. This was especially true in wet weather and very harsh racing environments. It wasn't unheard of for a car not to start after being washed, for example. Our upgrades and modifications made that a lot better, but still couldn't completely cure the design's shortcomings.

The second part of the test is with a completely redesigned engine management system, utilizing a new electrical harness and ECU based on the GM LS-series engine's ignition components. This setup eliminates the Optispark distributor and all of its associated problems.

Look at the two back-to-back runs to see a surprise. This not an inexpensive upgrade, but the gains are dramatic. Before we ran this test, you could not get us to believe that the factory LT1 spark output was deficient. But here's the test. We have redone it several times, and have always seen the same result. This is one of the best upgrades you can accomplish with your LT1/LT4 engine.

It's also interesting to look at power per cubic inch and torque per cubic inch:

	Optispark	*24X*
HP/ci	1.44	1.47
Torque/ci	1.26	1.32

CHAPTER 1

The 1992 LT1 engine followed the design of the traditional small-block Chevy engine, but introduced a few improvements related to cooling, intake manifold design, and ignition system.

The 1997 LS1 engine was a redesign of the traditional small-block Chevy engine. Its intake manifold and cylinder head design are unlike the early GM engines. This LS-series engine was assembled with a 5.3L truck long block, LS2 GTO intake manifold, and LS2 Corvette front accessories.

a desirable upgrade. Most sensors on these Vortec engines are compatible with Gen III PCMs.

Generation II, 1992–1997 LT1 and 1996–1997 LT4

General Motors changed the traditional V-8 cooling system and ignition system with the 1992 Corvette with the 5.7L LT1 engine. The higher horsepower LT4 engine was an option beginning in 1996. Compared to the L98 engine, minor changes were made to the sensors for fitment on these new engines. Functionally, many of the sensors remained the same. The ignition system is unique in that the engine control module (ECM) uses low- and high-resolution pulse counts from the distributor to determine engine position and ignition events. With the exception of this new distributor assembly and the pre–1996 knock sensor, the sensors on these engines are compatible with Gen III PCMs.

Generation III, 1997–2007 LS Series

A new engine design was introduced with the 1997 Corvette. The RPO "LS1" engine was also the beginning of a significantly improved engine management system. The one-coil-per-cylinder ignition system was managed by a 24-pulse signal produced by a unique reluctor wheel on the crankshaft to indicate true crankshaft position for ignition events. While Gen I and Gen II small-block engines relied on a distributor (and any variations due to timing chain slack and camshaft-to-distributor gear lash) to determine ignition events, Gen III engines have the ability to be controlled with the highest accuracy. This improved accuracy has been tested and revealed gains in both horsepower and torque. (See sidebar "John Schaefer LT1 Optispark vs. LS1 24x Ignition" on pages 10–11.)

Several variations of the LS1 were released in the 1998 Camaro and Firebird and 1999 light trucks and SUVs. The 1998–2002 Camaro and Firebird used a 5.7L engine similar to the Corvette; the trucks and SUVs were equipped with new 4.8L, 5.3L, and 6.0L variations of the 5.7L LS1. Because of the interchangeability of most hardware and electronics, all of these engines are referred to generally as "LS-series" engines.

Generation IV, LS Series

Although not discussed in detail in this book, the Gen IV engines increased crankshaft position signal accuracy with 58-pulse crankshaft and 4-pulse camshaft signals. These engines use different ECMs than Gen III engines and, due to hardware and software limitations, Gen IV ECMs cannot control cable throttle systems. Although Gen IV engines can be retrofitted with Gen III crankshaft and camshaft signals, the labor required (pulling the crankshaft) is not desirable.

CHAPTER 2

COMPARING GEN III CONTROLLERS

GM ECMs have come a long way since the introduction of the first multi-port injection V-8 ECM used in the 1985 TPI Camaro, Firebird, and Corvette. These early ECMs require a PROM (or "chip") that contains the engine's calibration data. While all TPI ECMs are for use with high-energy ignition (HEI) systems, which requires a single coil and distributor, there were a few ECM updates before the introduction of a new ECM and ignition system used with the 1992 LT1 Corvette engine. LT1 engines use a unique distributor assembly driven by the front of the engine's camshaft and output high- and low-resolution signals to the ECM (or PCM). All 1996 and newer vehicles have a flash-based PCM that is programmable through the vehicle's data link connector (DLC).

Tuned Port Injection ECMs

In general, all ECMs used with the Camaro, Firebird, and Corvette TPI engines require a single coil and distributor for engine operation. These early ECMs are a batch-fire system, meaning that injectors are not controlled individually (or sequentially). Since the TPI Camaro, Firebird, and Corvette were equipped with either a manual transmission or 700R4 automatic transmission, the only electronic control related to transmissions is 700R4 torque converter lockup. Due to limited calibration capabilities, these ECMs are not well suited for forced induction and high-horsepower engines. Despite the limitations, many continue to use these ECMs for most basic multi-port fuel injection engine installations.

LT1 PCMs

The 1992 Corvette introduced the LT1 engine and a new ECM that requires high- and low-resolution signals from within the distributor. This new distributor design, used through 1997, limits the LT1 ECM and PCM

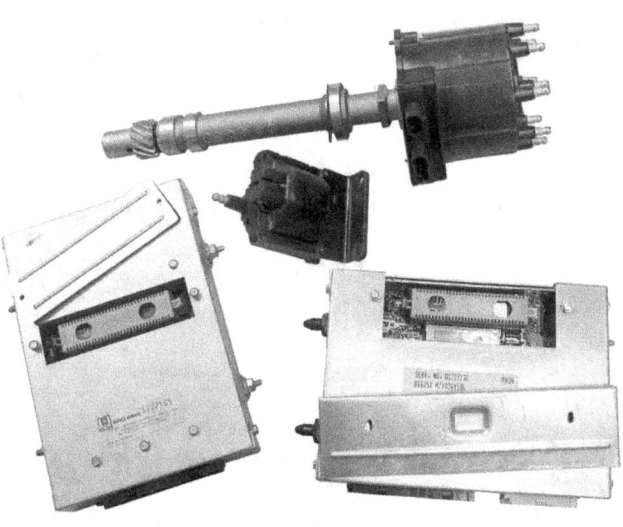

The earliest electronically controlled multi-port fuel injection for V-8 engines uses a PROM-based ECM and single coil with distributor ignition. The early TPI ECM (left) is shown with the cover removed to reveal the MEMCAL, which holds the PROM containing the engine calibration. The late TPI ECM (right) continued to use a MEMCAL, but relies on engine vacuum readings (through a MAP sensor) to calculate fuel delivery rather than measuring the amount of incoming air (through a MAF sensor). All TPI ECMs support only single coil and distributor ignition. All Corvette TPI engines use a large-cap distributor with coil on top (not shown).

GM GEN III LS-SERIES POWERTRAIN CONTROL SYSTEMS

as LT1 engine use only. In 1994 the 4L60-E transmission was a big leap forward in technology and requires the use of a PCM that handles both engine and transmission control. The 1994–1997 PCMs are desirable to the LT1 owner because they allow for custom transmission programming to adjust shift behavior. The OBD-II implementation in 1996 added a four-tooth crankshaft reluctor and crankshaft position (CKP) sensor within the engine timing cover for misfire detection.

Vortec PCMs

The Vortec 4.3L, 5.0L, 5.7L, and 7.4L engines received a significant ignition system update with the OBD-II implementation. The traditional HEI pickup was left behind and replaced with a CKP sensor that determined crankshaft position and was used for misfire detection. From within the timing cover, all Vortec 4.3L V-6 engines are fitted with a three-tooth crankshaft reluctor; all Vortec 5.0L, 5.7L, and 7.4L V-8 engines are fitted with a four-tooth crankshaft reluctor. Many of the PCMs used to control these Vortec engines offer support for 4L60-E and 4L80-E transmissions. Enthusiasts have been replacing these "black box" Vortec PCMs with the Gen III PCM for higher RPM capability and forced-induction support. (Read more about the Gen III PCM upgrade in Chapter 15, Project 5, on page 136).

Generation III Powertrain Control Modules

Not unlike the preceding PCMs, the Gen III PCMs were used to control and monitor the engine, transmission, emissions equipment, electric fans, charging system, and air conditioning system. While several updates and improvements were made to the Gen III PCMs, they can be used almost interchangeably for modern V-8 engine conversions. The versatility of the Gen III PCM makes it an excellent candidate for use as a standalone controller for just about any GM V-8 conversion.

512-Kilobyte PCM

The first Gen III PCM was introduced with the newly designed Gen III LS1 V-8 engine. This PCM (GM# 16238212) was used with the 1997 Corvette and was configured for electronic, drive-by-wire, throttle control. In 1998 the Camaro and Firebird received the LS1 engine and Gen III PCM, but it was configured for traditional cable throttle control using a throttle position sensor (TPS) and idle air control (IAC) valve.

What made this PCM unique to the LS1 engine was the 24-pulse crankshaft signal input. The PCM monitors the 24-pulse crankshaft signal to determine when to fire ignition coils and injectors. Early small-block and big-block Chevy engines do not produce this 24-pulse crankshaft signal. The wire harness for this PCM is the most unique among all Gen III–equipped vehicles. It shares the same wire harness connectors as all other, newer, 512-kb PCMs but it is pinned very differently.

In 1994 General Motors introduced a flash-based PCM in the Camaro, Firebird, and Corvette. This LT1 ECM is unique to the LT1 engines because it requires the high- and low-resolution signals from within the LT1 distributor. Although this early PCM is not fully OBD-II compliant, it has much in common with Gen III PCMs. GM trucks were fitted with an OBD-II compliant flash-based PCM in 1996 (not pictured). With no coil drivers, these early PCMs support only single coil and distributor ignition.

The Gen III PCMs were released in two different cases. The 1997–1998 PCMs (left) use the same wire harness connectors as other LS-series PCMs (right), but they are not pinned the same. The 1997–1998 PCMs are scarce and generally not commonly used with LS conversions. All other LS-series PCMs are plentiful and widely supported among engine tuners.

COMPARING GEN III CONTROLLERS

In 1999, the GM# 16238212 PCM was replaced with the GM# 09354896 PCM. These PCMs are not interchangeable and the wire harness was pinned differently. Vehicles using these PCMs included the Corvette, Camaro, Firebird, and full-size trucks. The full-size trucks were available with the 4.8L, 5.3L, and 6.0L engines. The only GM calibrations used with these PCMs were for Gen III engines, which were all equipped with a 24x crank reluctor. The Corvette continued to use an electronic throttle body, the Camaro and Firebird used a cable throttle body, and the trucks were available with either a cable or an electronic throttle body. The electronic throttle systems required a throttle actuator control (TAC) module, a small black module that communicates with the PCM to control the throttle body and cruise control system. The electronic throttle body and TAC module was different between Corvette and trucks.

The final update to the 512-kb series of PCMs was the introduction of the GM# 12200411 PCM in 2001. With the exception of the 2003 Corvette, this PCM was used through 2002. This PCM is considered the most desirable because of its versatility. General Motors used this PCM with Gen III engines (Corvette, Camaro, Firebird, and trucks), Gen I small-block engines (5.0L and 5.7L Express Van), and Vortec 4.3L V-6 engines (S10 pickup, Blazer, and Express Van).

General Motors released these PCMs with calibrations that support V-8 one-coil-per-cylinder ignition (24x crank signal only), V-8 single coil and distributor ignition (4x crank signal only), and V-6 single coil and distributor ignition (3x crank signal only). While this PCM was used with both cable and electronic throttle systems, electronic throttle is not available for engines with single coil and distributor ignition systems because General Motors never released such a configuration.

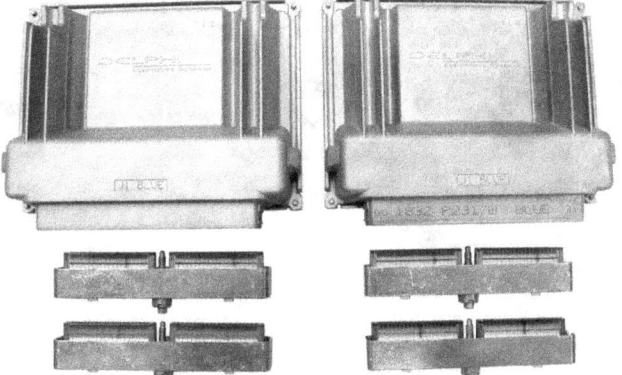

You must look closely at the PCM service number located on the bottom of each PCM. While the 1999–2000 PCMs are interchangeable with the 2001–2002 versions, the 2003s incorporate a few important changes. The 1999–2002 PCMs (left) use connectors with blue and red retainers, while the 2003-newer PCMs (right) use connectors with blue and green retainers. The red and green retainers are keyed differently. Not all 2003-newer PCMs support an IAC valve, a limitation that does not allow for a cable throttle body.

1-Megabyte PCM

General Motors released several different hardware numbers to identify the 1-mb Gen III PCMs, but any of them can be used with an engine equipped with a 24x crank signal. All 2003-newer Gen III PCMs (excluding the 2003 Corvette) were fitted with additional flash memory capacity. These 1-mb PCMs use the same harness connectors as the earlier 512-kb PCMs, but the color and key configuration of the removable retainers were changed. All 512-kb PCMs use one 80-cavity connector with two blue retainers and one 80-cavity connector with two red retainers. All 1-mb PCMs use one 80-cavity connector with two blue retainers and one 80-cavity connector with two green retainers. The 1-mb PCMs look

Notice the difference at the rear corner of these two 2003 PCMs. The one on the left (GM# 12582605) is missing the chip that handles the IAC stepper motor. The one on the right (GM# 12576106) includes the chip that handles the IAC stepper motor. Pay close attention to GM service numbers to be sure you have a PCM that works with your throttle type.

CHAPTER 2

Notice this PCM (GM# 12582605) is missing the chip that controls the IAC motor. This PCM does not allow for use of a cable throttle body. Avoid this GM service number if you plan to use a cable throttle with your engine.

This PCM (GM# 12576106) has the IAC chip installed. This PCM can be used with either a cable or electronic throttle body. This PCM is commonly found in the 2004 GTO and Express Van.

the same as the 512-kb PCMs and operate in much the same way.

Most 2003-newer Gen III engines are equipped with electronic throttle. The few cable throttle exceptions are found in the Express Van and 2004 GTO. The Corvette continued to use the same TAC module through the Gen III engine run, but the trucks received a new TAC module that is not interchangeable with the early version. Although all Gen III TAC modules use the same two harness connectors, they are not interchangeable.

Take caution to identify a 1-mb PCM that is compatible with your throttle system. Some 1-mb PCMs are unable to control the IAC valve on a cable throttle body. A visual inspection of the PCMs circuit board reveals whether the PCM is capable of controlling the IAC. Some 1-mb PCMs are not fitted with a driver (a chip located at the far corner of the circuit board). Other 1-mb PCMs, such as GM# 12586243, were used with both cable throttle engines (2004 GTO) and electronic throttle engines (2004 Corvette).

Moates 16-Bit Real-Time Emulation PCM

Craig Moates, a prominent GM enthusiast, developed an add-on emulation board that fits within the 1999–2003 512-kb PCMs and 2003–2007 1-mb PCMs. Rather than flash memory access through the serial data stream at the OBD-II diagnostic connector, the PCM's flash memory is tied to the tuner's laptop through a USB connection. This real-time tuning solution is compatible with EFILive and TunerCat OBD-II tuning software. The process of tuning an engine with this emulator is fantastic. Combined with EFILive, the tuner can watch engine parameters on a laptop PC and make instantaneous

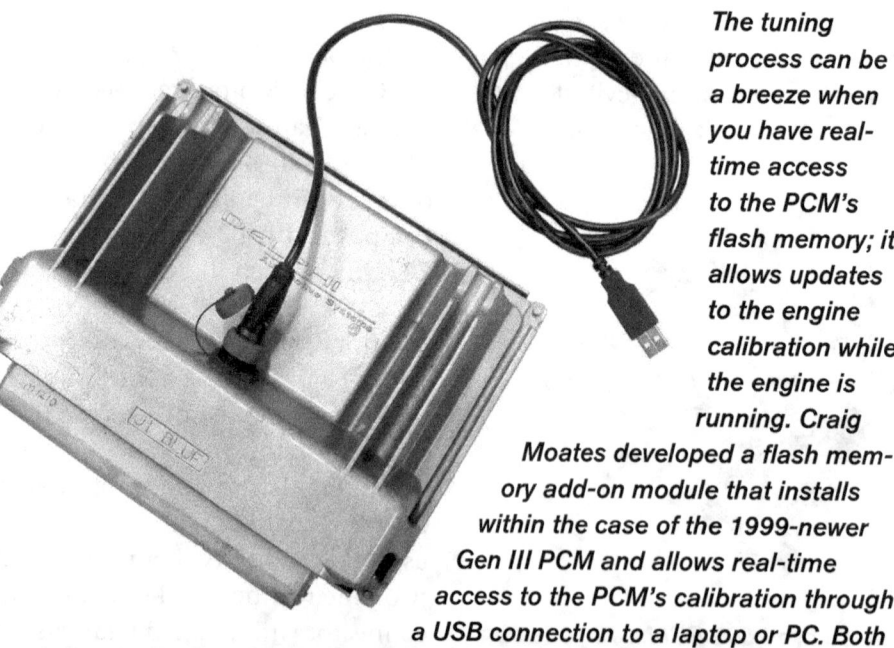

The tuning process can be a breeze when you have real-time access to the PCM's flash memory; it allows updates to the engine calibration while the engine is running. Craig Moates developed a flash memory add-on module that installs within the case of the 1999-newer Gen III PCM and allows real-time access to the PCM's calibration through a USB connection to a laptop or PC. Both EFILive and C.A.T.S. OBD-II Tuner have made a provision in their software for use of this PCM. Although the PCM can be permanently installed in a vehicle, it is most often used as a tool to quickly dial in the proper PCM calibration and then flash the final work into another PCM.

COMPARING GEN III CONTROLLERS

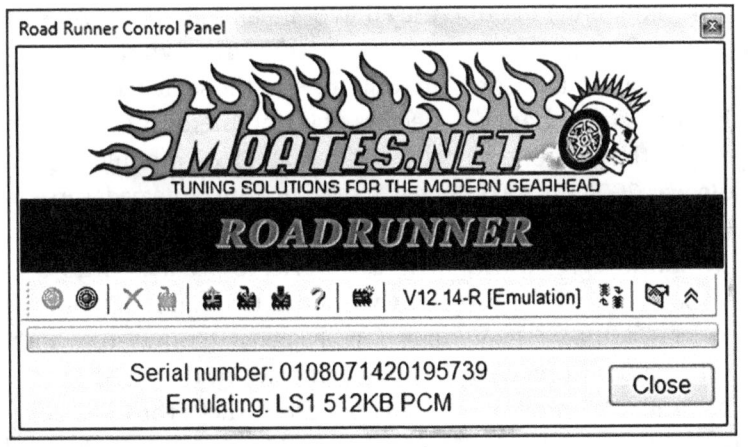

EFILive allows access to the Moates Emulation PCM through its tuning software. The user can retrieve a stored calibration, flash in a new calibration, or set the PCM for emulation mode to make real-time updates while the engine is running. If the setting option is enabled, the PCM makes instant changes as the tuner updates values within the tables in the tuning software; the vehicle experiences changes in engine/transmission behavior as updates are being made.

corrections to the calibration without a single hiccup from the engine.

EFILive has added a control panel to their software for toggling emulation, reading the calibration file from the PCM, applying calibration changes to the PCM, and rewriting the PCM's entire calibration content.

Throttle Actuator Control Modules

All Gen III electronics require a TAC module when using an electronic, drive-by-wire, throttle system. The responsibility of the TAC module is to receive inputs from the accelerator pedal position (APP) sensor plus TPS and operating parameters from the PCM (through two serial data lines) to control the throttle body motor.

Perhaps most significant to enthusiasts, the TAC module is responsible for cruise control operation. With the elimination of a throttle cable, cruise control module, cruise control cable, and all associated wiring and vacuum hoses, the engine bay is free of the extra clutter without cruise control compromise. The TAC module simply receives

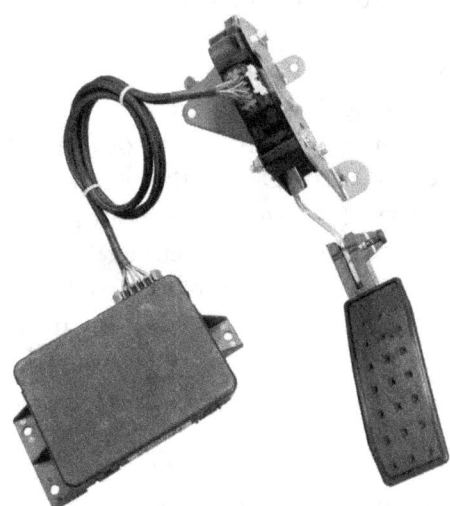

All Gen III engines equipped with an electronic throttle body use a TAC module for throttle and cruise control operation. This is a TAC module from a 2004–2005 Cadillac CTS-V and its APP sensor assembly (accelerator pedal). All TAC modules have two wire harness connections: one dedicated to the APP sensor and the other for power, ground, PCM communications, cruise control, and throttle operation.

No matter which TAC module you work with, it looks like one of these. The 1999–2002 GM truck TAC modules use the same black plastic housing (left) as all Corvette and LS6 Cadillac CTS-V TAC modules. The Corvette and LS6 Cadillac CTS-V share the same TAC module. In 2003 the trucks received an updated TAC module with an aluminum back plate (right). It is always best to keep matching electronic throttle components (TAC module, PCM, accelerator pedal, and TAC to pedal harness). A mismatch of electronic throttle components can cause a frustrating troubleshooting experience.

12V signals, the same as many early GM cruise control switches, to signal cruise control on/off, set/coast, and resume/accelerate driver requests.

With required brake and clutch switch signals, the PCM and TAC module know when to cancel cruise control operation. Compared to early, cable-driven, cruise control systems, the driver's experience is noticeably improved. With no vacuum actuator and cable, the acceleration lag experienced with early cruise control systems is replaced with a smooth, modern feel.

General Motors did away with the external TAC module with the introduction of the Gen IV E40 ECM. All Gen IV systems use electronic throttle and are controlled by the ECM. With no provision within the Gen IV ECMs for an IAC motor and the requirement of two throttle position signals, cable throttle is no longer an option with Gen IV ECMs. With the exception of the E67 ECM (and supported calibration), cruise control is a function of the body control module (BCM) and requires the controller area network (CAN) communication with the ECM for cruise control operation.

With the exception of the 2004 GTO and 2003–2006 van, all Gen III systems use a TAC module and electronic throttle body.

1997–2004 Corvette and 2004–2005 Cadillac CTS-V TAC

Electronic throttle was the only option with all C5 Corvettes; this meant the elimination of throttle and cruise control cables for a quick and responsive throttle and cruise control system. While there have been several hardware updates, all Corvette TAC modules are interchangeable. The last year for the Corvette to use a TAC module was 2004. In 2005, the C6 Corvette was released with a Gen IV E40 ECM that integrated the TAC within the ECM.

The 2004–2005 Cadillac CTS-V are fitted with the 2004 Corvette's LS6 engine, PCM, and TAC module. The CTS-V has a different throttle pedal, but its APP sensor is a functional equivalent to the Corvette's APP sensor.

Truck TAC for 512-kb PCMs

Electronic throttle was introduced with the 7.4L gasoline engine in the 1999 medium-duty GM trucks. Although these trucks share the same PCM as the 1997–1998 Corvette (which is also electronic throttle), the TAC module does not interchange. This first GM truck TAC module (GM# 19245410) was used with the 16238212 PCM.

The more common truck TAC module was introduced in 2000 (GM# 19245406). This TAC module was used through 2002 with Gen III engines equipped with electronic throttle. General Motors used this TAC module with two different PCMs: GM# 09354896 in 1999–2000 and GM# 12200411 in 2001–2002.

Truck TAC for 1-MB PCMs

With the 1-mb PCM came a new TAC module. The 2003–2007 truck TAC modules are identified easily as they have an aluminum back plate and plastic housing. While this TAC module accepts the same harness connectors, it is not interchangeable with the early truck TAC modules. However, it does use the same pedal assembly as the early drive-by-wire trucks. The early TAC-to-pedal harness uses nine wires (for three APP signals); the late TAC-to-pedal harness uses only six wires (for two APP signals).

The early truck throttle pedal assembly (GM# 15177923) is used with 2000–2005 trucks. An alternate pedal assembly (GM# 15264643) is used with 2004–2005 trucks. These pedal assemblies are quality pieces with a metal mount, metal arm, and traditional spring-loaded foot rest. The APP sensor contains three sensor signals that provide pedal position details to the TAC module (only two are used). The APP sensor is connected to the TAC module through a separate wire harness.

Reducing costs, General Motors began using a different throttle pedal (GM# 15107594) in the 2006–2007 trucks. Used with or without power adjust, this pedal assembly is plastic with a plastic arm and fixed foot rest. The APP sensor is built within the pedal assembly and contains only two sensors that provide pedal position details to the TAC module. The APP sensor is connected to the TAC module through a separate wire harness.

There are other truck pedals used with a power adjust. Because of their large size and extra electronics involved, however, they are not well suited for conversions.

CHAPTER 3

CRANKSHAFT AND CAMSHAFT SIGNALS AND IGNITION SYSTEMS

OBD-II compliance in 1996 brought a new ignition system to Vortec V-6 and Vortec V-8 engines. Engine position through a crankshaft sensor and reluctor wheel also meant improved ignition accuracy and misfire detection. Older HEI distributor ignition systems deliver spark and fuel based on distributor position. For these early systems, accuracy of spark and fuel delivery varies because the distributor gear must mesh with the camshaft and the camshaft must turn through the timing chain attached to the crankshaft sprocket. No doubt accuracy was close, but a signal from the crankshaft is the best way to determine the location of each piston. Ignition events based on crankshaft position means maximum horsepower and efficiency.

High-Resolution Crankshaft Signal

GM's 24-pulse crankshaft signal is a series of long (12 degrees) and short (3 degrees) pulses that are 15 degrees apart. This 24x pattern is generated from a crankshaft reluctor mounted on an engine's crankshaft and through a CKP sensor. GM's 24x crankshaft reluctors feature two rows of teeth that are out of phase. This dual row pattern requires a CKP sensor capable of dual input and single output.

The 24x crankshaft signal requires a 1x camshaft signal so the PCM can determine the stroke (intake or exhaust) of each piston based on its position during crankshaft rotation. Without a camshaft position signal, the PCM would have to guess between intake or exhaust stroke during engine startup.

The PCM supplies 12V high-reference and 0V low-reference signals to both crankshaft and camshaft sensors and receives back from each sensor a digital ON/OFF signal as each reluctor passes by its sensor.

24x Gen III

Although there are a variety of Gen III engines, every one has a crankshaft reluctor and sensor that produces a 24-pulse waveform (24x) used by the PCM to control spark and fuel events. This 24x signal represents crankshaft position. Because there are 720 degrees of crankshaft rotation to 360 degrees of camshaft

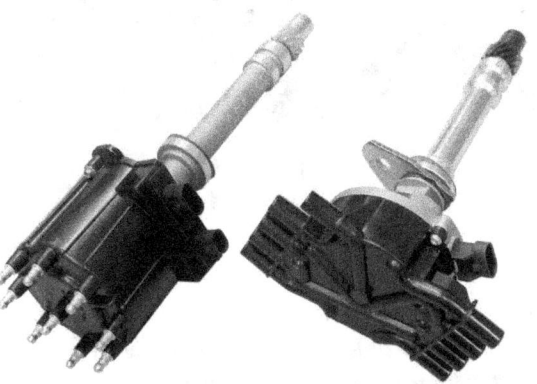

Early electronic fuel injection systems, such as on TBI and TPI engines, use an HEI distributor (left) with ignition module mounted to the base of the upper housing, within the cap. These early engines must rely on the distributor for setting base timing. The 1996–2002 Vortec V-6 and Vortec V-8 engines continue to use a distributor, but not for determining engine position. The Vortec distributor (right) is used to drive the oil pump, distribute spark, and provide the PCM with a camshaft position signal from the CMP sensor located within the cap.

GM GEN III LS-SERIES POWERTRAIN CONTROL SYSTEMS

CHAPTER 3

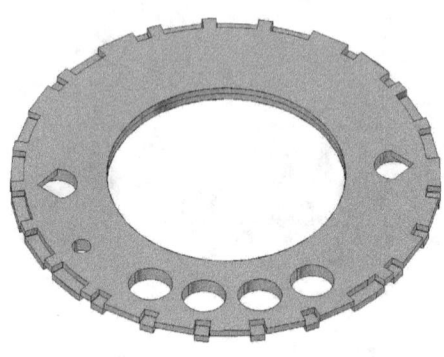

All LS-series engines are equipped with eight ignition coils: four mounted to a bracket on each valve cover.

The Gen III crankshaft reluctor wheel is mounted on the rear of the crankshaft and within the engine block. The outer diameter of the crankshaft reluctor is exposed through a hole in the side of the block above the starter. The CKP sensor seals the sensor hole and returns a 24-pulse signal to the PCM while the crankshaft is turning.

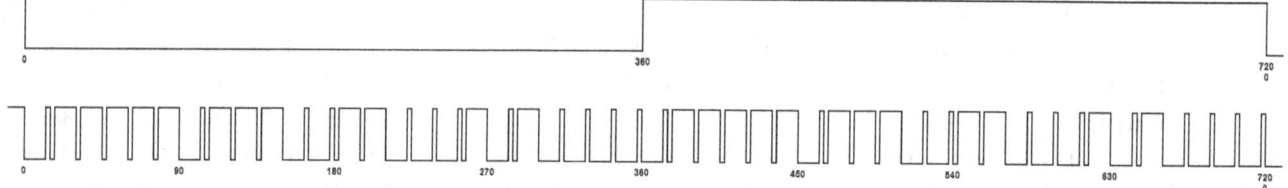

Vehicles equipped with Gen III engines use a PCM calibration that requires this 24x crankshaft and 1x camshaft waveform relationship.

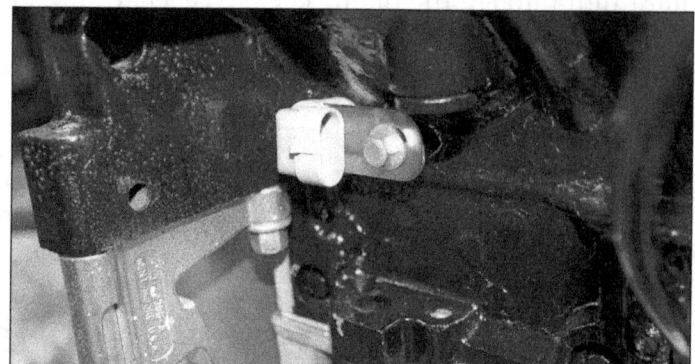

Identification of the crankshaft reluctor type (24x or 58x) is as easy as looking at the color of the CKP sensor mounted in the block above the starter. The black LS-series CKP sensor is used with a 24x crankshaft reluctor. What makes this sensor specific to the 24x reluctor is its ability to "read" a 24-pulse high/low signal (per 360 degrees crankshaft rotation) from the two rows of 24 teeth that are joined together, while out of phase, as one reluctor wheel.

The gray LS-series CKP sensor is used with a 58x crankshaft reluctor. This sensor is designed to "read" only one row of teeth from the crankshaft reluctor wheel. Where the 24x crankshaft reluctor is made up of two, out-of-phase rings, the 58x crankshaft reluctor contains only one row of 58 teeth. This gray CKP sensor is unable to properly produce a signal from GM's 24x crankshaft reluctor.

CRANKSHAFT AND CAMSHAFT SIGNALS AND IGNITION SYSTEMS

Gen III engines have a CMP sensor located at the rear of the engine where you commonly see a distributor for small-block Chevy engines. This CMP sensor gets its signal from a machined ring toward the rear of the camshaft. This sensor/reluctor pair generates a near 50-percent duty-cycle (on/off) high/low signal so the PCM can determine the stroke (intake or exhaust) for any given cylinder.

Gen IV engines mount the CMP sensor in the front timing cover and get a signal from the face of the camshaft timing sprocket. Early Gen IV engines are equipped with a 24x crankshaft reluctor and 1x camshaft reluctor. These engines use the same CMP sensor and timing cover as the later engines equipped with a 58x crankshaft reluctor and 4x camshaft reluctor. The CMP sensor output (1x or 4x) is determined by the signal surface area of the camshaft timing sprocket.

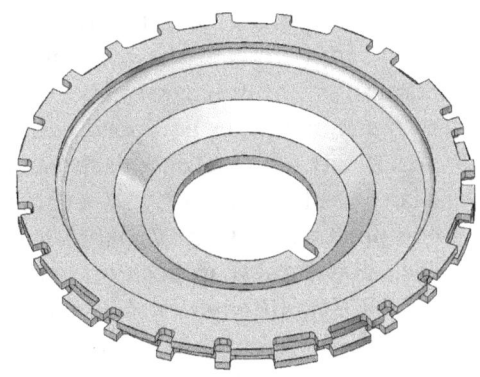

EFI Connection's 24x crankshaft reluctor design has a dual row of teeth and requires the use of a dual-input, single-output sensor. This reluctor installs in front of the crankshaft timing sprocket and is held firmly in place with the tightening of the crankshaft balancer bolt. The crankshaft signal solution requires a timing cover with provision for a CKP sensor.

rotation, a 1x signal from the camshaft allows the PCM to determine if a given piston is on the intake or exhaust stoke.

General Motors only used coil-per-cylinder ignition (eight ignition coils) with this 24x high-resolution crankshaft signal. Using the Gen III PCM with any other crankshaft signal does not allow for one coil for each cylinder. Unfortunately, the PCM calibration does not allow for remapping of the 24x encoded waveform to add or remove cylinders (ignition coils and injectors). However, if the engine firing order is mechanically changed, the PCM can be recalibrated for a new firing order. (See Chapter 7.)

EFI Connection's 24x LT1 conversion kit includes a crankshaft reluctor, crankshaft sensor, camshaft reluctor, camshaft sensor, and camshaft sensor housing. The camshaft sensor housing is installed on the face of the timing cover where the Optispark distributor used to reside. A 1996–1997 LT1 timing cover is required.

CHAPTER 3

Identifying a Gen III engine is easy; simply look at the color of the crankshaft position sensor above the starter. All engines equipped with a Gen III 24x reluctor use a black crankshaft position sensor; all engines equipped with a Gen IV 58x reluctor use a gray crankshaft position sensor.

All Gen III engines have a camshaft position sensor in the rear of the engine behind the intake manifold. All Gen IV 24x and 58x engines have a camshaft position sensor in the front timing cover. Gen IV 24x engines use an E40 ECM and can be found in the 2005 Corvette, 2005–2006 GTO, 2005–2006 Trailblazer, and 2005–2006 SSR. (This book does not cover Gen IV engines and electronics.)

EFI Connection 24x System

To introduce the LS-series coil-per-cylinder ignition system with Gen III PCM control to the Gen I small-block Chevy engine, EFI Connection designed a smaller diameter 24x crankshaft reluctor that installs within the 1996–2002 Vortec engine timing cover and uses a GM crankshaft position sensor. General Motors had already provided the required 1x camshaft signal through the 1996–2002 Vortec distributor, but EFI Connection's cast-aluminum distributor cap eliminates any spark plug wire provision on the distributor; it's function is to produce a camshaft position signal and drive the oil pump. The 24x crankshaft signal components and 1x camshaft signal components make the Gen I small-block Chevy engine ready for Gen III PCM control.

EFI Connection eliminated the problematic Optispark distributor used with all Gen II LT1 and LT4 engines by using the same 24x small-block reluctor and a 1996–1997 LT1 timing cover. The 1x camshaft posi-

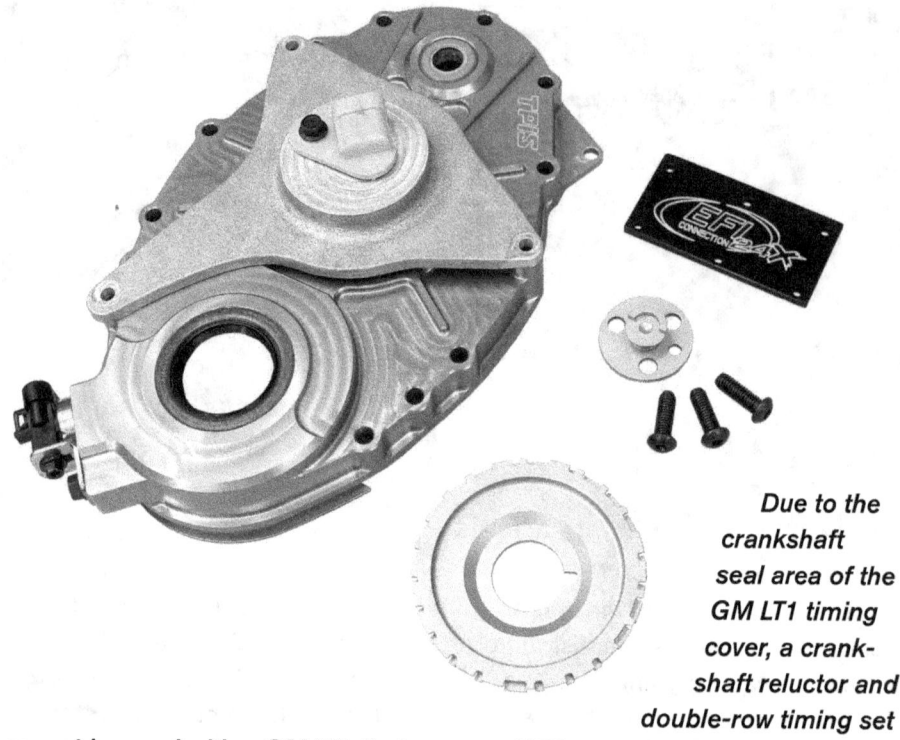

Due to the crankshaft seal area of the GM LT1 timing cover, a crankshaft reluctor and double-row timing set cannot be used with a GM LT1 timing cover. TPIS manufactures several anodized billet-aluminum timing cover solutions for use with EFI Connection's 24x small-block/LT1 crankshaft reluctor. The TPIS billet-aluminum timing covers are available with or without provision for the upper water pump driveshaft. A big-block Chevy diameter crank seal is also an option for engines requiring a larger-diameter crankshaft hub or balancer.

tion signal is achieved through EFI Connection's LT1 camshaft reluctor installed in front of the camshaft timing sprocket and the Gen IV camshaft position sensor installed in EFI Connection's cast-aluminum cam sensor housing. These LT1 camshaft signal components are installed in place of the Optispark distributor. The 24x crankshaft signal components and 1x camshaft signal components make the Gen II LT1 and LT4 engines ready for Gen III PCM control.

With the 24x crankshaft signal and the 1x camshaft signal, the Gen III PCM controls early V-8 engines just as it controls a Gen III engine. PCM calibration file selection requires a base calibration from a Gen III vehicle. This is significant because it allows for any LS-series vehicle hardware option (throttle type, transmission type, and so on). Tuners can choose from any Gen III base calibration file. Correcting the firing order requires the engine wire harness reassignment of injectors and coils 2 and 3 and 4 and 7.

In addition, the PCM requires a calibration update of the injector bank assignments table for proper fuel delivery (see 8-4 and 8-5 Chapter 7 for more details). The tuner works with this PCM just as he would with any LS-series engine.

Low-Resolution Crankshaft Signal

The Gen III PCM (GM# 12200411) was also used with the 2001–2002 Gen I small-block and

CRANKSHAFT AND CAMSHAFT SIGNALS AND IGNITION SYSTEMS

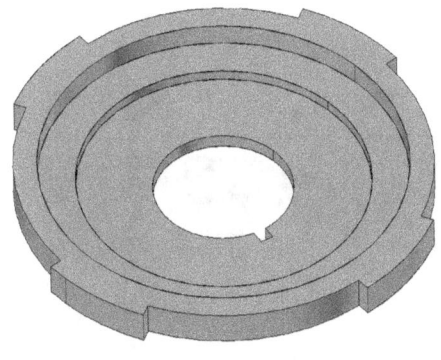

All 1996–2002 Gen I small-block engines found in production vehicles use a 4x crankshaft reluctor. This reluctor is installed on the crankshaft in the front timing chain cover. Combined with a CKP sensor, the PCM uses the signal to determine engine position.

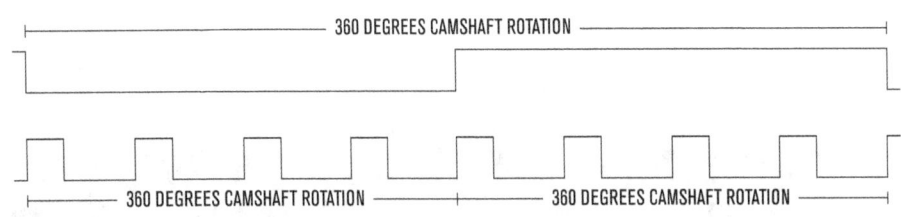

The PCM monitors the relationship of the crankshaft to the camshaft through a CKP sensor and a CMP sensor. The sensors return digital ON/OFF signals to represent engine position. This waveform is a visual representation of two complete revolutions of the crankshaft.

Vortec V-6 engines. While these engines are fitted with a low-resolution crankshaft signal, the crankshaft sensor principle is the same: a digital ON/OFF signal represents crankshaft location. General Motors never released a coil-per-cylinder ignition system that used a low-resolution crankshaft signal, meaning that the PCM cannot be recalibrated for coil-per-cylinder ignition with a low-resolution crankshaft signal. In addition, because General Motors did not use an electronic, drive-by-wire throttle system, only a cable throttle body is supported.

Gen I Vortec V-8

Since 1996, the Gen I small-block Vortec engines are equipped with a low-resolution 4x crankshaft signal and a 1x camshaft signal. This means all Gen I small-block Chevy engines are easily converted to PCM use (GM# 12200411) with the addition of a GM 4x crankshaft reluctor, CKP sensor, timing cover, and Vortec distributor. The 4x crankshaft signal is used by the PCM to identify piston pairs at top dead center (TDC). Combined with the 1x camshaft signal from within the Vortec distributor, the PCM determines the stroke for any given piston. Only single coil and distributor ignition are possible for an engine equipped with a low-resolution 4x crankshaft signal.

Vortec V-6

Since 1996, Vortec V-6 engines have been equipped with a low-resolution 3x crankshaft signal and a 1x camshaft signal. This means all early 4.3L V-6 Chevy engines are easily converted to PCM use (GM# 12200411) with the addition of a GM 3x crankshaft reluctor, CKP sensor, Gen I small-block Vortec timing cover, and Vortec distributor. The 3x crankshaft signal is used by the PCM to identify piston pairs at TDC. Combined with the 1x camshaft signal from within the Vortec distributor, the PCM can determine the stroke for any given piston. Only single coil and distributor ignition are possible for an engine equipped with a low-resolution 3x crankshaft signal.

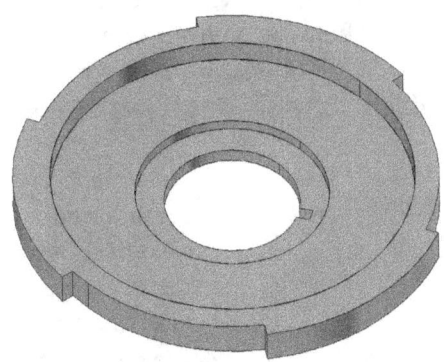

All 1996–2006 4.3L V-6 engines found in production vehicles use a 3x crankshaft reluctor. This reluctor is installed on the crankshaft in the front timing chain cover. Combined with a CKP sensor, the PCM uses the signal to determine engine position.

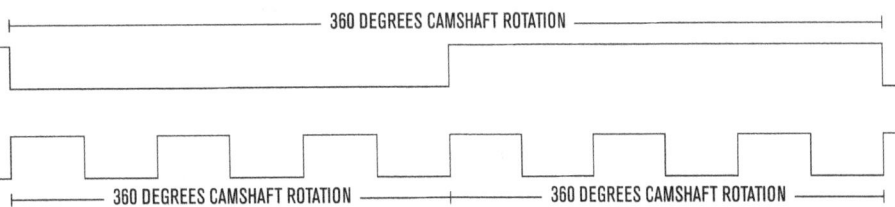

The PCM monitors the relationship of the crankshaft to the camshaft through a CKP sensor and a CMP sensor. The sensors return digital ON/OFF signals to represent engine position. This waveform is a visual representation of two complete revolutions of the crankshaft.

CHAPTER 4

TUNING SOFTWARE AND EQUIPMENT

Although Gen III PCMs are powerful control modules, they are of little use without tuning software to change engine (and transmission) operating parameters. You may find that the best results involve a blend of tuning services at an experienced dyno facility and final do-it-yourself tweaking using a popular scan-and-tune software package. The aftermarket offers all the tuning tools necessary for a successful LS1 PCM conversion.

GM Tuning

Prior to use in a production vehicle, each GM PCM is flashed with a calibration specific for its application. Vehicle options such as air conditioning, electric fans, transmission type, throttle type, etc. have different settings from one vehicle to another. Just as a new (or used) PCM installed into a production vehicle requires the latest GM calibration for that vehicle, a new (or used) PCM purchased for an engine/transmission conversion requires an initial calibration to be flashed into the PCM's memory that closely matches the features of the vehicle.

Service technicians have access to the latest vehicle calibrations through an online subscription-based service. This service is limited to flashing on-board modules with the latest GM calibrations. Gen III engine conversions always require calibration changes to a GM calibration, so this service is nothing more than a first step in preparing a PCM for an engine conversion. Unfortunately, service technicians having access to this GM service are often unwilling to use it for an enthusiast because it requires the vehicle to be present for a connection to the OBD-II DLC.

Software

GM's Technical Information System (TIS)—Service Programming System (SPS), (commonly referred to as TIS2Web) is an Internet utility used by service technicians to reprogram control modules with the latest GM calibration. The software is accessed through the Internet and opened as a Java applet launched on the technician's local laptop or desktop PC.

To reprogram a module, the technician first chooses the vehicle type (year, make, model, engine size). Then the technician enters the vehicle identification number (VIN), which provides a list of on-board

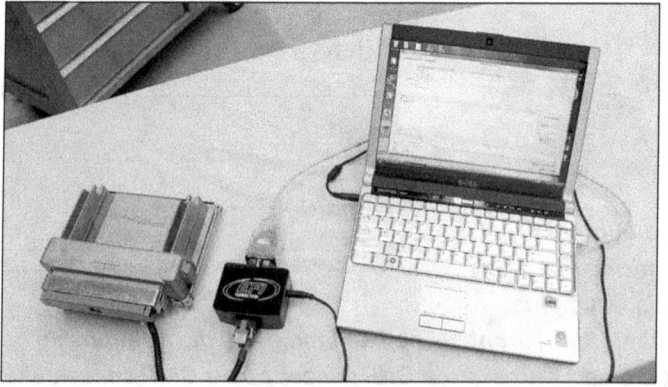

GM repair technicians use a web-based subscription service to access on-board control module calibrations. When an on-board module is replaced during service, the technician uses TIS2Web for service programming. Occasionally, a vehicle may receive a calibration update due to an undesirable performance behavior noted by owners of similar vehicles.

24   GM GEN III LS-SERIES POWERTRAIN CONTROL SYSTEMS

TUNING SOFTWARE AND EQUIPMENT

The Tech2 is the scan tool used by GM repair technicians to troubleshoot, diagnose, and reprogram on-board modules. Because of its price, many owners choose an alternative tool for retrieving and clearing OBD-II codes. (Photo Courtesy Keith McCord)

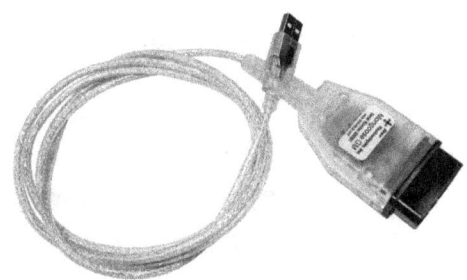

For TIS2Web on-board programming functions only, General Motors offers a calibration service that does not require an expensive Tech2. The Mongoose cable allows repair facilities to use TIS2Web.

modules available for programming. After choosing an on-board module for programming, the technician is prompted to select from among several available calibrations. The calibration data is temporarily downloaded to the local laptop or PC (so that an interruption in Internet service does not interrupt programming) and then the on-board module is programmed.

Hardware Interface

TIS2Web requires a J2534 programming interface such as the GM Tech2, Drew Technologies Mongoose cable, or other compatible programming interface. The programming hardware interface is a link between the vehicle's OBD-II diagnostic connector and a laptop or desktop PC. The Tech2 is a powerful handheld device used by GM service technicians for advanced vehicle diagnostics and programming. Note that the Mongoose cannot perform the advanced diagnostic procedures of the Tech2.

Custom Tuning and Data Acquisition

Preparing a PCM for use with any engine conversion requires custom programming. A new PCM does not contain a calibration ready for use and a PCM pulled from a used vehicle contains parameters preventing fuel delivery without satisfying vehicle antitheft system (VATS) requirements. VATS eliminator modules exist in the aftermarket but they do nothing more than supply the PCM with a signal to satisfy the VATS requirement and allow fuel delivery. Additional parameters must be changed for proper engine operation and appropriate diagnostic trouble code (DTC) processing and notification. See Chapter 15, Project 1, on page 112 for a list of DTCs after a Gen III PCM conversion.

PCM calibration data tables and parameters are used to mathematically apply injector and spark timing. A misconception is that the calibration data follows engine hardware (cubic inches, cylinder head specs, fuel injector size, and camshaft profile). In reality, engine hardware influences table and parameter settings that must be adjusted (by a tuner) for an engine to run properly. Incorrect calibration settings result in an engine that runs poorly.

Many owners choose to ship their PCM to a tuner who offers a mail-order calibration service. They typically fill out an order form with

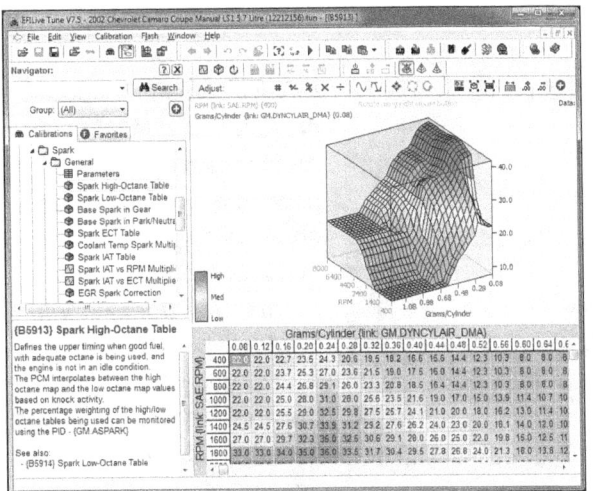

This Gen III PCM calibration table represents the main spark advance values when no detonation is present. The PCM switches to an equivalent low-octane spark table when knock is present. The PCM determines which values to use based on engine RPM and calculated airflow. The actual spark advance is based on other spark tables and parameters that take into consideration engine operating conditions such as coolant temperature and intake air temperature.

CHAPTER 4

questions related to engine hardware (cubic inches, cylinder head specs, fuel injector size, camshaft profile, etc) and send it along with the PCM.

The tuner opens a calibration from a vehicle he has previously tuned that had similar engine specs and uses it as a template for the new calibration.

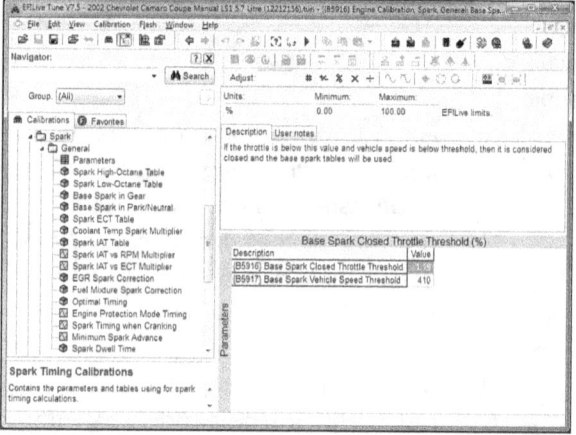

Gen III PCM calibration spark parameters are used in the calculation to determine actual spark advance. The PCM determines spark advance by adding, subtracting, or multiplying values with the main spark tables.

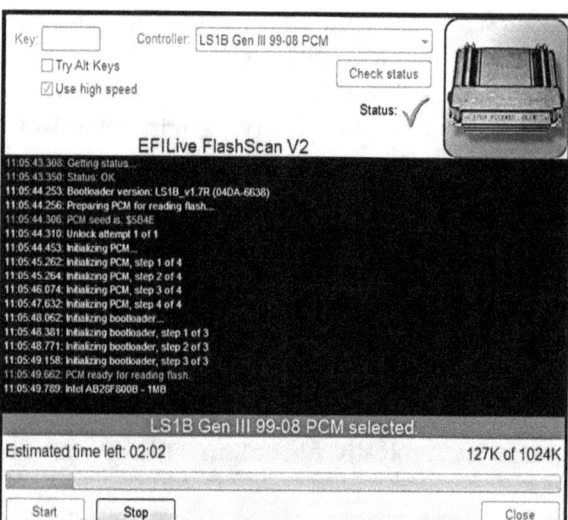

Here, the PCM calibration is being retrieved and then loaded into EFILive tuning software. The software goes through a series of checks to identify an attached interface cable and determine the readiness of the PCM. Retrieving the calibration stored in the PCM's flash memory takes only a few minutes with a GM PCM and only moments with an upgraded Moates.net emulation PCM.

EFILive can either update or replace the PCM flash memory. An update is used to make calibration changes only. If the operating system (OS) must be changed (for example throttle type or transmission type), a full flash is required. For Gen III PCMs, once the OS has been flashed into the PCM, only updates are required to finish the calibration work.

At best, the new calibration runs your engine as well as it did the previously tuned engine. However, because it is uncommon for one modified engine to be the same as the next, the new calibration may only serve to start the engine so the vehicle can be loaded on a trailer and taken to a local dyno tuning facility for final calibration work. Expect to have the dyno shop make final calibration changes using feedback from a wide-band oxygen (O_2) sensor and real-time data from a quality scan tool.

Tuning Software

The tuner's view into the PCM calibration is through a software application that presents the calibration data as tables and parameters. Only a few software applications are available that allow reading, viewing, and changing a Gen III PCM calibration.

The EFILive Tuning Tool (commonly referred to as simply EFILive) is one of the more popular software applications for Gen III tuning. Just as any other tuning software, EFILive allows you to "read" the calibration out of the PCM, view and edit a large set of tables and parameters, and "write" the updated calibration back to the PCM. While a Gen III PCM calibration has thousands of tables and parameters, tuning software exposes only a portion of these tables and parameters. The hidden tables and parameters are not necessary for engine conversions.

Gen III PCM tuning software allows the tuner to replace the PCM's current operating system and calibration segments with another vehicle's operating system and calibration segments. To put it another way, you can turn a 2002 Express Van PCM into a 2002 Corvette PCM. Because the PCM

TUNING SOFTWARE AND EQUIPMENT

service number (GM# 12200411) is the same for both vehicles, the calibration can be interchanged.

As an example, someone using an LS1 Corvette engine need not source the PCM directly from a Corvette. A tuner can simply begin with a calibration file pulled from a Corvette PCM, make necessary changes, and then perform a full flash into any PCM with a matching service number.

Gen IV ECMs cannot be fully overwritten with custom tuning software. If, for example, you are working with an LS2 engine pulled from a 2005 Pontiac GTO and source an ECM from a 2005 Corvette, the ECM must first be reprogrammed with GM's TIS2Web software using a 2005 GTO VIN. This replaces all calibration segments and turns the ECM into a 2005 GTO ECM. Without reprogramming the ECM with GM's TIS2Web, the GTO pedal assembly would not be compatible with the 2005 Corvette ECM calibration. Gen IV ECMs can only be used with engines equipped with a 58x crankshaft reluctor.

EFILive offers free custom operating system (OS) upgrades for features such as nitrous control and 3-bar forced induction support. Applying a custom OS begins by flashing (full write) the custom OS file supplied by EFILive. This enables features of the PCM that are not available with a GM calibration. A PCM calibration is then flashed (update only) into the custom OS-equipped PCM.

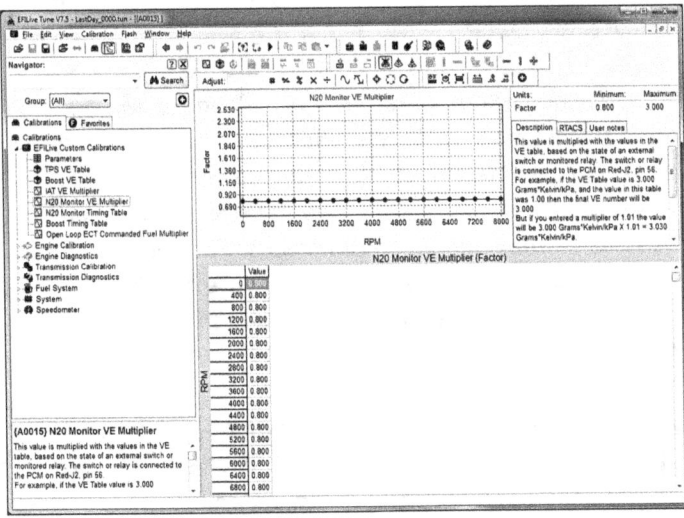

EFILive supports nitrous calibration through the activation of an arming switch. When the PCM sees the arming signal, it is ready to apply spark and fuel delivery multipliers when certain parameters (such as throttle position) are met.

Data Acquisition Software

Before making changes in tuning software, you should first monitor real-time data while the vehicle is running so the changes are based on actual operating conditions. Some tuning software packages include data acquisition software. EFILive's FlashScan Scan Tool software allows the user to choose standard and GM enhanced parameters (PIDs) for data monitoring and recording (see Chapter 14 for more details on PID selection). EFILive's FlashScan Scan

CHAPTER 4

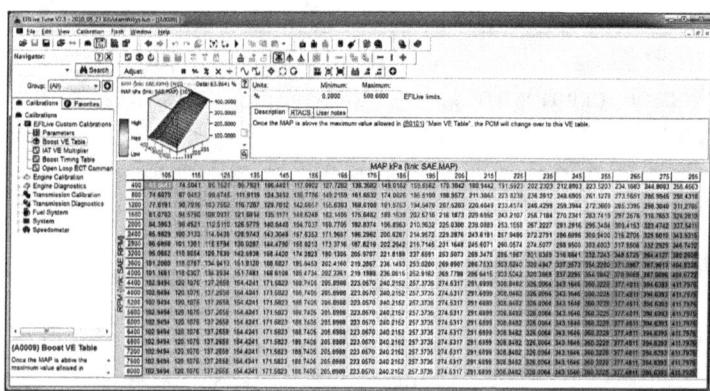

EFILive supports 2- and 3-bar MAP sensors and can account for forced induction (boost). The standard 1-bar MAP table (the Volumetric Efficiency table) is limited to a maximum MAP value of 105 kPa. Without the Boost VE table, tuning for a turbo or supercharged engine becomes difficult.

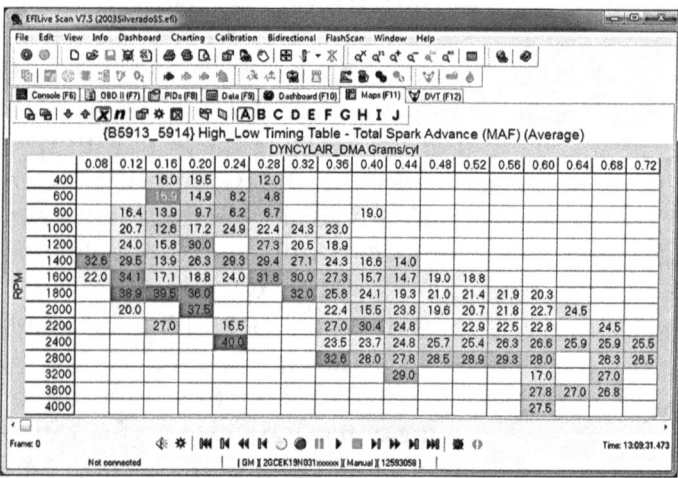

EFILive Scan software allows for customizable maps for logging data. These maps display data in columns, rows, and cells. To build a map, PID choices are available for rows, columns, and cells. Cell values at each row/column intersection may be toggled between averages and operation event counts. To focus on an issue, the table resolution may be defined for both rows and columns.

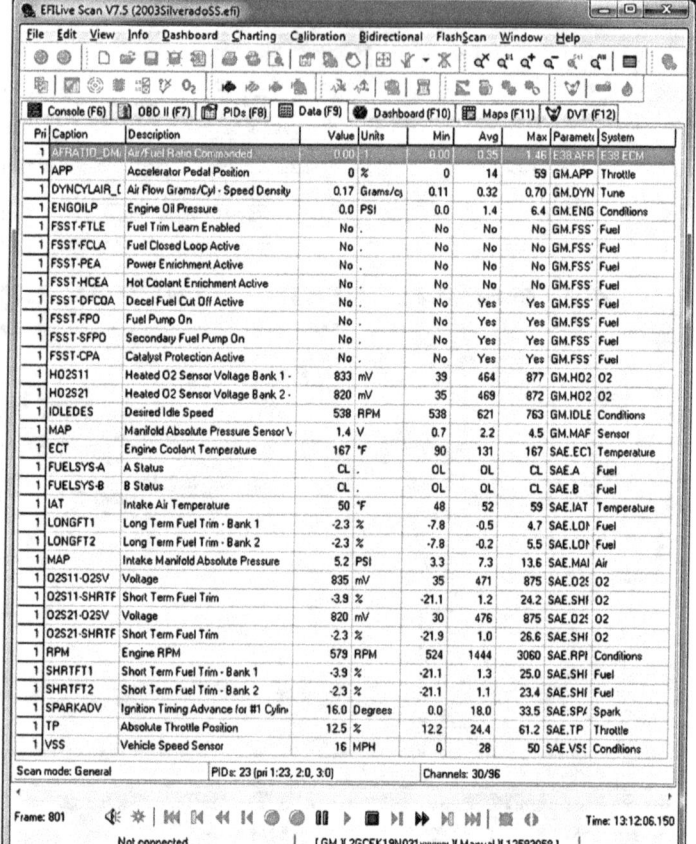

PID selection and data retrieval are standard among most OBD-II scan tools. EFILive presents meaningful descriptions and parameter identifiers for selected PIDs. PID values are shown in real-time and stored, per session, as minimums, maximums, and averages. Parameter names (such as SAE.RPM for engine speed) are helpful to identify which PID is necessary for data tracing through EFILive's tuning software.

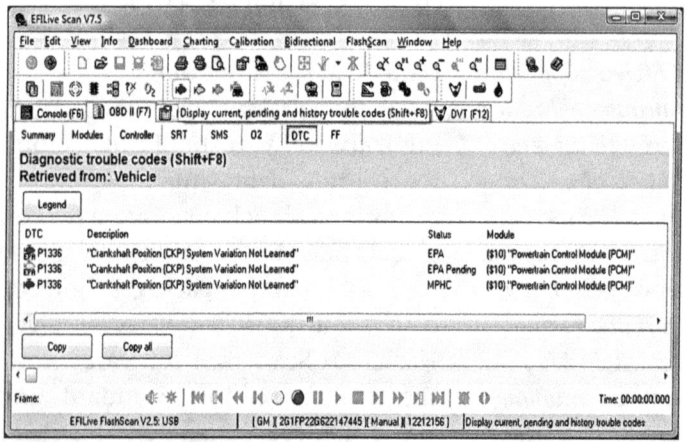

EFILive supports the retrieval and clearing of DTCs. This feature is common to OBD-II scan tools found at auto parts stores. Early OBD-I system DTCs could be cleared from memory by disconnecting the battery from the vehicle's wire harness. OBD-II DTCs are cleared through the use of an OBD-II scan tool, not by disconnecting the battery.

TUNING SOFTWARE AND EQUIPMENT

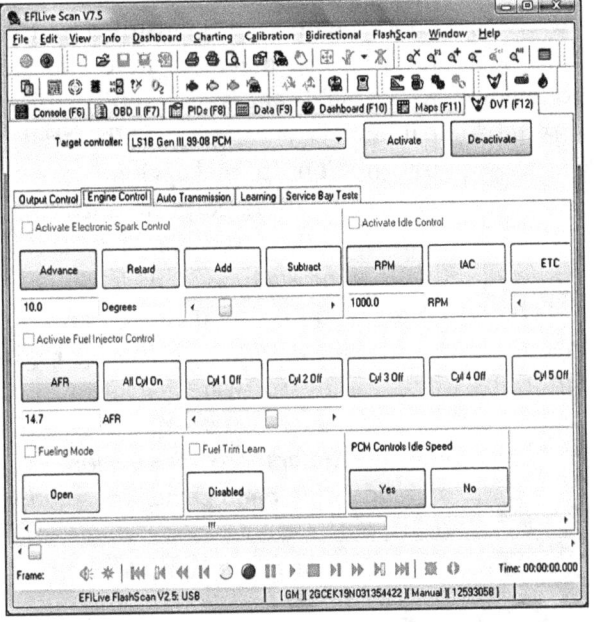

EFILive supports certain bi-directional service bay tests only offered through high-end OBD-II scan tools. Bi-directional controls are useful in many situations. As an example, when preparing to start an engine for the first time, it is helpful to know your fuel pump is generating the required system pressure with no leaks in the fuel lines. By toggling the fuel pump on while the engine is not running, you can safely check for any leaks.

EFILive is one of the few OBD-II tools that allow for CASE learning, which is a procedure required by the PCM when a timing cover, crank sensor, crankshaft reluctor, or PCM has been replaced.

Tool software also includes customizable maps for organizing and analyzing data, diagnostic trouble code retrieval, bi-directional service tests, and more.

Hardware Interface

The data communication between a laptop and the vehicle is processed through a hardware interface. Custom tuning software packages include an interface cable that is not interchangeable with other tuning packages. EFILive bundles a high-end interface cable that features an LCD display and keypad for data functions such as black box logging and diagnostic trouble code retrieval. Although not all interface cables feature an LCD display, most include inputs for adding data from external sensors such as a wide-band O_2 or thermocouple.

Handheld Tuners

Handheld tuners are simple devices that allow limited calibration changes to the PCM. These handy devices are tailored toward individual

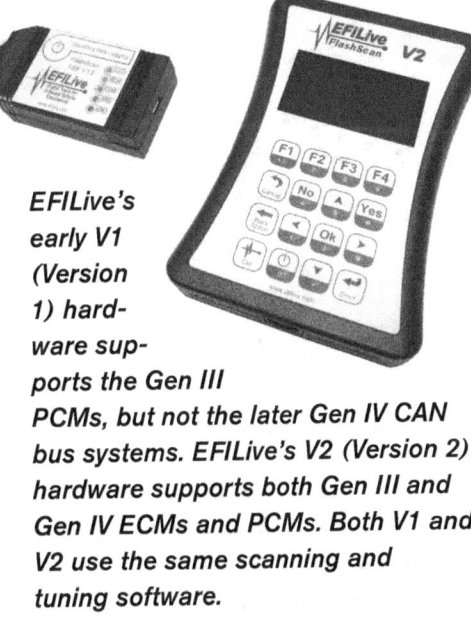

EFILive's early V1 (Version 1) hardware supports the Gen III PCMs, but not the later Gen IV CAN bus systems. EFILive's V2 (Version 2) hardware supports both Gen III and Gen IV ECMs and PCMs. Both V1 and V2 use the same scanning and tuning software.

HP Tuners' scan-and-tune package supports both Gen III and Gen IV ECMs and PCMs (bottom). The C.A.T.S. OBD-II Tuner is a tuning package only. Early versions of the C.A.T.S OBD-II Tuner supports the Gen III PCMs, (middle) but not the later Gen IV CAN bus systems. The later version of the C.A.T.S. OBD-II Tuner supports both Gen III and Gen IV ECMs and PCMs (top).

CHAPTER 4

vehicle use, as the device is locked to that vehicle once calibration changes are made. They allow updates related to spark timing, fuel delivery, idle speed, transmission shift behavior, and other basic parameters.

Before purchasing a handheld tuner, consider the modifications you want to make to your engine and transmission and consult a professional tuner to determine if the device is sufficient to fully tune your engine and transmission. An inexpensive handheld tuner may only be able to adjust the spark and fuel tables by 10 percent. Priced at nearly half the cost of a laptop tuning package such as EFILive FlashScan, you may be better off spending the extra money on a professional scan-and-tune package to gain much more access to the PCM and be able to monitor and log real-time data.

Tuning Equipment

Having the right tools for the job goes a long way in getting your Gen III PCM-controlled engine swap running well. A professional tuner has the equipment necessary for providing a quality tuning solution. Due to the high costs associated with some tuning equipment, you may choose to only purchase some of the equipment related to custom tuning and PCM data acquisition.

Laptop PC

Most modern tuning and data acquisition software are compatible with Microsoft Windows operating systems. For this reason, most tuners rely on either a laptop or desktop PC. With the OBD-II diagnostic connector located inside the vehicle, it is most common for tuners to use a laptop PC. Although most hardware cables rely on a USB connection, some require a serial port connection with a PC, so it is important to review the requirements of the tuning equipment before purchasing a PC.

Data Acquisition

Making changes to the PCM calibration requires knowledge about engine and transmission operation. You simply cannot make assumptions about engine and transmission performance to make accurate changes to the PCM calibration. While OBD-II parameters reveal much of the needed information to make changes to a PCM calibration, additional information is required from data acquisition equipment such as a wide-band O_2 sensor and dynamometer.

Scan-and-Tune Package: High-end tuning software packages such

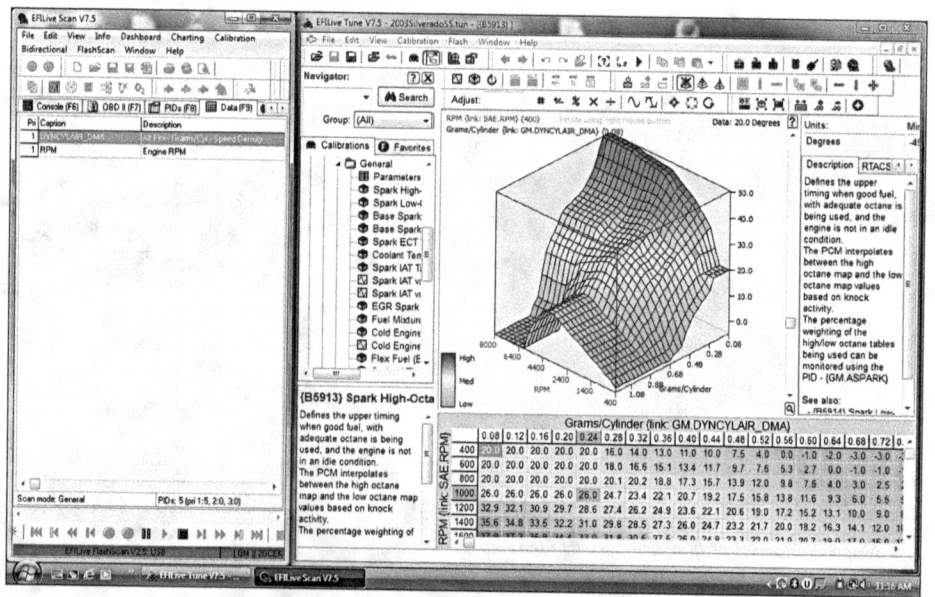

Innovate Motorsports offers a laptop or gauge wide-band O_2 sensor solution (LC-1, left) and a handheld wide-band O_2 sensor solution (LM-2, right). Either type is an important tool in the tuning process to determine how rich or lean the exhaust gases are. With no defects in engine hardware and use of a flow-matched set of injectors, the air/fuel ratio should be very similar for bank 1 and bank 2. Some technicians use a wide-band O_2 sensor in both bank 1 and bank 2 for increased accuracy. When you need to adjust the fueling for individual cylinders, a wide-band O_2 sensor (middle) may be installed after each exhaust port.

With both tuning software and scanning software open at the same time, you can monitor real-time data within the tuning software to recognize where the engine is operating within the tuning software's tables and parameters.

TUNING SOFTWARE AND EQUIPMENT

The DashDAQ XL is an advanced OBD-II scan tool that allows for retrieval of GM-specific DTCs. It also features generic and enhanced PID selection through customization of gauge settings, data logging, and GPS navigation. (Photo Courtesy Drew Technologies, Inc.)

Narrow-band O_2 sensors (left) are used by the Gen III PCMs to monitor an air/fuel ratio of approximately 14.7:1. The narrow-band O_2 sensors are unable to accurately indicate a wide range of air/fuel mixtures. Wide-band O_2 sensors (right) are capable of indicating a wide range of air/fuel mixtures, which is a requirement of the custom PCM tuning process.

as EFILive, HP Tuners, and LS1Edit include data logging scan software. Having both tuning and scanning software in one package is very convenient. EFILive presents users with the ability to monitor real-time data within the tuning software to identify where the engine is operating within the graphical representation of the PCM's calibration.

Low-end tuning software packages such as Tuner Cat OBD-II Tuner and JET Performance Dynamic Spectrum Tuner only offer tuning software and require additional tools for monitoring data logging. If you are already familiar with standalone scanning equipment you may find the lower cost of these tuning packages to be attractive. Comparatively, with integrated real-time data logging, some scan-and-tune packages have more features to offer within the tuning software.

Tuners not using a scan-and-tune suite use some other method of data retrieval. Drew Technologies offers the DashDAQ, a high-end scan tool for OBD-II vehicles. By default, the DashDAQ comes with standard OBD-II PID monitoring and has the addon option of enhanced GM PIDs. Up to two analog and two digital input devices can be added for additional monitoring.

Wide-Band O_2 Sensor: The Gen III PCMs use two narrow-band O_2 sensors to determine if the engine is operating at a 14.7:1 air/fuel ratio. One O_2 sensor is located in the exhaust for each bank of cylinders. Due to its design, a narrow-band O_2 sensor returns a signal voltage between 0 and 1V that can only indicate rich or lean based on a target air/fuel ratio of 14.7:1, which is an air/fuel ratio ideal for idle, moderate acceleration, and cruise conditions. To tune for heavy acceleration, wide open throttle (WOT), and lean cruise, an air/fuel ratio other than 14.7:1 must be targeted, which is a job for a wide-band O_2 sensor. For this reason, any professional tuner relies on one or more wide-band O_2 sensors during the tuning process. Once the PCM has been calibrated, wide-band O_2 sensor(s) are removed.

Engine or Chassis Dynamometer: A dynamometer (or dyno) is a tool used by professional tuners to operate the engine (on an engine dyno) or vehicle (on a chassis dyno) through its RPM range to receive feedback data, apply calibration changes, and test applied calibration changes. Not all dynos have the ability to apply a load to the engine/vehicle through the RPM range, so in some cases fully tuning the PCM may require a load-bearing dynamometer. A common use for any dyno is to determine peak horsepower and torque. Tuners who

This engine dyno is used by TPIS to break in new engines, tune engine controllers, and test for maximum horsepower and torque. An engine dyno allows the tuner to operate an engine in a safe, controlled setting while making changes to the engine controller's calibration settings. By applying a load to the engine, the tuner can adjust calibration settings for operating conditions that are not possible without installing the engine into a vehicle and going for a drive.

CHAPTER 4

A chassis dyno (this one used by Smokey's Dyno & Performance) allows the tuner to simulate certain driving conditions by applying a load to the rotating drum being turned by the vehicle's wheels. This load is transferred through the drivetrain to the engine and allows the tuner to adjust calibration settings for operating conditions that are not possible without driving on the road.

use a dyno ought to pay just as much attention to cold-start and idle tuning as they do to WOT tuning.

Emulation PCM: Flashing a PCM with an updated calibration takes about 30 seconds and requires the engine to be stopped (ignition off) and then restarted after the programming process has been completed. An efficient alternative is to use an emulator that allows direct access to the PCM's flash memory through a USB connection with a laptop PC. The Moates.net 16-Bit Realtime Emulation PCM is used by both professionals and enthusiasts with either EFILive or Tuner Cat software to make quick work of reprogramming an LS-series PCM. (See Chapter 4 for more information on tuning software.)

Benchtop Programming Cable

Many tuners find reasons to reprogram PCMs out of the vehicle. Professional tuners sell calibrations through mail-order PCM tuning services. The Gen III PCMs require a 12V battery, switched ignition, ground, and a serial data circuit for programming. Many wire harness shops offer benchtop programming harnesses to power up and reprogram the PCM outside the vehicle. If you are in the market for such a solution, consider your current and future programming needs before making a purchase.

Most Gen III PCM benchtop programming harnesses are fully sufficient to reprogram the PCM out of the vehicle using a simple 12V power supply hookup. These harnesses pass through the 12V battery, switched ignition, ground, and serial data circuit. An OBD-II diagnostic connector is included for the programming interface cable connection. Some benchtop programming harnesses include a convenient AC to DC regulated 12V power supply.

A high-end benchtop programming solution, such as EFI Connection's Professional Series OBD-II Programming System, uses an enclosed circuit board to support J1962 compliance. The J1962 specification is implemented by automobile manufacturers as a standardization of the OBD-II connector cavity assignments. What this means is that as long as manufacturers continue to implement the J1962 specification, this benchtop programming solution is compatible with all 1996-newer OBD-II interface cables and programming equipment.

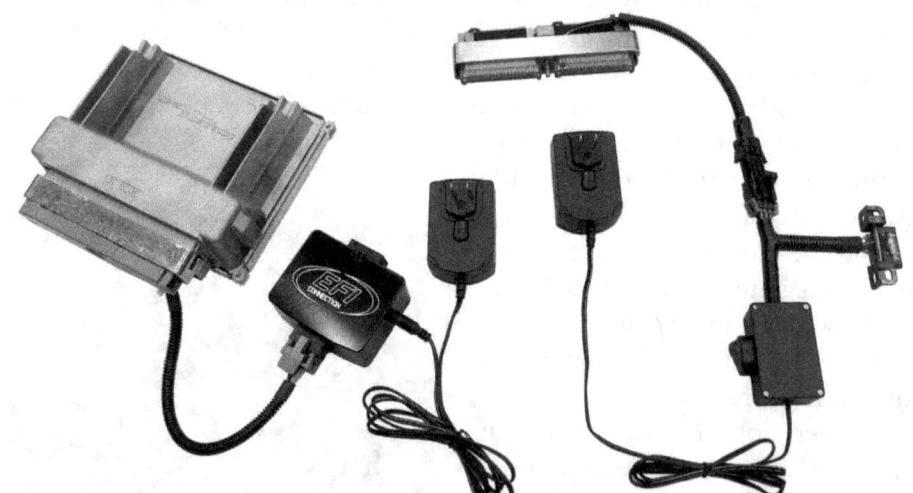

EFI Connection offers a few different solutions for powering an ECM or PCM outside a vehicle. A hobbyist solution (right) is specific to Gen III and Gen IV GM systems while a professional solution (left) supports the SAE J1962 OBD-II recommendation for all vehicle manufacturers.

CHAPTER 5

SENSORS AND INPUTS

Vehicles are equipped with a variety of sensors that are used by the PCMs to perform their intended functions. Since the introduction of GM electronic fuel injection, the sensors have changed in form, but not function. In most cases, early GM sensors are directly compatible with the Gen III PCMs. They all have significant importance to the PCM.

Throttle Position Sensor

The purpose of a TPS is to indicate to the PCM the angle of the throttle blade. For cable throttle systems, this sensor directly represents the driver's expectations related to acceleration and deceleration. At closed throttle, the TPS supplies a signal of approximately .5V to indicate idle and a signal of up to 5V to indicate WOT. The PCM commands additional fueling during WOT by entering the power enrichment (PE) mode.

Early sensors have slotted mounting holes that allow the sensor to be mechanically zeroed; that is, set to a specified low voltage (approximately .5V) at closed throttle to indicate 0 percent TPS to the PCM. Late sensors

General Motors has used a variety of TPSs with its engines. They generally all perform the same function of returning a voltage signal to the PCM to reference throttle angle. Shown here, the top left TPS is used with 1996-newer Vortec V-6, Vortec V-8, Ram Jet 350, and many Gen III engines. The middle left TPS is used with 1992–1997 LT1 and Ram Jet 502 engines. The top right TPS is used with the 5.0L and 5.7L TPI engines.

It is not safe to assume that a replacement TPS is accurate based on looks alone. For each of these sensors, there are look-alike sensors with the same housing, but they are not compatible. As an example, the early TBI sensor looks like the TPI sensor, but they are specific to their application.

The 1999–2002 truck TPS (bottom left) is mounted on the throttle body toward the bank 1 side of the engine because the truck throttle body has the electronic motor toward the bank 2 side of the engine. The 1999–2002 Corvette TPS (bottom right) is mounted on the throttle body toward the bank 2 side of the engine because the Corvette throttle body has the electronic motor toward the bank 1 side of the engine. These sensor housings each contain two sensors. As the throttle is opened or closed, the sensors operate with opposite voltage changes. Although the truck and Corvette TPS look the same, they are not interchangeable.

CHAPTER 5

are nonadjustable and if TPS voltage at closed throttle is within an allowable range, the PCM auto-zeros the TPS signal (percentage of calculated throttle angle).

The LS1 and LS6 Corvette throttle body was also used with the LS6 engine in the 2004–2005 Cadillac CTS-V. This throttle body looks similar to the 1999–2002 truck throttle body, but is not interchangeable as the TPS and actuator motor are on opposite sides of the housing. The Corvette throttle body has a six wire TPS mounted toward the bank 2 side of the engine and an electronic motor toward bank 1 side of the engine.

TPI Throttle Position Sensors

The early TPS (1985–1989) allows for adjustment so that a closed throttle signal can be adjusted to a recommended .54V and sweep to more than 4.0V at WOT. The late TPS (1990–1992) is not designed to be adjustable because the ECM auto-zeros the TPS. This TPS uses a different harness connector than the LT1 and LS-series sensors.

LT1 Throttle Position Sensors

The LT1 throttle body changed to accept a new style of TPS. General Motors installed nonadjustable sensors. The aftermarket has adjustable sensors available to allow for signal adjustment if, after an aftermarket throttle body upgrade, the PCM cannot auto-zero the TPS. An adjustable TPS may be appropriate for poorly manufactured aftermarket throttle bodies known to require TPS adjustment. This type of TPS housing uses a different connector than the early TBI and TPI sensors.

LS-Series Throttle Position Sensors—Cable

The LS-series (4.8L, 5.3L, 5.7L, 6.0L, and 8.1L) TPS is nonadjustable and uses the same harness connector as the LT1 sensor. This TPS is interchangeable among 1999–2002 LS-series engines with the exception of electronic throttle systems.

LS-Series Throttle Position Sensors—Electronic

Early LS-series throttle position sensors for electronic throttle systems are unlike any TPS used with a cable throttle system. Electronic throttle systems use an APP sensor, TAC module, and TPS to electronically operate the throttle blade. For these systems, the TPS is used by both the PCM and the TAC module to indicate throttle angle. These sensors vary in appearance, but have the task of reporting two opposite voltages. (See Chapter 8 for more information about electronic throttle systems.)

While the LS2 throttle body is considered Gen IV equipment, it is electronically compatible (and often used as an upgrade) with the LS1/LS6 Corvette and 2004–2005 LS6 Cadillac CTS-V. All Gen IV GM throttle bodies have integrated TPSs. In the event that a TPS goes bad, the entire throttle body assembly needs to be replaced.

EFI Connection's 52 mm, 58 mm, and Mono Blade electronic TPI, LT1, and Ram Jet 502 throttle bodies are essentially an LS1/LS6 Corvette throttle body in a new housing. These throttle bodies are built from new LS1/LS6 Corvette throttle bodies. A replacement TPS can be obtained through General Motors through service as any LS1 or LS6 Corvette.

The throttle body used with 1999–2002 GM trucks looks similar to the LS1/LS6 Corvette throttle body, but is not interchangeable because the TPS and actuator motor are on opposite sides of the housing. This truck throttle body was used with the 7.4L engine in 1999–2000 medium duty trucks and 1999–2002 trucks equipped with electronic throttle.

SENSORS AND INPUTS

Throttle Position Sensor

Application	Cavity	Wire Color	Function
5.0L/5.7L TPI	A	Black	Low Reference
	B	Dark Blue	Signal
	C	Gray	5V Reference
LT1, LS-Series	A	Gray	5V Reference
	B	Black	Low Reference
	C	Dark Blue	Signal
1997–2004 Corvette, 2004–2005 CTS-V	A	Dark Green	5V Reference
	B	Purple	Low Reference
	C	Dark Blue	Sensor 1 Signal
	D	Yellow/Black	5V Reference
	E	White	Low Reference
	F	Pink	Sensor 2 Signal
1999–2002 5.3L, 6.0L, 7.4L Electronic Throttle	A	Gray	5V Reference
	B	Black	Low Reference
	C	Dark Green	Sensor 1 Signal
	D	Light Blue/Black	5V Reference
	E	Black/White	Low Reference
	F	Purple	Sensor 2 Signal

With the IAC housing removed from the bottom of the throttle body assembly, you can see the IAC passage. The pintle, attached to the electronic valve, is moved in one direction or the other to allow engine vacuum to pull air through the IAC passage. Sometimes this passage is dirty with carbon buildup and must be cleaned to restore proper function. The passage at the bottom here is for engine coolant. The warm coolant temperature keeps the throttle body from sticking in very cold weather conditions, but General Motors ultimately eliminated the coolant passage in newer throttle bodies.

Idle Air Control Valve

Cable-driven throttle systems require air to bypass the closed throttle blade(s) for an engine to idle well. The amount of air required is adjusted by the PCM through the IAC valve. The IAC is an electrical valve that moves a pintle (pin/bolt) one direction or the other to add or subtract airflow around the throttle blade(s) through a small passage within the throttle body housing. Although some IAC valves appear to look the same, they vary in pintle shape and spring tension. It is important that the IAC valve matches the housing. The LS-series PCMs control all TPI, LT1, and LS1 IAC valves. The only exception is PCMs from vehicles not equipped with cable throttle.

Electronic throttle systems do not use an IAC valve. The Gen III electronic throttle systems use the TAC module to add or remove throttle blade angle to adjust the amount

These are just a few GM IAC valves. The TPI engine IAC valve (left) has a slightly different conical pintle shape than the others. Also unique to the TPI (and 1992–1993 LT1) is the harness connector. Clearly, the LT1 engine IAC valve (middle) cannot be used with the LS-series engine IAC valve (right) because the pintle design is different. The LT1 and LS1 IAC valves accept the same harness connector.

of incoming air at idle. The Gen IV systems have throttle control built within the ECM; they also adjust the throttle for idle. Because the throttle area is so much larger than an idle air passage, electronic throttle systems can adjust the amount of incoming air more quickly than cable throttle systems. For engines with aggressive camshafts, this means better control of the engine at idle.

TPI IAC Valves

At first glance, all TPI IAC valves appear to be the same. However, the late TPI IAC valves do not interchange with the early TPI throttle body lower IAC housings. Be sure that the IAC valve matches the year, make, and model of your throttle body.

LT1 IAC Valves

The late TPI IAC is used with 1992 and 1993 LT1 engines. This IAC is functionally the same as the 1994–1997 IAC valves, but they do not interchange due to the differences in the throttle body lower IAC housings. The 1994 IAC stands alone while the 1995–1997 IAC is interchangeable. The late LT1 IAC valve interchanges with the Ram Jet 502.

Gen I Vortec Truck IAC Valves

General Motors used the same IAC from 1996 to 2005 for the 4.3, 5.0, and 5.7L Vortec trucks. This IAC does not interchange with LT1

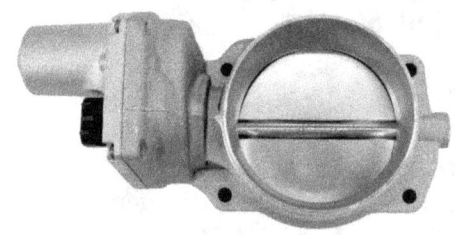

Electronic throttle bodies, such as this LS2 throttle body, have no IAC passage. Rather than use a redundant motor to add or remove air during idle, the TAC system uses its IAC function to rapidly open and close the throttle blade angle for a smooth idle. Consider how much more quickly an electronic throttle body can adjust idle airflow for engines fitted with an aggressive camshaft.

or LS1 throttle bodies. Having the same throttle body housing as the Vortec engines, the Ram Jet 350 IAC interchanges with the Gen I Vortec truck IAC.

Gen III IAC Valves

Among the Gen III IAC valves (4.8, 5.3, 5.7, 6.0, and 8.1L), the only one that stands alone is for the 1998–1999 Camaro and Firebird. All other IAC valves are interchangeable.

Ram Jet 350 IAC Valves

The Ram Jet 350 uses the same throttle body housing as the Gen I Vortec truck. The IAC valve interchanges with the Gen I Vortec throttle bodies.

This Ram Jet 502 throttle body is essentially the same housing as the LT1 throttle body. Between the two 48-mm throttle openings and toward the bottom of the hourglass-shaped feature is a hole that mates to the IAC passage in the lower IAC housing. On the other side of the throttle blades is a passage that receives engine vacuum. When the IAC valve is closed, the engine vacuum cannot pull air through the IAC passage. As the PCM commands the IAC valve open, the engine receives additional air through the IAC passage. Notice the Ram Jet 502 lower IAC housing is not designed for coolant flow.

Ram Jet 502 IAC Valves

The GM Ram Jet 502 throttle body uses the same IAC as the 1995–1997 LT1 engines.

Engine Coolant Temperature Sensor

The PCM relies heavily upon the temperature of the engine. The engine coolant temperature (ECT)

Idle Air Control (IAC) Valve

5.0L/5.7L TPI and Early LT1			1994-up LT1 and LS Series		
Cavity	Wire Color	Function	Cavity	Wire Color	Function
A	Light Blue/White	IAC Coil A High	A	Light Green/Black	IAC Coil B Low
B	Light Blue/Black	IAC Coil A Low	B	Light Green/White	IAC Coil B High
C	Light Green/White	IAC Coil B High	C	Light Blue/Black	IAC Coil A Low
D	Light Green/Black	IAC Coil B Low	D	Light Blue/White	IAC Coil A High

SENSORS AND INPUTS

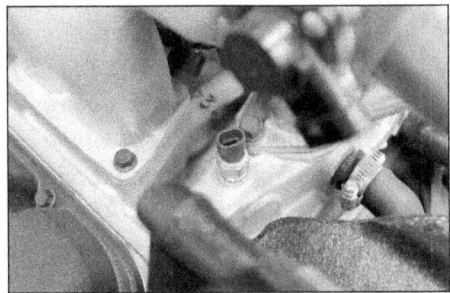

ECT sensors were commonly located in the front intake manifold coolant passage near the thermostat housing. This was convenient for cast-aluminum manifolds, but impossible for LS-series engines due to the intake manifold design. This Ram Jet 502 engine has an ECT sensor within the intake manifold front coolant passage. LT1 engines locate the ECT sensor in the front of the water pump. LS-series engines locate the ECT sensor in the bank 1 cylinder head.

The TPI ECT sensor (left) has a steel housing and is installed in the front of the intake manifold. The LT1 ECT sensor (right) is functionally the same, but has a brass housing. Featuring the same 3/8-inch, 18 NPT thread, the replacement TPI sensor is now the same as the LT1 ECT sensor.

LS-series engines have a M12 x 1.5 threaded hole in the cylinder head for the installation of an ECT sensor. The 1998 F-Body instrument cluster requires a sending unit for measuring engine coolant temperature. Rather than install a sending unit in the cylinder head, General Motors used a three-wire ECT (left) that serves the function of a sensor (for the PCM) and a sending unit (for the coolant temperature gauge). The most common ECT sensor (right) is used with all other LS-series engines. LS-series vehicles fitted with this two-wire sensor use the PCM's data stream output to display the calculated engine coolant temperature.

sensor is commonly located in either the intake manifold or the cylinder head and measures the temperature of engine coolant. The PCM uses the ECT signal for turning on and off electric fans, ignition timing, fueling, and many other functions.

ECT with 3/8-Inch, 18 NPT Thread

The most common ECT sensor among Gen I engines installs into a 3/8-inch, 18 NPT threaded hole in the engine's intake manifold. The Gen II (LT1) uses this sensor, but it is located in the front of the water pump. This sensor is used with all TPI, LT1, and Gen I Vortec engines.

Engine Coolant Temperature (ECT) Sensor

TPI/LT1/LS-Series

Cavity	Wire Color	Function
A	Black	Low Reference
B	Yellow	Signal

ECT with 1/4-Inch, 18 NPT Thread

While not used with any Gen I, II, or III engine, Delphi sensor # 12146911 is functionally the same as the sensor used with Gen I and II engines, but installs into a 1/4-inch, 18 NPT threaded hole.

ECT with M12 x 1.5 Thread

All Gen III engines have an M12 x 1.5 thread in the cylinder head for the ECT sensor. There are two sensors: one for the 1998 Camaro/Firebird and one for all other Gen IIIs. The ECT sensor used with the 1998 Camaro and Firebird has a built-in sending unit for the coolant temperature gauge in the instrument cluster. These sensors are functionally the same as the sensor used with Gen I and II engines.

Air Temperature Sensor

The intake air temperature (IAT) sensor is used by the PCM to determine the temperature of the air entering the engine. This temperature data is used to determine fuel and spark calibrations. In most applications, the IAT is located ahead of the throttle body and in the airstream.

TPI engines, however, locate a manifold air temperature (MAT) sensor in the bottom of the upper plenum. The IAT and MAT produce the same signals and are used in the same way with the PCM. Because a sensor mounted in the aluminum plenum becomes heat soaked, a better location for the sensor is ahead of the throttle body.

CHAPTER 5

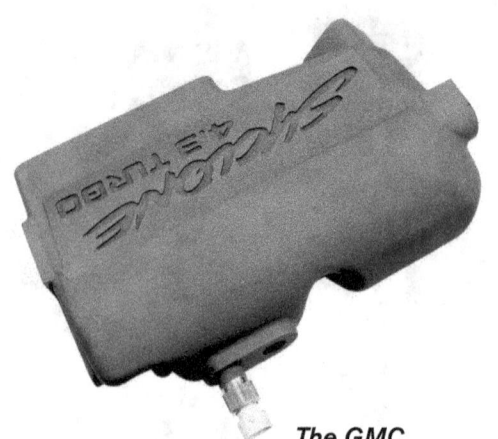

The GMC Syclone measures the temperature of incoming air through an IAT sensor mounted in the upper aluminum plenum. The TPI engine does the same. Because of heat soak through the aluminum intake manifold, the most accurate reading of incoming air temperature is in the airstream and ahead of the throttle body.

Intake Air Temperature Sensor

A variety of IAT sensors are used among the many GM fuel-injected engines. These sensors differ in form only, as their function remains the same. The GM IAT sensors may be used interchangeably. The late IAT sensors are located within the mass airflow (MAF) sensor assembly. If a MAF sensor is your preference, it is easiest to use a MAF sensor with integrated IAT. For speed density configurations (no MAF sensor), there are several sensors to choose from, so finding the right sensor to fit your intake air tubing should be easy.

Intake Air Temperature (IAT) Sensor

TPI/LT1/LS-Series

Cavity	Wire Color	Function
A	Black	Low Reference
B	Tan	Signal

General Motors has used a variety of IAT sensors. The LS1 IAT sensor (top left) requires a grommet or rubber intake tubing for installation. Some GM vehicles use an IAT with a wide flange and foam seal (top middle). Some TPI engines use a sensor with a brass housing and visible thermistor (top right); other TPI engines use a sensor with a steel housing and sealed thermistor (bottom left). The sensor with a steel housing can be replaced by a sensor with a brass housing (bottom right). The two bottom sensors are used interchangeably as an ECT sensor.

Manifold Air Temperature Sensor

The MAT sensor is used with TPI engines to determine the temperature of air entering the engine. This brass sensor has a 3/8-inch, 18 NPT thread and is located in the bottom of the upper plenum. The Camaro and Firebird use the same ECT sensor as the MAT sensor while most Corvettes use a similar brass sensor with a visible thermistor. Although the signals are the same, these two sensors are not interchangeable without changing the harness connector. These sensors become heat soaked as the aluminum intake manifold increases in temperature.

Many TPI owners relocate the MAT sensor ahead of the throttle body or replace it with an IAT sensor ahead of the throttle body. The MAT sensor signal is the same as the IAT signal.

Mass Airflow Sensor

The MAF sensor is used by the PCM to directly measure weight (or mass) of air that enters the engine to control fuel delivery. The MAF signal, measured in hertz (Hz), is interchangeable among the LT1 and LS1 sensors. The early 1985–1989 TPI MAF sensor is not compatible with the LS-series PCM. In fact, the Gen IV MAF sensors are also compatible with the LT1 and Gen III PCMs.

TPI MAF Sensor (1985–1989)

The TPI MAF sensor outputs a 0–5V analog signal to the ECM. This signal is not compatible with the Gen III PCMs.

Three-Wire MAF Sensor (1994–2002)

The common three-wire MAF sensor was introduced with the 1994 LT1 vehicles. It can be found in many 1996–2002 vehicles, including Camaro, Firebird, Corvette, and GM trucks. This sensor measures 78 mm in airflow diameter.

Five-Wire MAF Sensor (2000–2007)

Perhaps the most desirable MAF sensor for Gen III LS engine conver-

SENSORS AND INPUTS

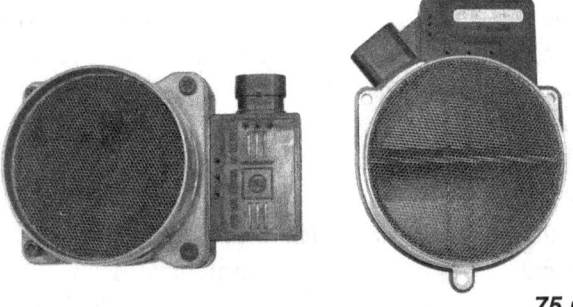

Several MAF sensors have been used with LS-series PCMs. The first LS1 MAF sensor (top left) was introduced in 1994 for use with the LT1 engine. This three-wire sensor has an inside diameter of approximately 75 mm and was used with the 1994–2000 Corvette, 1994–2002 F-Body, and 2004 GTO.

A larger sensor was introduced with the 1999 LS-series truck engines and has an inside diameter of approximately 85 mm (top right). This MAF sensor incorporated an IAT sensor, a convenience for finding a difficult location for an external IAT sensor.

In 2006, a slot-type five-wire MAF (bottom) was used with the Corvette. The slot-type MAF can be custom mounted by welding an aluminum boss (GM# 19166574) to an aluminum intake tube. Although these MAF sensors are compatible with the LS-series PCMs, MAF frequency table calibration changes are required.

The three-wire GM MAF sensor introduced with the 1994 LT1 engine was also used with LS1 engines. These sensors are interchangeable. The inside diameter measures approximately 75 mm. TPIS offers a new aluminum housing for this MAF to increase airflow by more than 300 cfm.

Slot-Type MAF Sensor

The LS7 6.2 and 7.0L Corvette engine introduced a five-wire MAF sensor that inserts in the side of the intake air tubing ahead of the throttle body. This sensor outputs a frequency that is compatible with the Gen III PCMs. It may be mounted in any size of inlet tubing ahead of

sions is the five-wire version that was introduced with the 2000 GM trucks. Its extra two wires are used for the internal IAT sensor. Having the IAT within the MAF housing is very convenient. This sensor is also used with the 2001–2007 Corvette and 2005–2006 GTO. The inside airflow diameter of this sensor measures 85 mm. Engine calibrations that were set for the earlier 78-mm MAF requires updates to the MAF frequency table for proper fuel delivery.

All GM trucks with a Gen III engine use a five-wire MAF sensor with an inside diameter that measures approximately 85 mm. The extra two wires are used with the integrated IAT sensor. This MAF sensor was also used with the LS1 and LS6 Corvette and LS6 Cadillac CTS-V.

The common 85-mm truck and Corvette MAF sensor contains an internal thermistor that provides the IAT signal to the PCM. The IAT is clearly visible in the MAF sensor housing. By using the IAT sensor within the MAF housing, there is no need for an external IAT to be mounted in the airstream ahead of the throttle body.

Mass Airflow (MAF) Sensor

LT1/LS1

Cavity	Wire Color	Function
A	Yellow	Signal
B	Black/White	Ground
C	Pink	12V Ignition

LS-Series Truck and 2001-up Corvette

Cavity	Wire Color	Function
A	Purple	IAT Low Reference
B	Tan	IAT Signal
C	Black/White	Ground
D	Pink	12V Ignition
E	Yellow	MAF Signal

CHAPTER 5

Commonly referred to as the LS3 MAF sensor, the slot-type MAF sensor was introduced with the LS7 engine in the 2006 Z06 Corvette (and later with the LS3 engine in the 2008 Corvette). This sensor is functionally the same as the 85-mm five-wire MAF sensor, but requires MAF frequency table calibration changes for proper use.

the throttle body. For big-cubic-inch engines and/or forced induction, this sensor is a good choice.

Manifold Absolute Pressure Sensor

The manifold absolute pressure (MAP) sensor measures manifold pressure. Its signal is used by the PCM to control fuel delivery and ignition timing. The Gen III PCMs rely heavily on the use of a MAF sensor for fuel delivery; if the MAF fails, the PCM looks to the MAP sensor to calculate fuel delivery.

It has become rather common for engine conversions to eliminate the MAF sensor and for tuners to calibrate the PCM for MAP use only, otherwise known as "speed density." This system requires several factors to calculate fuel delivery, where a mass airflow system uses a direct measurement from the MAF.

Most MAP sensors are suitable for up to 1-bar intake manifold pressure. Without a supercharger or turbocharger, intake manifold pressures do not exceed 1 bar. The turbocharged GMC Syclone and Typhoon, along with the supercharged 3.8L Grand Prix GXP, require a 2-bar sensor because the turbocharger is capable of generating more than 1-bar pressure within the intake manifold. When forced-induction pressures exceed 2 bar, such as with the 1989 Turbo Trans Am, a 3-bar sensor is required.

Remote-Mount MAP Sensors

The most universal 1-bar MAP sensor is GM# 12569240. It is mounted to a bracket on the side of the 1990–1992 TPI plenum and uses a vacuum hose elbow connection to a fitting in the intake manifold plenum chamber. This sensor can be mounted to a vehicle's firewall while using a vacuum hose connection to a fitting on the intake manifold. If you supercharge or turbocharge your engine, a 2-bar MAP (GM# 12569241) supports up to about 14.7-psi boost, and a 3-bar MAP (GM# 12223861) supports up to about 29.7-psi boost. These 2- and 3-bar MAP sensors use the same housing as the 1-bar MAP sensor, but because the connector key configuration is not the same, the 1-bar green harness connector must be changed to the orange harness connector.

Be careful to choose the proper MAP sensor for your engine configuration. The PCM simply sees 0–5V from the MAP sensor. Regardless of MAP sensor (1-, 2-, or 3-bar), the output range is 0–5V. Choosing a 3-bar

Manifold Absolute Pressure (MAP) Sensor

Late TPI and LT1

Cavity	Wire Color	Function
A	Black	Low Reference
B	Light Green	Signal
C	Gray	5V Reference

LS-Series

Cavity	Wire Color	Function
A	Black	Low Reference
B	Light Green	Signal
C	Gray	5V Reference

The early GM MAP sensor (top) has a provision for being mounted just about anywhere it fits. All that is required is a vacuum hose from the intake manifold plenum to the sensor. This sensor is found on 1991–1992 TPI engines and 1992–1997 LT1 engines.

The LS1/LS6/LS2 MAP sensor (bottom left) is sealed to the intake manifold with a rubber seal. The MAP sensor used with the LS-series engine in the GM trucks (bottom middle) are functionally the same as the LS1/LS6/LS2 MAP sensor. The LS3 intake manifold accepts a different sensor (bottom right) that is not physically interchangeable with the other LS-series MAP sensors.

Although the signal to the PCM is basically the same, it is best to choose the sensor you want to use before tuning your PCM to avoid any potential differences in the signal voltage range.

SENSORS AND INPUTS

The remote-mount MAP sensor is mounted directly to the LT1 and Ram Jet 502 intake manifold using a rubber seal (GM# 1635948). This rubber seal may also be used with 2- and 3-bar remote-mount MAP sensors. Other applications do not require this seal, as a vacuum hose may be installed between the MAP sensor and a fitting on the intake manifold.

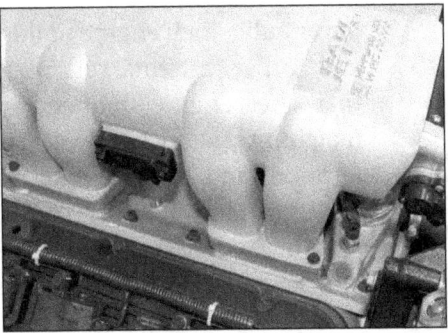

The Ram Jet 502 accepts the TPI and LT1-type MAP sensor with a mounting boss on the side of the intake manifold. A rubber seal (GM# 1635948) is used to seal the MAP to the intake manifold vacuum hole. For forced-induction applications, the Ram Jet 502 MAP can be changed out for a 2- or 3-bar sensor.

MAP sensor when MAP values do not exceed a 2-bar MAP sensor's range results in loss of lookup table resolution/definition for proper fueling.

Be sure to take advantage of a PCM custom operating system upgrade when using a 2- or 3-bar MAP sensor so that the PCM works best with the 0–5V range of the MAP sensor.

Manifold-Mount MAP Sensors

The manifold-mount MAP sensors are available in three different housings. The earliest MAP sensor is the same as the remote-mount TPI sensor, but is used with a seal. The OBD-II 4.3, 5.0, and 5.7L Vortec engines use a sensor housing that is also found on the 4.8, 5.3, and 6.0L LS-series truck engines. The sensor housing used with the LS1 Camaro, Firebird, Corvette, and GTO attaches slightly differently than the LS-series truck sensor.

The LT1 engines use the same remote-mount 1-bar MAP sensor as the TPI engine. However, the sensor is bolted to the front of the intake manifold and sealed with a rubber seal (GM# 1635948). General Motors used this same design with the Ram Jet 502 intake manifold.

For supercharged or turbocharged engines, a 2-bar MAP (GM# 12569241) supports up to about 14.7-psi boost, and a 3-bar MAP (GM# 12223861) supports up to about 29.7-psi boost. These 2- and 3-bar MAP sensors are a direct fit to the LT1 and Ram Jet 502 intake manifold, but because the connector key configuration is not the same, the 1-bar green harness connector has to be changed to the orange harness connector.

The OBD-II 4.3, 5.0, and 5.7L Vortec engines use the same sensor as the 4.8, 5.3, and 6.0L LS-series engines. These intake manifolds use plastic attaching tabs that break if you are not careful. The Ram Jet 350 engine also uses this MAP sensor, but is attached to the side of the intake manifold with a metal bracket. For supercharged or turbocharged engines, a 2-bar MAP (GM# 12615136) supports up to about 14.7-psi boost, and a 3.3-bar MAP (GM# 12623671) supports up to about 30-psi boost. These 2- and 3-bar MAP sensors are a direct fit to these truck-type intake manifolds and Ram Jet 350 intake manifold, and do not require a harness connector change.

The LS1, LS6, and LS2 intake manifolds use their own MAP sensor. It mounts to the intake manifold with one plastic clip. The MAP sensor is found at the rear of the LS1 and LS6 intake manifolds. The LS2 intake manifold relocates the MAP sensor to the front of the intake manifold with a plastic attaching clip.

For supercharged or turbocharged engines, a 2-bar MAP (GM# 12615136) supports up to about 14.7-psi boost, and a 3.3-bar MAP (GM# 12623671) supports up to about 30-psi boost. These 2- and 3-bar MAP sensors require slight modification to the housing to fit one of these intake manifolds. A harness connector change is not needed.

With the LS3 engine, General Motors introduced a Bosch MAP sensor in the same location as the LS2 manifold, but with an attaching bolt. While electronically compatible with the LS1/LS6/LS2 MAP sensor, the LS3 MAP sensor is not a direct fit to the early intake manifolds, uses a different harness connector, and its pin configuration is unique.

Knock Sensor

Knock sensors are used by the PCM to reduce ignition timing if detonation occurs. With varying frequencies produced by the engine, the knock sensor vibrates to generate a small voltage that is interpreted by

CHAPTER 5

The single-wire, resonant-type knock sensors are used with TPI, LT1, and LS-series engines. Because the knock sensor is designed for the application in which it is used, they are not all interchangeable.

The two-wire, flat-response-type knock sensors are used with Gen IV engines (left) and Vortec V-6 engines (right). The 1999-newer Gen III PCMs can accept the signal of either type of knock sensor.

larger-cubic-inch engine builds, and other aftermarket parts that alter engine frequencies, matching a knock sensor, its location, and PCM calibration details can be difficult.

There are two types of knock sensors used with the LS-series PCMs: resonant and flat response. The resonant sensor is a single-wire connection to the PCM and the flat-response sensor is a two-wire connection to the PCM.

Resonant Knock Sensor

The single-wire resonant knock sensor was introduced with early small-block engines. This sensor typically threads into one of the coolant plug holes near the center of the block just above the oil pan. TPI engines use only one knock sensor and, with the exclusion of the Camaro and Firebird, LT1 engines use two knock sensors. The sensors look the same, but are not interchangeable. LS-series engines use a similar knock sensor with a straight M10x1.5 thread. In the LS-series engine, resonant knock sensors are found under the intake manifold.

Flat-Response Knock Sensor

The two-wire, flat-response knock sensor requires either an attaching bolt

or stud for attachment to the engine. The flat-response knock sensor was introduced with the 2005 LS2 engine and with the 2001 4.3L Vortec engine. With proper calibration changes and a little engine wiring work, the early LS-series PCM can be configured to use the flat-response knock

The LS-series resonant knock sensors (left) are installed in the intake manifold valley cover and use an M10x1.5 thread. The Gen I and Gen II small-block resonant knock sensor (right) is typically installed near the bottom of the engine block in one of the 1/4-inch, 18 NPT threaded coolant drain holes.

The two-wire, flat-response knock sensor was used with the GM# 12200411 PCM and 2001–2002 4.3L V-6 engines. For SBC, LT1, BBC, and 4.3L V-6 installations where flat-response sensors are desirable, a mounting stud can be installed in the coolant drain hole. Gen IV LS-series engines accept the flat-response sensors on the sides of the engine block.

the PCM as normal (no ignition timing retard necessary) to severe (retard ignition timing by predetermined amount).

For best results, the knock sensor(s) should be located where detonation-related frequencies can be detected. The sensor should be of a design that accurately generates the appropriate voltages to the PCM when those frequencies occur. With the introduction of aftermarket valvetrain upgrades,

Resonant Knock Sensor

TPI, LT1, Gen III LS Series

Cavity	Wire Color	Function
A	Dark Blue	Signal

Flat-Response Knock Sensor

Gen IV LS Series

Cavity	Wire Color	Function
A	Blue	Signal
B	Gray	Return

The Gen IV engines attach the flat-response knock sensors to the engine block with a metric bolt. The through-hole diameter of the flat-response knock sensor does not allow for bolt attachment to a small-block coolant drain hole. Fortunately, and because the MEFI-5 ECM requires flat-response knock sensors, the marine market offers a mounting stud that allows for installation of flat-response knock sensors on a traditional small-block or big-block engine. As shown on this Ram Jet 502 engine, the flat-response knock sensor is attached to the engine using a mounting stud in a lower 1/4-inch, 18 NPT threaded hole.

sensors. It's a convenience for LS2 engine swaps into LS1 vehicles.

Oxygen Sensor

The purpose of an O_2 sensor (often abbreviated O_2S) is to generate a signal voltage to the PCM that represents the air/fuel ratio. The target air/fuel ratio for engines burning pump gas is 14.7 parts air to 1 part fuel. This balanced reaction of combustion is referred to as the stoichiometric point. This is where the engine burns fuel most cleanly while generating low emissions.

But don't write this off as being important for emissions only. A controlled 14.7:1 ratio keeps an engine clean. You can also hear the engine run well at idle when it is producing exhaust gases at the stoichiometric point. During the tuning process, and while at idle, as the fuel calibration is changed to target the stoichiometric point, the engine begins to sound unstrained and RPM increases.

Closed-Loop Operation

Upon engine startup, the PCM does not immediately use the O_2S signals to adjust the injector pulse times. This operation is called "open loop" because the feedback from each O_2S is ignored while the PCM calculates injector pulse times based on calibrated values. After a predetermined amount of time and engine coolant temperature, the PCM enters "closed loop" and monitors the O_2S signals. In closed loop, the PCM applies fuel trims to each bank of injectors in an effort to achieve the point of stoichiometry.

When the O_2S signal voltage is low (below 450 millivolts, or mV), the PCM detects a lean air/fuel mixture and adjusts the injector pulse times to add more fuel to the bank of cylinders that is running lean. When the O_2S signal voltage is high (above 450 mV), the PCM detects a rich air/fuel mixture and adjusts the injector pulse times to take away fuel to the bank of cylinders that is running rich. At an O_2S signal voltage of 450 mV, the PCM zeros the fuel trims and does not apply adjustments to the injector pulse times.

There are two types of fuel trims: short-term fuel trim (STFT) and long-term fuel trim (LTFT). The PCM uses STFT to make quick, and continuously changing, percentage adjustments to the delivered amount of fuel by adjusting fuel injector pulse times while targeting the stoichiometric point. LTFT is less responsive than STFT and is used to make broader air/fuel mixture adjustments to compensate for wear and tear type conditions; for example, a small air leak from an intake manifold gasket.

For safety, STFT and LTFT have limits. It may seem beneficial to allow the fuel trims to replace calibrated fuel delivery values, so that a camshaft upgrade would not require custom tuning. However, over time O_2S performance degrades (slow response) or even fails, so this could lead to the demise of an engine that is controlled by a bad O_2S. Although the advertisements of aftermarket engine control units (ECUs) may seem to suggest it, no engine computer can (fully) tune itself.

Heating Circuit

All Gen III production vehicles have four heated oxygen sensors (HO_2S). Each sensor is electronically heated because the internal zirconia-sensing element only generates voltage when it is hotter than about 600 degrees F. The exhaust temperatures alone may not keep each HO_2S hot enough, especially when the engine is operating at idle for an extended amount of time.

Early LS-series production vehicles use 12V ignition and a battery ground to heat each O_2S. Later LS-series production vehicles use 12V ignition and a PCM-applied ground to heat each O_2S. With the PCM monitoring the O_2S heating circuit, a malfunction can be diagnosed through any OBD-II scan tool.

CHAPTER 5

Placement of Oxygen Sensors

The terms bank 1 and bank 2 refer to a set of engine cylinders. Bank 1 represents the side of the engine that begins with cylinder 1, or cylinders 1, 3, 5, and 7. Bank 2 represents the side of the engine that begins with cylinder 2, or cylinders 2, 4, 6, and 8.

Each bank contains two HO_2S: one before the catalytic converter and one beyond the converter. Each HO_2S before the converter is used by the PCM for fuel trims and each HO_2S beyond the converter is used to monitor the change in air/fuel mixture through the converter for emissions purposes.

Most "off road only" vehicles eliminate each rear HO_2S when catalytic converters are not installed.

The PCM only knows engine oil pressure through the use of an oil pressure sensor. Its purpose is to return a voltage that represents the engine oil pressure. Engines that have a 1/4-inch, 18 NPT threaded oil passage hole can use the 8.1L sensor (left). Engines that have a M16x1.5 threaded oil passage hole can use the LS-series sensor (right). They are functionally the same.

Oil Pressure Sensor

The oil pressure sensor is a three-wire sensor that returns a 0–5V signal to the PCM representing engine oil pressure.

Do not confuse it with an oil pressure sender used with the oil pressure gauge only, or an oil pressure switch that allows electrical current to pass when oil pressure exists.

The oil pressure sensor is used by the PCM for calibration logic and to broadcast the engine oil pressure through the OBD-II data stream to be used by the instrument cluster (not all vehicles) and displayed through an OBD-II scan tool.

Although the oil pressure sensor is not required by the PCM, it is a useful signal to have available through a scan tool. For engines on a test stand or dynamometer, this sensor eliminates the need for a separate oil pressure gauge. When using scanning software such as from EFILive, the oil pressure PID can be selected among the other PIDs that are monitored while the engine is running.

M16 x 1.5 Threads

The first oil pressure sensor was used with the 1997 Corvette. Until 2003, all other LS-series engines were fitted with an oil pressure sender used by the instrument cluster. The oil pressure sender was eliminated in 2003, and the sensor became standard with LS-series engines. For retrofits, the oil pressure sensor can be removed and replaced with an oil pressure sender compatible with the vehicle's oil pressure gauge.

The oil pressure sensor is located at the rear of the engine near the intake manifold. All LS-series engines have M16x1.5 threads for the oil pressure sensor.

1/4-inch, 18 NPT Threads

A sensor with a 1/4-inch, 18 NPT thread was used with the 2003–2007 8.1L engines. This sensor is an excellent solution for any early small- or big-block Chevy engine. For small-block installations at the rear of the engine, a 1/4- to 1/8-inch, 18 NPT adapter is required.

Vehicle Speed Sensor

The vehicle speed sensor (VSS) is a magnetic pickup used by the PCM to indicate vehicle speed. The sensor is commonly mounted in the transmission tailshaft housing and gets its signal from a toothed ring installed on the transmission output shaft. The early VSS (TPI and early LT1) mated to a plastic gear that meshed with another gear on the transmission output shaft.

Calibrating the VSS after a tire size change or gear ratio change used to be a big deal with TPI engine computers. The early TPI engine computer required a 2,000-pulse-per-mile signal and the late TPI engine computer required a 4,000-pulse-per-mile signal. To achieve these signals, you had to install a different set of internal VSS gears or use an aftermarket VSS interface module. The LS-series PCMs accommodate all of these GM VSS signals because the pulse count, tire size, and gear ratio are configurable within the PCM.

Oil Pressure Sensor		
LS-Series		
Cavity	Wire Color	Function
A	Black	Low Reference
B	Gray	5V Reference
C	Tan/White	Signal

SENSORS AND INPUTS

For transmissions that are set up with a mechanical speedometer drive only, a dual-purpose VSS can be used to drive the speedometer cable and generate a signal for the PCM to use to calculate wheel speed.

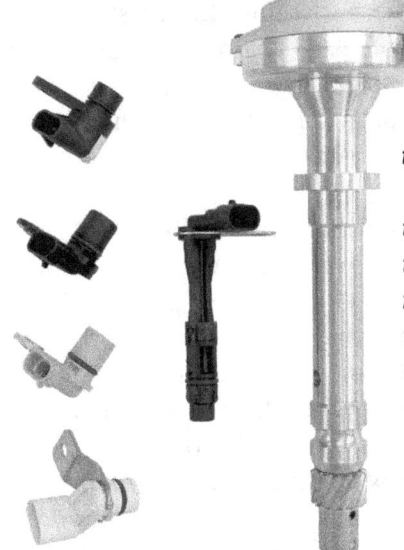

General Motors has used several different CMP sensors that perform the same function. The early 8.1L engines use a CMP sensor (top left) mounted in the front timing cover.

The late 8.1L engines used a different timing cover and camshaft timing sprocket that required a different CMP sensor (second from top left). The late 8.1L CMP was updated with a new housing and then used with the Gen IV engines in the front timing cover.

All Gen III engines use a CMP sensor (third from top left) mounted in the rear of the engine above the camshaft.

The Gen IV LS4 engine requires a CMP (bottom left) in a different location than all other Gen IV engines.

The Vortec V-6 and Vortec V-8 engines use a CMP sensor (middle) mounted within a distributor assembly. EFI Connection offers a cast-aluminum cap (right) that eliminates spark plug provision and keeps dirt and debris out of the distributor housing.

In situations where you do not know the pulse count from the VSS, use a chassis dynamometer to calibrate the PCM's VSS input. As long as you know tire size and gear ratio, the pulse count can be changed so that the VSS PID value matches the wheel speed of the dynamometer. Your local tuning facility can assist with VSS calibration.

Camshaft Position Sensor

The camshaft position (CMP) sensor supplies a 50-percent duty-cycle signal from the camshaft to the PCM to indicate the stroke (intake or exhaust) for any given cylinder. When the ignition key is turned the engine is started, the PCM monitors engine speed (RPM) and expects to see an increase in RPM to indicate that the engine has started. If this RPM increase does not occur, and the engine has not started, the PCM considers the cam signal faulty and assumes the opposite stroke in another effort to start the engine.

Symptoms of a bad CMP sensor or misalignment of the cam reluctor wheel include backfiring while cranking the engine to start and/or extended cranking before the engine starts. In addition, the PCM may set a DTC related to the cam sensor.

The PCM supplies a 12V reference, low reference, and receives a signal. General Motors offers several Hall effect (magnetic trigger) sensors; the following sensors perform the same function.

Rear-Mount CMP Sensor

Early LS-series engines have a CMP at the rear of the engine where a distributor is traditionally located. The sensor gets its signal from the camshaft. Although the harness connector is the same as the front-mount CMP, the connector cavity assignments are not the same.

Front Timing Cover CMP Sensor

Late LS-series engines have a CMP mounted in the front timing cover. The sensor gets its signal from

Camshaft Position (CMP) Sensor

Gen III LS-Series

Cavity	Wire Color	Function
A	Brown/White	Signal
B	Pink/Black	Low Reference
C	Red	12V Reference

Gen IV LS-Series

Cavity	Wire Color	Function
A	Red	12V Reference
B	Pink/Black	Low Reference
C	Brown/White	Signal

Vortec V6 and Gen I Vortec V8

Cavity	Wire Color	Function
A	Pink/Black	Low Reference
B	Brown/White	Signal
C	Red	12V Reference

CHAPTER 5

The Vortec V-6 and Vortec V-8 distributors contain a CMP sensor that gets its signal from a reluctor pressed onto the distributor shaft. This half-moon reluctor passes through the CMP sensor to return a 50-percent duty-cycle signal to the PCM that indicates the stroke (intake or exhaust) for any given cylinder.

Several CKP sensors have been used to read a signal from a reluctor mounted on the engine crankshaft. The 8.1L engine's CKP (left) is installed at the rear of the engine and ahead of the flywheel to return a 24x signal to the PCM.

All Gen III engines have a CKP sensor (middle) located just above the starter to return a 24x signal to the PCM.

Vortec V-6 and Vortec V-8 engines have provision for a CKP sensor (top right) in the bottom of the front timing cover to return a 3x (for V-6) or 4x (for V-8) signal to the PCM.

The 1999–2000 medium-duty truck 7.4L engine crankshafts are fitted with a 24x reluctor and CKP sensor (bottom right) in the bottom of the timing cover.

a pattern cast into the camshaft timing sprocket. The harness connector is the same as the rear-mount CMP; the connector cavity assignments are not the same.

Vortec Distributor CMP Sensor

The 1996–2002 Vortec distributor outputs the same 50-percent duty-cycle signal as the Gen III engines. The Vortec distributor requires proper orientation adjustment so that its signal falls correctly within the 24x crank signal. This CMP uses a different harness connector and its cavity assignments are different than the LS-series CMP.

Crankshaft Position Sensor

The CKP sensor outputs a square waveform to the PCM to indicate crankshaft position. Although there is no PID to monitor crankshaft location, the engine-speed (RPM) PID value is generated from the CKP sensor signal. The PCM supplies a 12V reference, low reference, and receives a signal voltage. General Motors offers several Hall effect sensors; the CKP sensors in this book perform the same function.

Gen III Engines

All LS-series CKP sensors are located in the side of the engine block, just above the starter. The CKP sensor gets its signal from a reluctor ring that is pressed onto the back of the crankshaft. (See Figure 5.1.)

The 1997 Corvette LS1 engine introduced a crankshaft reluctor that generates a 24-pulse square waveform to be used by any Gen III PCM to control a V-8 engine. The CKP sensor reads from this 24x reluctor, which has two rows of 24 teeth that are out of phase. The resulting signal consists of two different width pulses (12 and 3 degrees) that are 15 degrees apart.

Gen VII 8.1L Big-Block Engines

The 2001–2007 8.1L Vortec engines use the same PCM as the Gen III engines and have the same 24x crank signal requirement. The CKP sensor is located at the rear of the block, just ahead of the transmission,

Fig. 5.1. Early LS-series engines are fitted with a 24x crankshaft reluctor and CKP sensor capable of generating a 24-pulse signal (per 360 degrees of engine revolution) while the engine is rotating. This 24x signal is required by the PCM for engine operation.

SENSORS AND INPUTS

and extends toward the crankshaft to read a 24x signal from the crankshaft reluctor.

4.3L Vortec V-6 Engines

The 1996–2007 4.3L Vortec V-6 engines have a CKP sensor mounted in the timing cover. This CKP sensor reads from a three-tooth crank reluctor (3x) that is pressed onto the front snout of the crankshaft. (See Figure 5.2.)

All 4.3L Vortec V-6 engines use a single coil and distributor because the low-resolution 3x signal does not allow for coil-per-cylinder ignition.

The 2001–2002 4.3L Vortec V-6 vehicles use the same PCM as the 2001–2002 LS-series vehicles (GM# 12200411).

5.0L and 5.7L Vortec V-8 Engines

The 1996–2002 5.0L and 5.7L Vortec V-8 engines have a CKP sensor mounted in the timing cover. This CKP sensor reads from a four-tooth crank reluctor (4x) that is pressed onto the front snout of the crankshaft. (See Figure 5.3.)

All 5.0L and 5.7L Vortec V-8 engines use a single coil and distributor as the low-resolution 4x signal does not allow for coil-per-cylinder ignition.

The 2001–2002 5.0L and 5.7L Vortec V-8 vehicles use the same PCM as the 2001–2002 LS-series vehicles (GM# 12200411).

LT1 Engines

The 1996–1997 LT1 engines have a CKP sensor mounted in the timing cover. This CKP sensor reads from the same four-tooth crank reluctor (4x) that is used with the 5.0L and 5.7L Vortec V-8 engines. (See Figure 5.4.) Although the LT1 PCM looks to the Optispark distributor for crankshaft position, the 4x CKP signal is used for misfire detection.

7.4L Vortec V-8 Engines

The 1996–2000 7.4L Vortec V-8 engines have a CKP sensor mounted in the timing cover. Light-duty trucks (with engine RPO code L29) use a four-tooth crank reluctor (4x) pressed onto the front snout of the crankshaft. (See Figure 5.5.)

All L29 7.4L Vortec V-8 engines use a single coil and distributor because the low-resolution 4x signal does not allow for coil-per-cylinder ignition.

The 1999–2000 medium duty trucks (with engine RPO code L21) use a dual-pattern 24x crank reluctor with teeth that are out of phase. (See Figure 5.6.) This 24x signal is identical to the Gen III LS-Series and Gen VII 8.1L big-block crank signal.

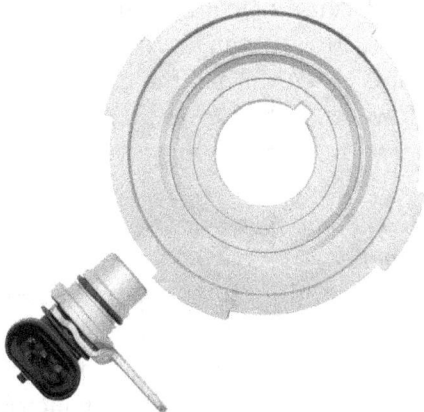

Fig. 5.4. The 1996–1997 LT1 engines are equipped with the same 4x crankshaft reluctor as the 1996-newer small-block engines. The CKP sensor is unique to the LT1 as the harness is routed toward the front (rather than the side) of the engine. The LT1's unique hub and balancer configuration creates clearance to allow for this 90-degree sensor. The 4x crankshaft signal is used for misfire detection and is not required by the PCM for engine operation. The LT1 PCM relies on the optical sensors within the Optispark distributor for engine operation.

Fig. 5.2. The 4.3L V-6 engines found in 1996-newer GM vehicles are equipped with a 3x crankshaft reluctor and a CKP sensor that is shared with the 1996-newer V-8 engines. This 3x signal is required by the PCM for engine operation.

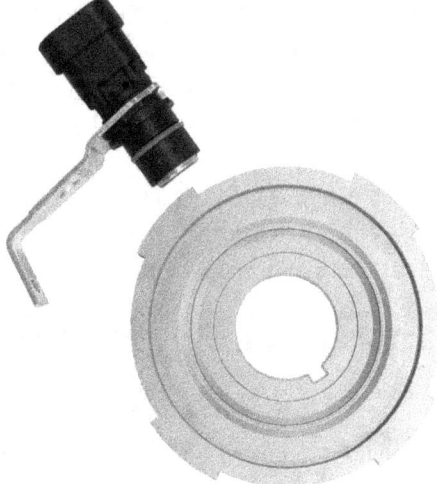

Fig. 5.3. The 5.0L and 5.7L V-8 engines found in 1996-newer GM vehicles are equipped with a 4x crankshaft reluctor and a CKP sensor that is shared with the 1996-newer V-6 engines. This 4x signal is required by the PCM for engine operation.

CHAPTER 5

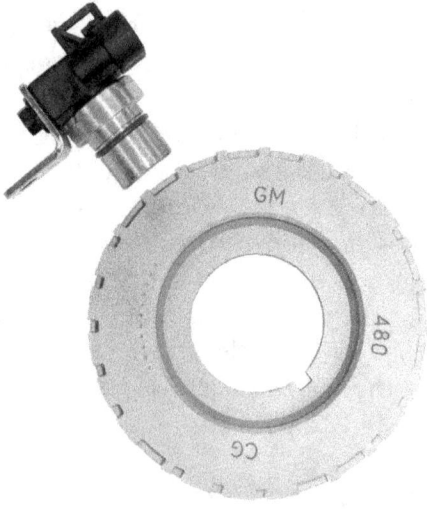

Fig. 5.5. Most 7.4L V-8 engines in 1996-newer GM vehicles are equipped with a 4x crankshaft reluctor and a CKP sensor that is shared with the 1996-newer small-block engines. This 4x signal is required by the PCM for engine operation.

Fig. 5.6. Some 1998-newer 7.4L V-8 engines are equipped with a 24x crankshaft reluctor and a CKP sensor capable of generating a 24-pulse signal (per 360 degrees of engine revolution) while the engine is rotating. This 24x signal brings LS fuel management and one-coil-per-cylinder ignition to the 7.4L V-8 engines.

Fig. 5.7. EFI Connection designed a 24x crankshaft reluctor for small-block and LT1 engines. This reluctor is used with a GM CKP sensor to produce a 24x signal (per 360 degrees of engine revolution) while the engine is rotating. This 24x signal brings LS fuel management and one-coil-per-cylinder ignition to early small-block and LT1 engines.

Because of crank reluctor differences, the L21 engines use a different CKP sensor than the L29 engines. However, both L29 and L21 engines share the same timing cover.

Gen I Small-Block and Gen II LT1 Engines

To bring coil-per-cylinder ignition to the small-block and LT1 engines, EFI Connection designed two similar 24x crankshaft reluctors that produce the CKP sensor signal requirement of the Gen III PCMs.

For Gen I small-block engines, this crank reluctor is used with the 1996–2002 5.7L Vortec timing cover and 7.4L L21 CKP sensor. (See Figure 5.7.) For LT1 engines, this crank reluctor is used with the 1996–1997 LT1 timing cover and 7.4L L21 CKP sensor.

The 1996–1997 LT1 timing cover has limited clearance near the crankshaft seal, so one reluctor design allows for the LT1 timing cover and the GM single-row timing set.

The 1996–2002 5.7L Vortec timing cover has additional clearance near the crankshaft seal and allows for the other 24x crank reluctor that can be used with double-row timing sets.

TPIS has designed billet-aluminum timing covers for both

Crankshaft Position (CKP) Sensor

Gen III LS-Series

Cavity	Wire Color	Function
A	Dark Blue/White	Signal
B	Yellow/Black	Low Reference
C	Light Green	12V Reference

24x 7.4L (RPO L21)

Cavity	Wire Color	Function
A	Dark Blue/White	Signal
B	Yellow/Black	Low Reference
C	Light Green	12V Reference

3x Vortec V6 & 4x Vortec V-8

Cavity	Wire Color	Function
A	Light Green	12V Reference
B	Yellow/Black	Low Reference
C	Yellow	Signal

SENSORS AND INPUTS

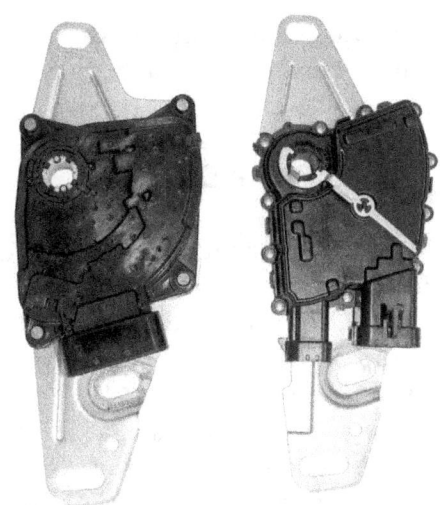

The early gear select switch (right) was used on 4-speed automatic transmissions through 2003. The late gear select switch (left) was used with 2004 and newer 4-speed automatic transmissions. The switches are functionally the same and even interchange with the transmission case, but require different harness connectors. Installing a gear select switch on a transmission not originally equipped with one (such as the LT1 F-Body 4L60-E) requires a longer gear select shaft to be installed.

small-block and LT1 engines that have adequate clearance for double-row timing sets and any EFI Connection 24x crank reluctor.

Accelerator Pedal Position Sensor

The APP sensor is only used with electronic throttle systems. The APP signals are received by the TAC module to indicate the angle of the accelerator pedal. The APP sensor receives several 5V references, several low references, and outputs two or three 0–5V signals.

With the exception of the 2005–2006 E40 engine computers (Corvette and GTO), all APP signals are received by the TAC module. The E40 engine computer has the TAC built within and directly receives two APP signals. (See Chapter 8 for more information about the APP sensor.)

Park/Neutral Indicator

The park/neutral (P/N) indicator signal is a ground signal from a gear select switch that is used by the PCM to determine if the vehicle is in park/neutral or in gear. A ground signal indicates park or neutral, and an open signal indicates that the vehicle is in gear.

The PCM uses the P/N input for idle characters and as a requirement to perform the crankshaft variation learn procedure. The P/N signal is only required for automatic transmissions. The only LS-series vehicles with a P/N signal are the 1998–2002 LS1 Camaro and Firebird. The LS1 Camaro and Firebird have a P/N switch attached to the gear select lever in the center console. All other LS-series vehicles are equipped with a gear select switch on the side of the transmission case that indicates not only P/N, but also the selected gear.

When using a P/N switch, the calibration must be set to expect the P/N-only signal. If your base calibration is from a truck or Corvette, you must change the gear select type to P/N only. This setting is not available in all tuning software packages.

Gear Select Switch

The gear select (PRNDL) switch is mounted to the side of the transmission case. The transmission's gear select lever passes through the PRNDL switch. The PRNDL signal is based on a combination of four wires that, depending on the selected gear, output either a ground signal or an open signal. This combination of ground/open signals is used by the PCM to determine the selected gear.

When using a PRNDL switch, the calibration must be set to expect the PRNDL signals. Base calibrations from a Camaro or Firebird must be adjusted to change the gear select type to PRNDL. This setting is not available in all tuning software packages.

Although the same gear select switch was used across the same model year, not every vehicle used the switch in the same way. For example, some wire harnesses use the neutral safety switch for starter crank inhibit and some wire harnesses use the neutral safety switch for a starter relay control signal.

Early Gear Select Switch

The first transmission-mounted gear select switch carries GM# 24229422. This early PRNDL can be found as early as 1995 on 4L60-E and 4L80-E transmissions. This switch is easily identifiable as it has two connections. The four cavity harness connector provides the PCM with a combination of ground signal wires to indicate the selected gear. The seven-cavity harness connector provides neutral safety, P/N indicator, and backup lamp signals.

Many of these switches, and their harness connectors, are considered unusable (cannot be modified or used in other applications) since adhesive at the connections has bonded the harness connectors to the switch assembly.

Late Gear Select Switch

A revised switch assembly was introduced in 2004 and carries GM# 24221125. This switch assembly is

CHAPTER 5

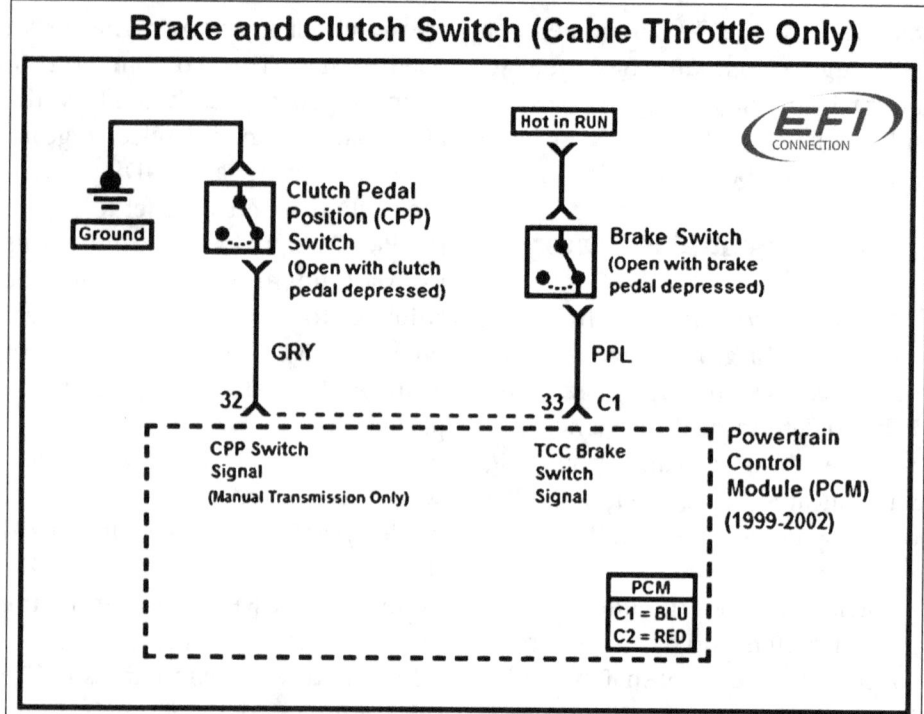

Fig. 5.8. The brake and clutch pedal switches are mounted to the brake and clutch pedal mounting brackets and are used by the PCM to determine the state of the brake and clutch pedals. The PCM uses the brake switch signal for transmission and cruise control operation, and the clutch pedal signal for cruise control operation.

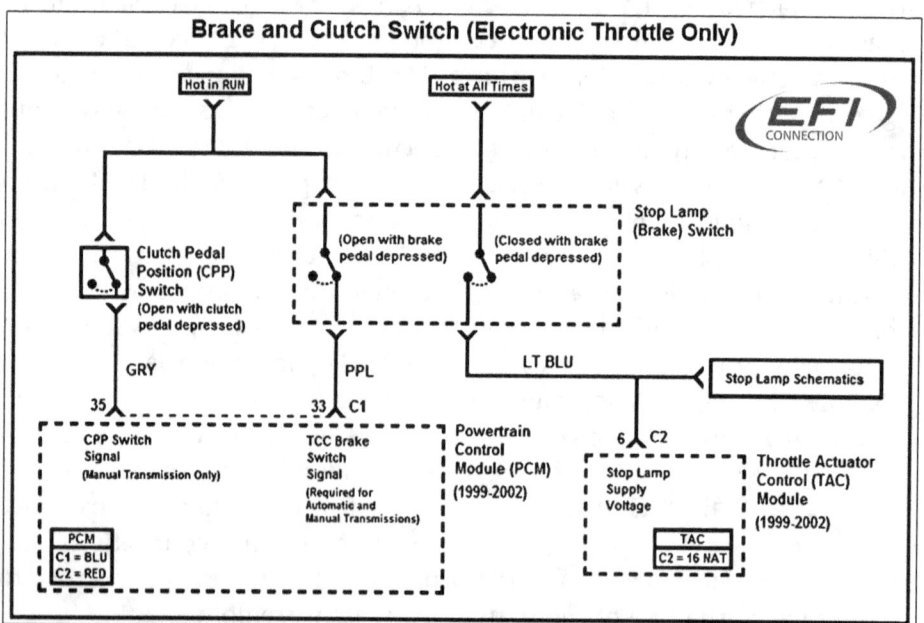

Fig. 5.9. Electronic throttle systems require the brake and clutch pedal position signals for cruise control operation. When the brake or clutch pedal is depressed, the TAC module disables cruise control operation. The TAC module also requires a second brake switch signal that receives 12V with the stop lamps.

functionally the same as the early switch assembly but it accepts an improved lever lock type connection.

Brake Switch

The brake switch has been used since the 1980s to control 700R4 torque converter clutch (TCC) lockup. In these early applications, the brake switch receives 12V ignition power and passes 12V to the TCC solenoid when the brake pedal is not depressed. With the brake pedal depressed, the TCC solenoid loses power and inhibits TCC application.

Rather than providing 12V to the TCC solenoid, the LS-series PCMs receive this brake switch signal and apply additional logic to TCC control.

Cable Throttle Systems

For applications with cable throttle, this switch is only required with 4L60-E and 4L80-E transmissions. For manual transmission installations, this switch is not used. (See Figure 5.8.)

Electronic Throttle Systems

For applications with electronic throttle, regardless of transmission type (automatic or manual), the brake switch signal is used by the TAC system for cruise control logic. When the brake pedal is depressed, cruise control is disabled. Without this brake switch signal, cruise control is inhibited. (See Figure 5.9.)

Clutch Pedal Position Switch

For vehicles fitted with a manual transmission, a clutch pedal position (CPP) switch is used to control deceleration fuel cut-off (DFCO) events.

SENSORS AND INPUTS

For such vehicles also fitted with an electronic throttle, the TAC system uses the CPP signal for cruise control logic. When the clutch pedal is depressed, cruise control is disabled. Without the CPP signal, cruise control is inhibited.

12V Ignition Signal

Some vehicles are equipped with a clutch switch that passes 12V ignition to the PCM. These vehicles require 12V ignition power when the clutch pedal is not depressed. The circuit is open when the clutch pedal is depressed. This signal is not received at the PCM in the same pin location as vehicles equipped with a CPP ground signal. (See Figure 5.9.)

Ground Signal

The LS1 Camaro and Firebird are equipped with a clutch switch that passes a ground signal to the PCM. The PCM requires ground when the clutch pedal is not depressed. The circuit is open when the clutch pedal is depressed. This signal is not received at the PCM in the same pin location as vehicles equipped with a CPP 12V ignition signal. (See Figure 5.8.)

Fuel Enable Control

The Camaro and Firebird require a 5V 50Hz pulse width modulated (PWM) signal to the PCM's fuel enable circuit to disarm the antitheft system and allow the PCM to command fuel delivery. Other vehicles with a Gen III PCM use Class 2 communications for disarming antitheft.

For Camaro and Firebird only, the early 1998 PCM receives this signal at pin 11 of the red connector and 1999–2002 PCMs receive this signal at pin 30 of the red connector. VATS bypass signal generators are widely available on the market, but they do nothing more than satisfy this antitheft signal requirement. Because conversions always require custom tuning, your tuner can disable the VATS at that time within the calibration—if for nothing more than to disable unneeded DTCs.

Sensor Part Numbers and Interchange

The Gen III PCM is compatible with many GM sensors. This chart is a summary of the sensors used with the common GM vehicles equipped with 4.3L V-6, 5.0L, 5.7L, 7.4L, and LS-series engines. With several types of the same sensor (like coolant temperature or IAT), finding a sensor with a mounting configuration that suits your application is often easy.

Throttle Position Sensor

Year	Model	Engine (liters)	Part Number	LS-Series PCM Support
1985–1989	Camaro, Firebird, Corvette	5.0, 5.7	17111606	Yes
1990–1992	Camaro, Firebird, Corvette	5.0, 5.7	17112368	Yes
1991–1993	Syclone, Typhoon	4.3	17112368	Yes
1992–1993	Corvette	5.7	17106682	Yes
1993	Camaro, Firebird	5.7	17106682	Yes
1994–1995	Corvette	5.7	17113077	Yes
1994–1997	Camaro, Firebird, Impala	5.7	17106680	Yes
1996	Corvette	5.7	17106680	Yes
1996–2005	Trucks, Vans	4.3, 5.0, 5.7	17123852	Yes
1999–2002	Trucks (Cable Throttle)	4.8, 5.3, 6.0	17123852	Yes
1999–2002	Trucks (Electronic Throttle)	5.3, 6.0	17114083	Yes
1998–2002	Camaro, Firebird	5.7	17123852	Yes
2004	GTO	5.7	17123852	Yes
	Ram Jet 350	5.7	17123852	Yes
	Ram Jet 502	8.2	17106682	Yes

Sensor Part Numbers and Interchange CONTINUED

IAC Valve

Year	Model	Engine (liters)	Part Number	LS-Series PCM Support
1985–1992	Camaro, Firebird	5.0, 5.7	25527077	Yes
1985–1988	Corvette	5.7	25527077	Yes
1989–1993	Camaro, Firebird, Corvette	5.0, 5.7	17112193	Yes
1991–1993	Syclone, Typhoon	4.3	17112193	Yes
1994	Camaro, Firebird, Corvette, Impala	5.7	17113099	Yes
1995–1997	Camaro, Firebird, Corvette, Impala	5.7	17113188	Yes
1996–2005	Trucks, Vans	4.3, 5.0, 5.7	17113209	Yes
1999–2002	Trucks	4.8, 5.3, 6.0	17113598	Yes
1998–1999	Camaro, Firebird	5.7	17113391	Yes
2000–2002	Camaro, Firebird	5.7	17113598	Yes
2004	GTO	5.7	17113598	Yes
	Ram Jet 350	5.7	17113209	Yes
	Ram Jet 502	8.2	17113188	Yes

Engine Coolant Temperature Sensor

Year	Model	Engine (liters)	Part Number	Mount	LS-Series PCM Support
1985–1997	Camaro, Firebird	5.0, 5.7	15326386	3/8-inch, 18 NPT	Yes
1985–1996	Corvette	5.7	15326386	3/8-inch, 18 NPT	Yes
1996–2005	Trucks, Vans	4.3, 5.0, 5.7	15326386	3/8-inch, 18 NPT	Yes
1997–2005	Corvette	5.7, 6.0	19236568	M12 x 1.5	Yes
1998	Camaro, Firebird	5.7	12551708	M12 x 1.5	Yes
1999–2002	Camaro, Firebird	5.7	19236568	M12 x 1.5	Yes
2004–2005	GTO	5.7, 6.0	19236568	M12 x 1.5	Yes
1999–2005	Trucks	4.8, 5.3, 6.0	19236568	M12 x 1.5	Yes
2006	SSR, Trailblazer SS	6.0	19236568	M12 x 1.5	Yes
	Ram Jet 350	5.7	15326386	3/8-inch, 18 NPT	Yes
	Ram Jet 502	8.2	15326386	3/8-inch, 18 NPT	Yes

Intake Air Temperature Sensor

Year	Model	Engine (liters)	Part Number	Mount	Other Description	LS-Series PCM Support
1985–1991	Corvette	5.7	15326386	3/8-inch, 18 NPT	Interchanges with ECT	Yes
1985–1992	Camaro, Firebird	5.0, 5.7	15326386	3/8-inch, 18 NPT	Interchanges with ECT	Yes
1985–1991	Corvette	5.7	25036751	3/8-inch, 18 NPT	Visible Thermistor	Yes
1985–1992	Camaro, Firebird	5.0, 5.7	25036751	3/8-inch, 18 NPT	Visible Thermistor	Yes
1992–2000	Corvette	5.7	12160244	Grommet	Short Housing	Yes
1993–2002	Camaro, Firebird	5.7	12160244	Grommet	Short Housing	Yes
1996–2005	Truck, Van	4.3, 5.0, 5.7, 7.4	12160244	Grommet	Short Housing	Yes

SENSORS AND INPUTS

Mass Airflow Sensor

Year	Model	Engine (liters)	Part Number	LS-Series PCM Support
1985–1989	Camaro, Firebird, Corvette	5.0, 5.7	19187357	No
1994–2000	Corvette	5.7	19207203	Yes
1994–2002	Camaro, Firebird	5.7	19207203	Yes
1996–2000	Trucks, Vans	4.3, 5.0, 5.7	19208521	Yes
2001–2002	Vans	4.3, 5.0, 5.7	19208522	Yes
1999–2002	Trucks	4.3, 5.0, 5.7	19207203	Yes
2004	GTO	5.7	19207203	Yes
2000–2006	Trucks	4.8, 5.3, 6.0	15904068	Yes
2001–2007	Corvette	5.7, 6.0	15904068	Yes
2005–2006	GTO	6.0	15904068	Yes
2006	SSR, Trailblazer SS	6.0	15904068	Yes
2006–2012	Corvette	6.2, 7.0	15865791	Yes

Manifold Absolute Pressure Sensor

Year	Model	Engine (liters)	Part Number	Pressure	Manifold Type	LS-Series PCM Support
1990–1997	Camaro/Firebird	5.0, 5.7	12569240	1 Bar	Remote Mount	Yes
1990–1996	Corvette	5.7	12569240	1 Bar	Remote Mount	Yes
	Ram Jet 502	8.2	12569240	1 Bar	Remote Mount	Yes
1991–1993	Syclone, Typhoon	4.3	12569241	2 Bar	Remote Mount	Yes
1989	Firebird Turbo Trans Am	3.8	12223861	3 Bar	Remote Mount	Yes
1997–2008	Corvette	5.7, 6.0	12614970	1 Bar	LS-Series Car	Yes
1998–2002	Camaro/Firebird	5.7	12614970	1 Bar	LS-Series Car	Yes
2004–2006	GTO	5.7, 6.0	12614970	1 Bar	LS-Series Car	Yes
2006	SSR, Trailblazer SS	6.0	12614970	1 Bar	LS-Series Car	Yes
1996–2002	Trucks, Vans	4.3, 5.0, 5.7	12614973	1 Bar	LS-Series Truck	Yes
1999–2007	Trucks	4.8, 5.3, 6.0	12614973	1 Bar	LS-Series Truck	Yes
	Ram Jet 350	5.7	12614973	1 Bar	LS-Series Truck	Yes
2004–2007	Grand Prix GTP	3.8	12615136	2 Bar	LS-Series Truck	Yes
2007–2010	Truck	6.6L Diesel	12623671	3.3 Bar	LS-Series Truck	Yes

Knock Sensor

Year	Model	Engine (liters)	Part Number	Type	Mount	LS-Series PCM Support
1996–2002	Express Van	5.0	10456287	Resonant	1/4-inch, 18 NPT Male	Yes
1996–2002	Express Van	5.7	10456288	Resonant	1/4-inch, 18 NPT Male	Yes
1997–1998	Corvette	5.7	19236388	Resonant	M10, 1.5	Yes
1998	Camaro, Firebird	5.7	19236388	Resonant	M10, 1.5	Yes
1999–2004	Corvette	5.7	12589867	Resonant	M10, 1.5	Yes
1999–2002	Camaro, Firebird	5.7	12589867	Resonant	M10, 1.5	Yes
1999–2006	Trucks, Van	4.8, 5.3, 6.0	12589867	Resonant	M10, 1.5	Yes
2004	GTO	5.7	12589867	Resonant	M10, 1.5	Yes
2001–2005	Blazer, S-Series, Express Van	4.3	21024981	Flat Response	Through Hole	Yes

Sensor Part Numbers and Interchange CONTINUED

Knock Sensor (CONTINUED)

Year	Model	Engine (liters)	Part Number	Type	Mount	LS-Series PCM Support
2005	Corvette	6.0	12623730	Flat Response	Through Hole	Yes
2005–2006	GTO	6.0	12623730	Flat Response	Through Hole	Yes
2006	SSR, Trailblazer SS	6.0	12623730	Flat Response	Through Hole	Yes

Oil Pressure Sensor

Year	Model	Engine (liters)	Part Number	Type	Mount	LS-Series PCM Support
1997–2008	Corvette	5.7, 6.0, 6.2, 7.0	12616646	Sensor	M16 x 1.5	Yes
2003–2008	Truck, Van	4.8, 5.3, 6.0	12616646	Sensor	M16 x 1.5	Yes
2003–2006	SSR, Trailblazer SS	5.3, 6.0	12616646	Sensor	M16 x 1.5	Yes
2004–2006	GTO	5.7, 6.0	12616646	Sensor	M16 x 1.5	Yes
2003–2007	Truck	8.1	12574403	Sensor	1/4-inch, 18 NPT	Yes

Camshaft Position Sensor

Year	Model	Engine (liters)	Part Number	Location	LS-Series PCM Support
1997–1998	Corvette	5.7	12560229	Rear Block	Yes
1998	Camaro, Firebird	5.7	12560229	Rear Block	Yes
1999–2002	Camaro, Firebird	5.7	12561211	Rear Block	Yes
1999–2004	Corvette	5.7	12561211	Rear Block	Yes
1999–2006	Truck, Van	4.8, 5.3, 6.0	12561211	Rear Block	Yes
2004	GTO	5.7	12561211	Rear Block	Yes
2003–2004	SSR	5.3	12561211	Rear Block	Yes
2005	Corvette	6.0	12591720	Front Timing Cover	Yes
2005–2006	GTO	6.0	12591720	Front Timing Cover	Yes
2005–2006	SSR, Trailblazer SS	6.0	12591720	Front Timing Cover	Yes
1996–2005	Truck, Van	4.3, 5.0, 5.7, 7.4	10485432	Distributor	Yes

Crankshaft Position Sensor

Year	Model	Engine (liters)	Part Number	LS-Series PCM Support
1997–2005	Corvette	5.7, 6.0	12560228	Yes
1998–2002	Camaro, Firebird	5.7	12560228	Yes
1999–2006	Trucks, Van	4.8, 5.3, 6.0	12560228	Yes
2003–2006	SSR, Trailblazer SS	5.3, 6.0	12560228	Yes
2004–2006	GTO	5.7, 6.0	12560228	Yes
1999–2000	Medium Duty Truck	7.4	10456248	Yes
1996–2002	Trucks, Van	4.3, 5.0, 5.7, 7.4	12596851	Yes

Gear Select Switch

Year	Model	Transmission	Part Number	LS-Series PCM Support
1995–2003	All Models, Excluding Camaro, Firebird	4-Speed Automatic	24229422	Yes
2004–2008	All Models	4-Speed Automatic	24221125	Yes

CHAPTER 6

PCM SIGNAL OUTPUTS

Production GM vehicles rely on the PCM to provide signal outputs to control the engine, gauges, electric fans, emissions equipment, air conditioning, and other equipment.

Engine Control Output

The basic purpose of any engine computer is to correctly deliver fuel and initiate ignition events for any engine operating condition. To do this correctly, engines are fitted with many sensors that provide measurable real-time operating data. Combined with calibrated parameters, the sensor values are used by the engine computer to activate the injector and ignition-coil control signals.

Ignition Coils

All Gen III engines are fitted with eight ignition coils. Each coil is responsible for delivering spark to its assigned cylinder. The engine computer must determine spark angle, or degrees Before Top Dead Center (BTDC), to activate each ignition coil through the ignition control (IC) circuit. As part of this complicated calculation, the engine computer considers engine speed (CKP input), coolant temperature (ECT input), intake air temperature (IAT input), knock sensor values (KS input), throttle position (TPS input), vehicle speed (VSS input), transmission gear (P/N input), and more. To prevent weak spark, the engine computer also controls the ignition coil charge time (or dwell time) before firing. (See Figure 6.1.)

LS-Series Ignition Coil Output: LS-series engines have eight individual coils. To release a coil's charge when an ignition event is requested, the engine computer commands the

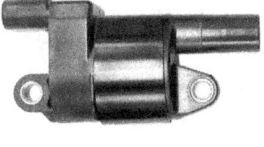

LS-series ignition coils are interchangeable. As an example, you can swap a 2002 Corvette ignition coil bracket assembly (ignition coils, mounting bracket, and coil harness) with a 2008 Corvette ignition coil bracket assembly. General Motors has designed each ignition coil pack harness to be universal to any LS-series engine wire harness. General Motors has used a variety of ignition coils with LS-series engines.

GM# 12558948 ignition coil (bottom left) is only used with the LS1 and LS6 engine in the Camaro, Firebird, Corvette, and Cadillac CTS-V.

GM# 12573190 ignition coil (middle left) and GM# 12611424 ignition coil (top left) are used with 2005-newer cars, trucks, and vans.

GM# 10457730 ignition coil (bottom right) and GM# 12558693 (top right) are used with 1999–2007 trucks and vans.

CHAPTER 6

IC coil output circuit low (toward 0V). This energizes the ignition coil and causes the spark plug to produce spark. All ignition coils on LS-series engines operate in the same way. Changing a set of eight ignition coils for a different set of eight ignition coils may require (or at the very least, benefit from) changes to the engine computer's spark calibration, including the spark dwell time table. (See Figure 6.1.)

Vortec V-6 and Gen I Small-Block Vortec V-8 Ignition Coil Output: The only Gen III PCM that General Motors used with the Vortec V-6 and Gen I small-block Vortec V-8 engines is the 2001–2002 (GM# 12200411). These engines only offer single coil and distributor ignition. Comparing wire schematics between an LS-series engine and Vortec V-6 or Vortec V-8 engine reveals that the same IC circuit controlling ignition coil 1 on the LS-series engines is used to control the ignition control module (ICM) of the Vortec V-6 and Gen I small-block Vortec V-8 engines. (See Figure 6.2.) The ICM causes the ignition coil to fire based on IC circuit signal pulses.

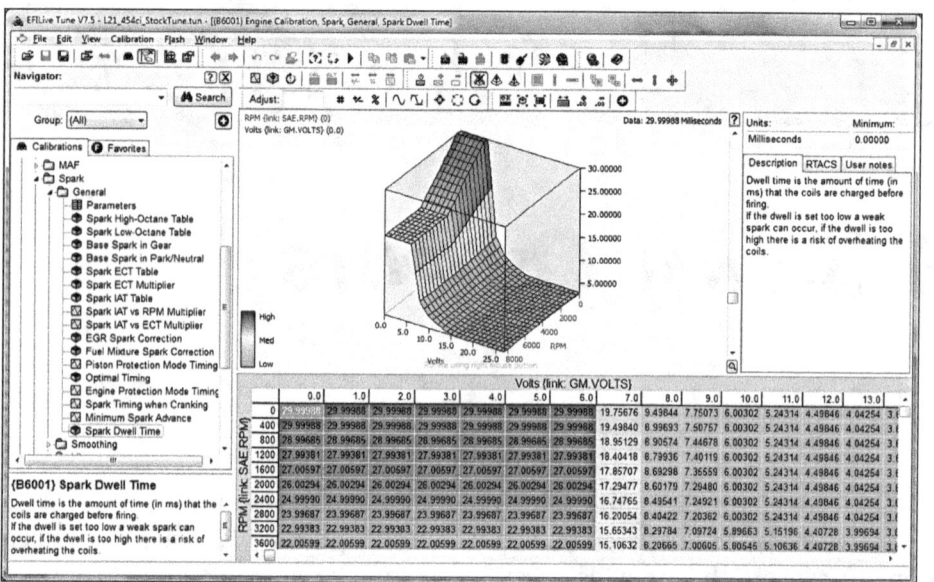

Fig. 6.1. This table represents lookup values for the amount of time the ignition coils are charged before the PCM sends a signal to fire them. If the dwell time is too long, the ignition coils may overheat. If the dwell time is too short, a weak spark (and loss of power) may result.

This LS1 and LS6 GM coil bracket assembly is installed on all 1999-newer LS1 and LS6 engine valve covers. A coil bracket assembly includes a formed steel bracket, four ignition coils, and a wire harness. With a variety of LS-series ignition coils, not all coil mounting positions and brackets are the same. However, General Motors has designed all coil pack wire harnesses to universally plug into any LS-series engine wire harness.

Fuel Injector Control

By 1996 all GM V-6 and V-8 engines were fitted with one injector for each cylinder. The engine computer controls each fuel injector through an internal switch (or driver), which applies a ground signal to each fuel injector. With 12V ignition power at each injector while the engine is running, the fuel injector driver applies ground, opening each injector to allow fuel to pass through the injector and into the engine cylinder.

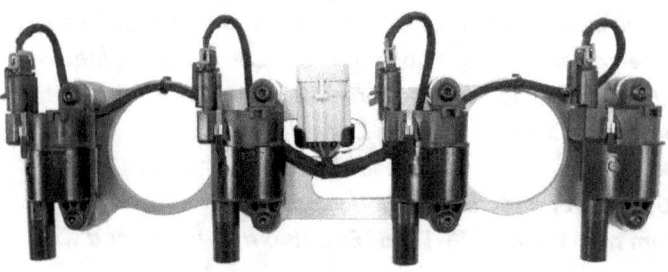

EFI Connection offers a coil bracket assembly that uses GM# 12573190 ignition coils. The coil bracket cleanly fits Gen I small-block and Gen II LT1 engine center bolt valve covers. The layout allows clearance for oil fill, PCV, and breather. The wire harness is specific to the bracket and ignition coil layout, but universally plugs into any LS-series engine wire harness. For engines with perimeter-bolt valve covers, bosses can be welded to the surface of the valve cover for attachment.

PCM SIGNAL OUTPUTS

The engine computer controls the pulse width (or duration) and sequencing of each injector driver. The engine computer determines fuel injector sequencing based on crankshaft position (CKP) and camshaft position (CMP). Pulse widths are calculated from inputs such as air mass (MAF input), manifold pressure (MAP input), throttle position (TPS input), intake air temperature (IAT input), coolant temperature (ECT input), engine speed (CKP input), and more.

The firing order is hardwired to the engine computer, but the bank assignment of each injector is defined within the engine computer's calibration. (See Chapter 7 for more about the firing order.)

Fuel Pump Relay Control

The fuel pump is controlled by the engine computer through a relay. The relay coil is grounded and the engine computer supplies a 12V power source to the relay coil. This switches battery power to the fuel pump. When the ignition switch is turned to the ON position, the PCM cycles the fuel pump on for several seconds to pressurize the fuel rails. The fuel pump only runs when the engine computer sees a signal from the CKP sensor indicating that the crankshaft is rotating.

Malfunction Indicator Lamp Control

Knowing that a malfunction is occurring (or has occurred) can be critical. The malfunction indicator lamp (MIL) in the instrument cluster is used to indicate that a malfunction has occurred. In a production GM vehicle, the MIL receives 12V power through the gauges fuse. The engine computer applies a ground to

Since 1996, the Vortec V-6 and Vortec V-8 engines have used a single coil, ignition module, and distributor. The 2001–2002 GM vehicles with Vortec V-6 and Vortec V-8 engines use the same PCM (GM# 12200411) as the vehicles with LS-series engines. Engine operation requires a four-pulse (for V-8) crankshaft signal (reluctor and sensor at bottom), one-pulse camshaft signal from within a Vortec distributor (right), a single coil and ignition module (middle), GM# 12200411 PCM (left), and a base PCM calibration that supports a low-resolution crankshaft signal with single coil and distributor (like a 2001 5.7L Express Van calibration). Vortec V-6 engines require a three-pulse crankshaft signal and supporting PCM calibration (like a 2001 4.3L S-10 calibration).

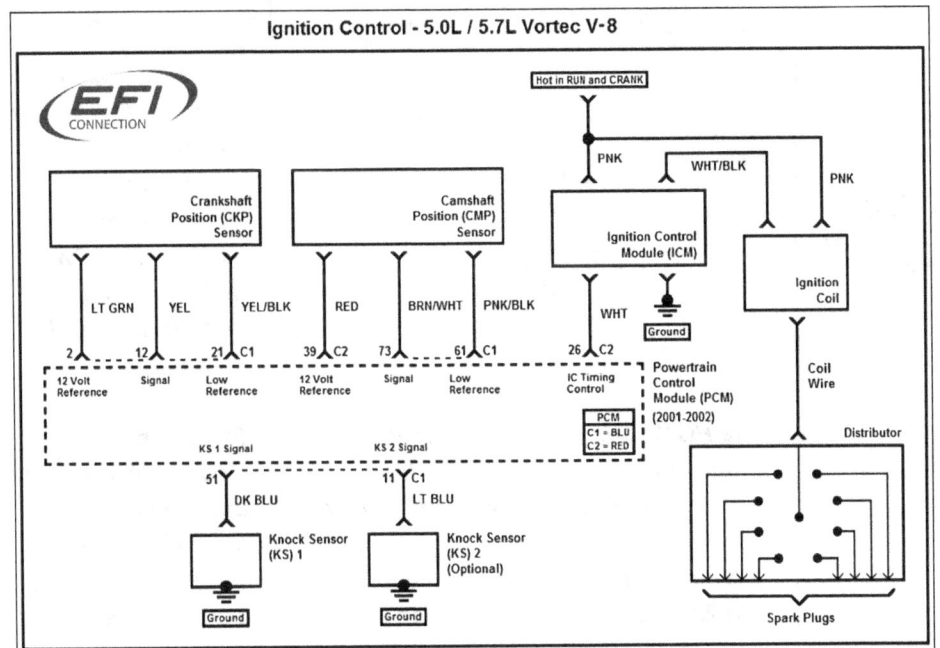

Fig. 6.2. The V-8 and V-6 Vortec ignition system components have remained unchanged since 1996. All 1996-newer Vortec V-8 and V-6 engines use the same ignition module, ignition coil, CKP sensor, and CMP sensor. Due to the variations in engine size, and for accuracy, several different knock sensors have been used. Because only the PCM has been changed throughout the years, the 2001–2002 Gen III PCM (GM# 12200411) may be used with any 1996-newer V-8 and V-6 Vortec engine.

CHAPTER 6

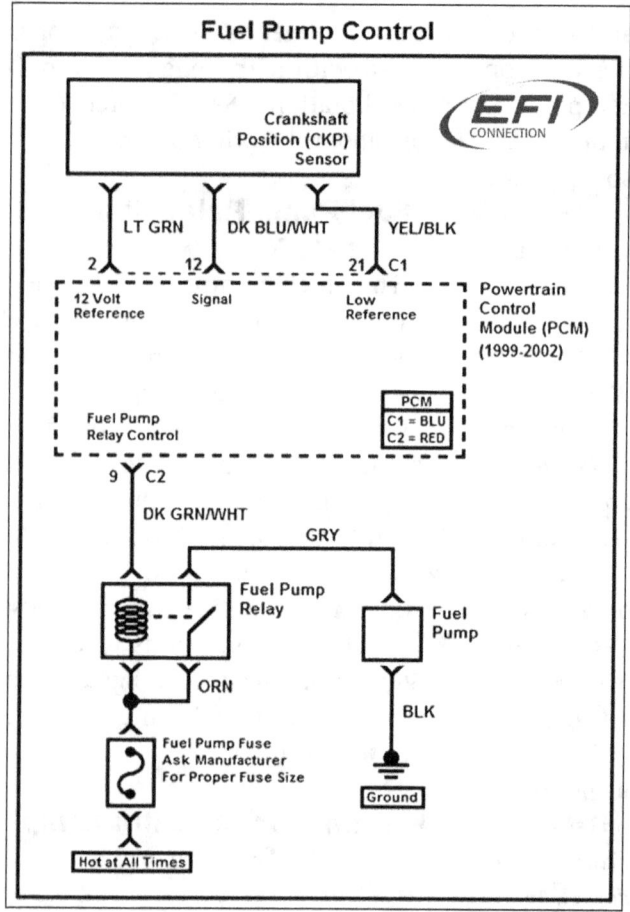

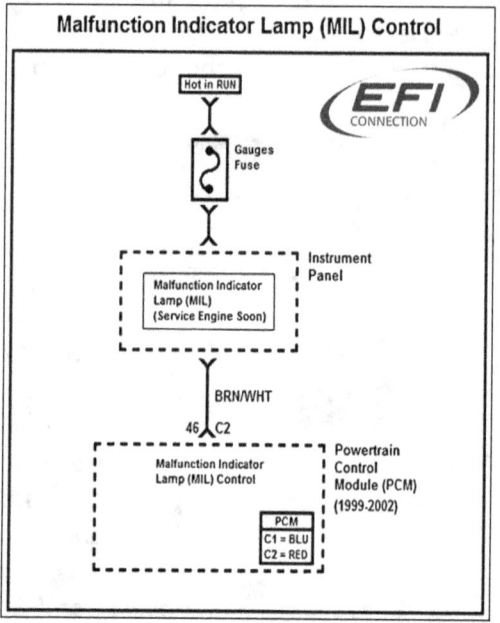

The fuel pump is turned on through a relay because the PCM cannot handle the current. When the ignition key is turned on, the PCM turns the fuel pump relay on for several seconds to prime the fuel system. The PCM does not command the fuel pump to run again until a signal is received from the CKP sensor.

The PCM controls the illumination of the MIL by applying a ground to the bulb. Ignition power is received at the bulb from the gauges fuse. The MIL is important because it may be the first indicator that there is a problem with engine or transmission performance.

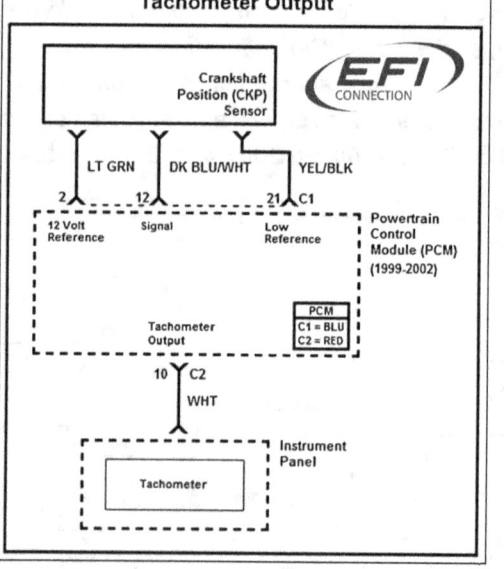

The PCM calculates engine speed (RPM) based on the signal it receives from the CKP sensor. The RPM signal is then output to the tachometer.

The PCM uses the VSS and calibration data to determine how many pulses to output for each of the VSS outputs. Most production GM vehicles only use the primary VSS output, which is most often used for the speedometer. The secondary VSS output, for example, can be used with any third-generation F-Body to satisfy the 2,000-pulse-per-mile cruise control module VSS signal input requirement.

PCM SIGNAL OUTPUTS

the control circuit to illuminate the lamp. When the cause of a malfunction has been fixed, the MIL can be reset by clearing stored DTCs or by running the engine or transmission through several cycles as defined in the calibration.

Tachometer Output

The engine computer provides a tachometer output for monitoring engine speed. For LS-series engines, one revolution per minute (RPM) equals one set of 24 crankshaft signal pulses. For Gen I small-block Vortec and Gen VI big-block Vortec engines, one rpm equals one set of four crankshaft signal pulses. For Vortec V-6 engines, one rpm equals one set of three crankshaft signal pulses. The engine computer calibration allows for adjustment to the output signal for compatibility with many tachometers.

Vehicle Speed Output

Two VSS outputs are available with Gen III PCMs. These VSS outputs are defined in the PCM calibration as primary and secondary. For production GM vehicles, the primary VSS output is often used for the speedometer and the secondary VSS output is often used for the antilock brake system (ABS). The pulse count for each VSS output is configurable within the PCM calibration.

Electric Fan Control

While all Gen III PCMs support electric fan control, not all production GM vehicles with a Gen III PCM have electric fans. The PCM controls two output signals based on coolant temperature (ECT input), vehicle speed (VSS input), and air conditioning inputs. General Motors uses these two outputs with three relays to operate two electric fans in low/high-speed operation by switching between series and parallel operation. (See Chapter 11 for more information about electric fan operation.)

Air Conditioning Control

The PCM is solely responsible for controlling the A/C compressor clutch through a relay. The A/C compressor clutch relay coil and switch receive 12V ignition power with the key in the ON position. Based on the A/C request input, A/C compressor clutch supply voltage input, A/C pressure sensor input, engine speed (RPM input), throttle angle (TPS

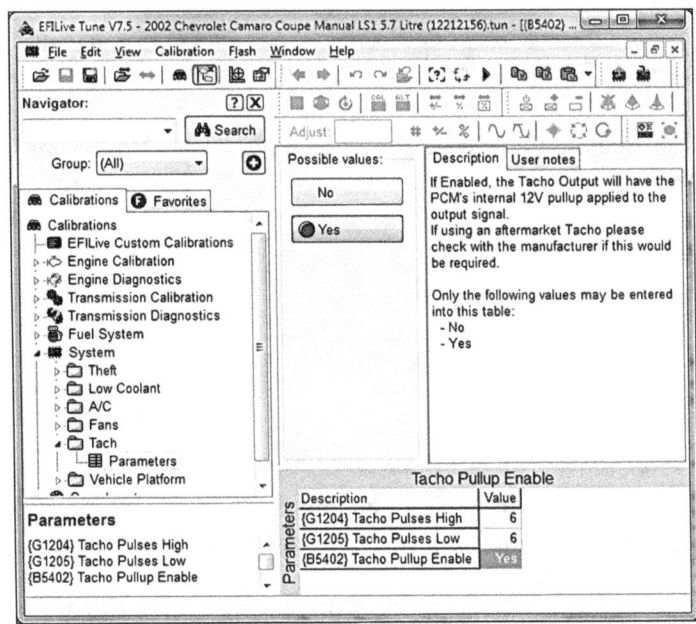

The number of output pulses for the tachometer is configurable. As shown here, the tachometer in a 2002 LS1 Camaro instrument cluster requires the Tacho Pulses High and Tacho Pulses Low values of "6."

As another example, a Gen III PCM installation into an LT1 Camaro requires Tacho Pulses High and Tacho Pulses Low values of "3" and Tacho Pullup Enable set to "Yes."

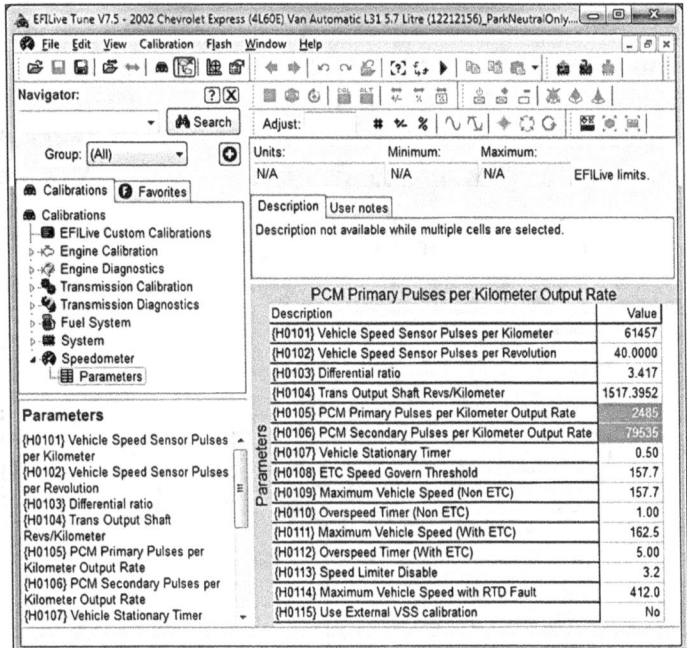

Using EFILive, from Calibration > Speedometer > Parameters, you find the primary VSS output (calibration {H0105}) and the secondary VSS output (calibration {H0106}). These values should be set after the VSS tooth count, tire size, and gear ratio have been properly set in the PCM calibration file.

CHAPTER 6

input), and intake air temperature (IAT input), the PCM applies a ground to the control circuit to switch 12V power to the A/C compressor clutch. (See Chapter 11 for more information about A/C operation.)

Generator Control

Gen III PCMs have the ability to control generator load on the engine through a turn-on signal output. In addition, some vehicles use a generator field duty cycle signal input to the PCM to monitor the duty cycle (ON/OFF) of the generator. Generator load on the engine is calculated based on a PWM signal from the generator. Many conversions disable PCM generator control, but it may be beneficial to retain or enable this feature to adjust engine idle speed to compensate for high generator loads.

When the PCM is not used to control the generator, DTCs P1637 and P1638 need to be disabled. If you forget to disable these DTCs, they appear in the list of active DTCs when you scan the PCM through the DLC.

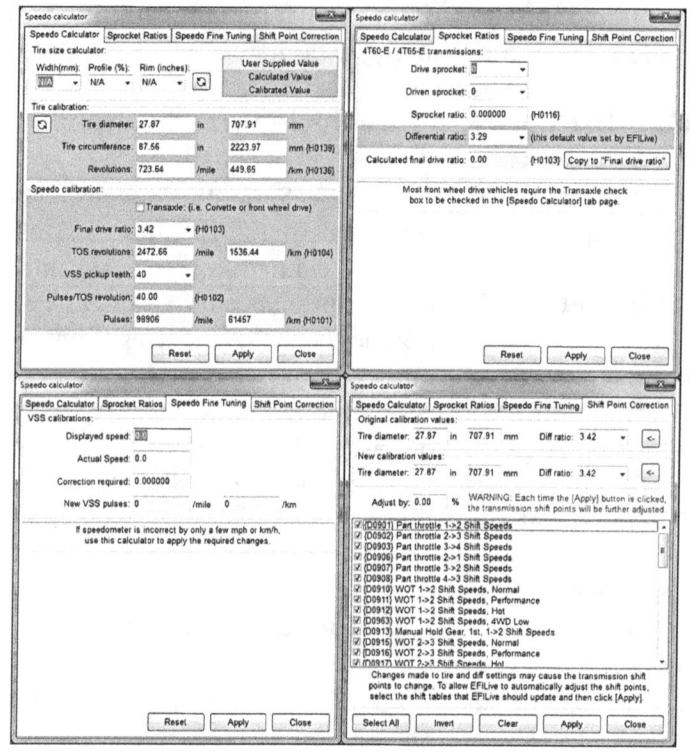

EFILive's Speedo Calculator is accessed from Calibrations > Speedometer > Parameters > Speedo Calculator.

The Speedo Calculator tab presents tire size, gear ratio, and number of teeth on the VSS pickup reluctor. The Sprocket Ratios tab is related to front-wheel-drive transmissions.

The Speedo Fine Tuning tab is most accurately used while the vehicle is on a chassis dyno to make fine adjustments to the value displayed on the speedometer.

The Shift Point Correction tab allows a percentage adjustment to the shift tables after a tire size or gear ratio change.

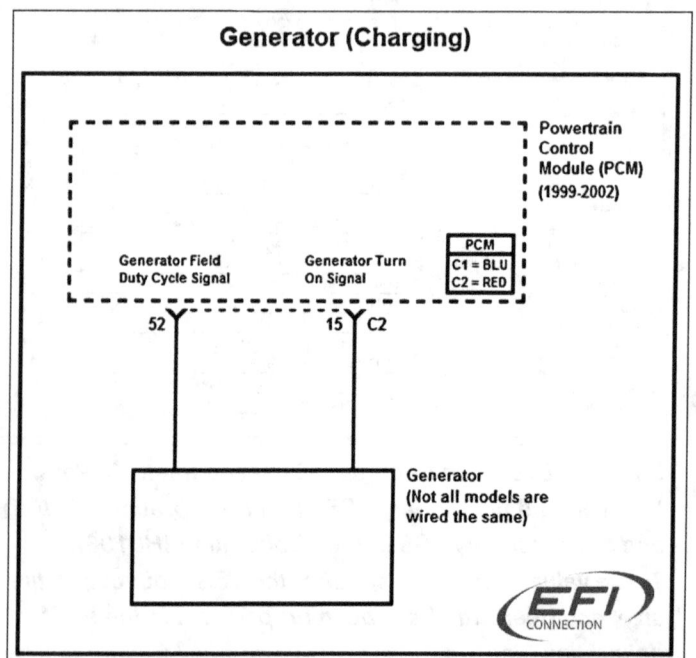

Production vehicles with Gen III PCMs use the PCM to control the generator. Although the generator turn-on signal output is always used, the generator field duty cycle signal is not.

Most commonly the Camaro and Firebird use only the generator turn-on signal; trucks and vans use both the generator turn-on signal and the generator field duty cycle signal; the Corvette uses both PCM signals plus a 16-gauge battery wire (in generator connector cavity A).

Be sure to consider which generator you are working with and your instrument panel charge lamp requirement when wiring your generator.

60   GM GEN III LS-SERIES POWERTRAIN CONTROL SYSTEMS

PCM SIGNAL OUTPUTS

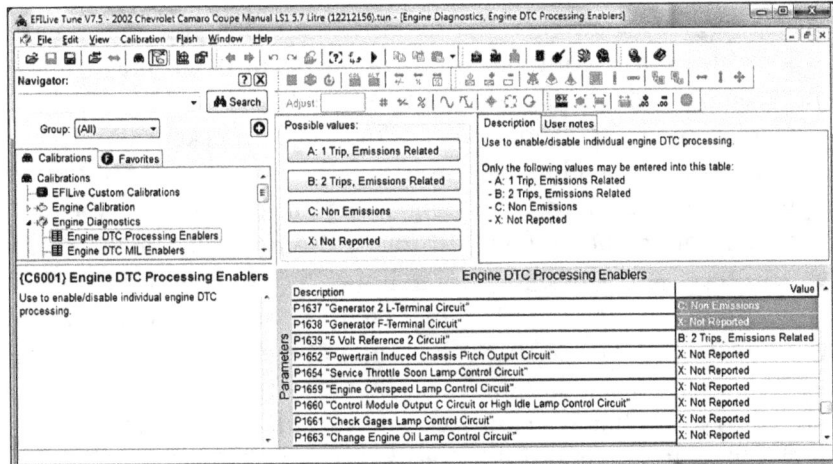

When the PCM is not used to control the generator, there are a few DTCs that need to be disabled. There are two parts to disabling these DTCs: processing enablers and MIL enablers. By setting DTCs P1637 and P1638 to "Not Reported" within the processing enablers, the PCM ignores the processing of these DTCs.

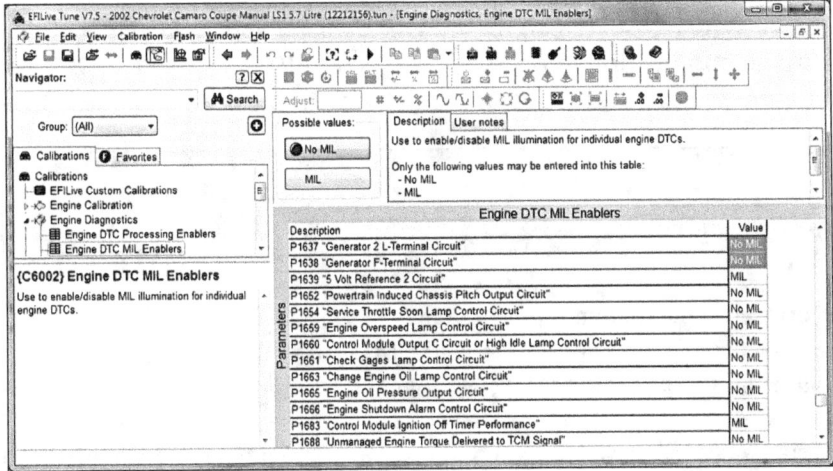

By setting DTCs P1637 and P1638 to "No MIL" within the MIL enablers, the PCM does not apply ground to the MIL control circuit (the MIL does not illuminate).

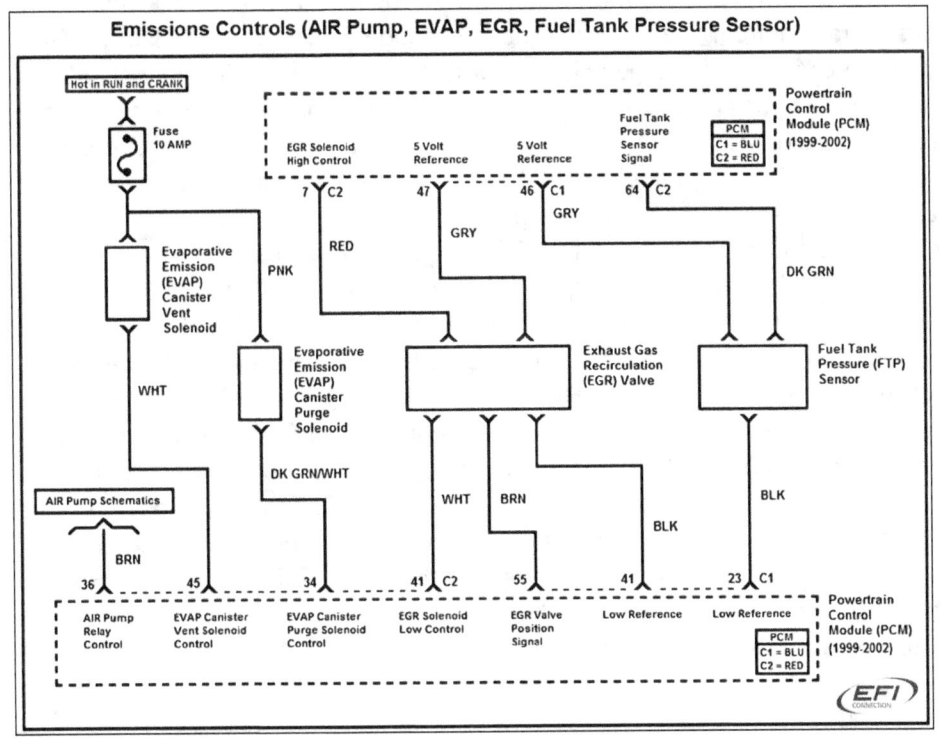

Although the PCM is capable of controlling AIR, EGR, and EVAP, using the PCMs emissions controls does not necessarily mean emissions compliance in your state or county. Before removing emissions equipment, check with your local emissions laws. Removing emissions components also requires turning off (or disabling) the DTC processing enablers and DTC MIL enablers within the PCM calibration.

GM GEN III LS-SERIES POWERTRAIN CONTROL SYSTEMS

CHAPTER 6

Emissions Control

Gen III PCMs are emissions control *capable*, but may not be emissions *compliant*. Your state has specific emissions laws for on-road vehicles that you must adhere to for emissions compliance. After checking with your local emissions testing station, you may find that emissions compliance for your conversion simply means adding a charcoal canister and purge line, or you may find that emissions compliance requires all relevant emissions control of your engine's original vehicle.

EVAP Canister Purge Solenoid

Today's vehicles are equipped with an evaporative emissions (EVAP) control system. Its primary function is to control a charcoal canister purge solenoid. This canister stores fuel vapor and is connected to the fuel tank through a hose.

The engine computer controls the purge solenoid during engine operation to purge the charcoal canister of fuel vapor. Intake manifold vacuum pulls the fuel vapor from the charcoal canister so it can be burned in the combustion process. The PCM applies logic to the operation of the purge solenoid so the purge routine does not create a rich or lean condition.

The PCM checks EVAP purge solenoid performance by monitoring fuel tank pressure (or vacuum) through the fuel tank pressure sensor. If fuel tank vacuum is more than expected within a predetermined amount of time, the PCM knows that the EVAP purge solenoid is leaking engine vacuum to the fuel tank and sets a DTC.

EVAP Canister Vent Solenoid

The EVAP vent valve allows fresh air to enter the EVAP canister. The

EVAP Operation

An effective method of containing, and later consuming, fuel tank gasoline vapors is the charcoal canister. Used since the 1970s, it has the ability to absorb and safely store a large volume of gasoline vapors while the engine is not operating. The charcoal canister is located between the fuel tank and the engine. A hose from the fuel tank to the canister allows the vapors to transfer from the fuel tank to the canister. A hose from the canister to the engine's intake manifold allows the vapors to transfer from the canister to the engine's airstream during certain engine operation.

Early vehicles with electronic fuel injection use an ECM-controlled EVAP canister purge solenoid to open and close the canister-to-engine vapor passage (or hose). The ECM opens and closes the solenoid at predetermined engine operating conditions. The transfer of vapors from the canister and into the engine allow for the gasoline vapors to be burned in the normal combustion process.

Early implementations of the EVAP system had no way of detecting a leak or blockage in the hose connecting the fuel tank to the canister or detecting a solenoid that had stuck open or closed. Leak detection was achieved through the addition of a fuel tank pressure sensor and EVAP vent solenoid so that the ECM could run diagnostic tests that reported a leak in the EVAP system.

To detect a leak, the ECM uses the EVAP purge solenoid and EVAP vent solenoid to charge the EVAP system with a predetermined amount of vacuum. If appropriate vacuum cannot be achieved, the PCM sets a DTC to indicate that a leak (such as a faulty or missing gas cap, damaged purge line, damaged charcoal canister, faulty EVAP purge solenoid, or faulty vent solenoid) is present. When appropriate vacuum is achieved, the ECM turns off the EVAP purge solenoid to seal vacuum in the EVAP system. The ECM then uses the fuel tank pressure sensor to monitor loss of vacuum.

The EVAP vent passage is tested for restrictions by turning off the EVAP vent solenoid (which opens the EVAP vent passage) and EVAP purge solenoid (which prevents engine vacuum from being applied to the EVAP system). By monitoring the fuel tank pressure sensor signal during normal operation of the EVAP system, the PCM should see a rapid decrease in EVAP system pressure while the vent passage is open. If this rapid decrease in EVAP system pressure does not occur, the PCM sets a DTC to indicate that there is a fault with the EVAP vent solenoid, a blockage in the vent line, or a blockage in the charcoal canister.

PCM SIGNAL OUTPUTS

vent valve is normally open, but is closed when the PCM-controlled vent solenoid is activated. Closing the vent valve allows the PCM to test the EVAP lines for any leaks. To activate the vent solenoid, the PCM applies a ground.

EGR Solenoid Control and Valve Position Signal

The exhaust gas recirculation (EGR) valve introduces exhaust into the intake manifold to be burned in the combustion process, effectively lowering exhaust temperatures by diluting the air/fuel mixture. Because high exhaust temperatures generate nitrogen (NOx) emissions, the effect is lower levels of NOx. Production LS-series engines without an EGR valve perform an EGR function through the camshaft profile with valve timing that accomplishes a similar effect.

The PCM supplies a 5V reference and ground to the EGR solenoid to open and close the valve through a PWM signal. EGR valve position is monitored by the PCM through a sensor within the EGR valve assembly. The PCM runs diagnostic tests to determine if the valve is operating as it is commanded.

The EGR valves used with the Gen III PCM are unlike the early vacuum-operated EGR valves. The LT1 EGR valve (left) opens when vacuum is applied through the electrical solenoid. (Notice the vacuum lines from the solenoid to the engine and from the solenoid to the EGR valve assembly.) Newer engines use an electronically controlled EGR valve (right) with an internal sensor. Early engines being converted for Gen III PCM use either need a custom EGR solution or the elimination of the EGR valve.

AIR Pump Control

Secondary air injection (referred to as AIR, an acronym for "air injection reactor") is a method of injecting fresh air into the exhaust stream. A similar method was implemented before electronic fuel injection as a means of lowering emissions through a more complete combustion of exhaust gases.

With the addition of the catalytic converter and modern PCM logic, the AIR system now serves the purpose of injecting fresh air into the exhaust steam during cold starts to effectively raise the exhaust temperatures at the catalytic converter, bringing the converter up to temperature faster for efficient burn of otherwise rich exhaust mixture. During normal

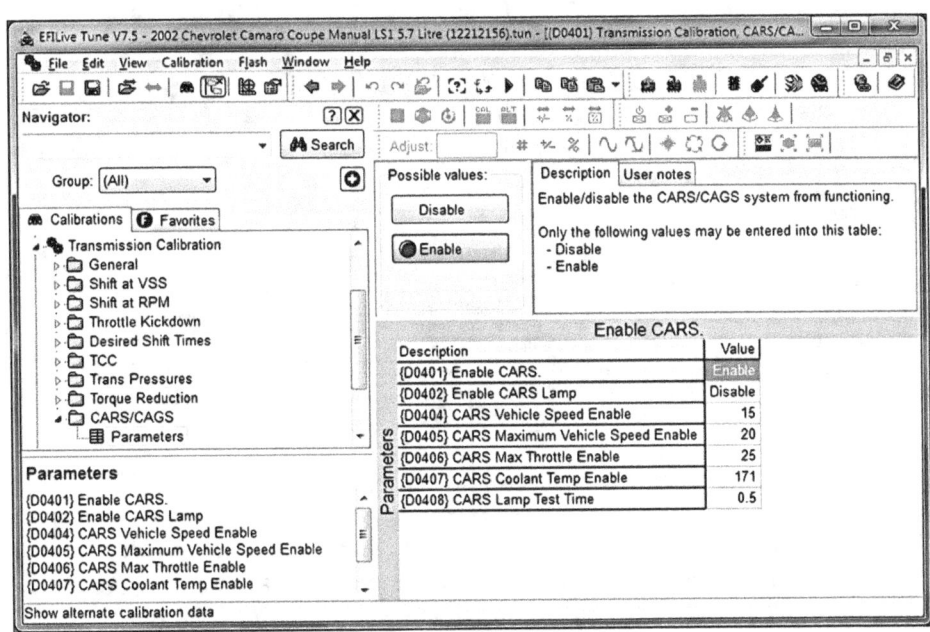

Skip shift calibration options can be found in EFILive through Transmission Calibration > CARS/CAGS > Parameters.

CHAPTER 6

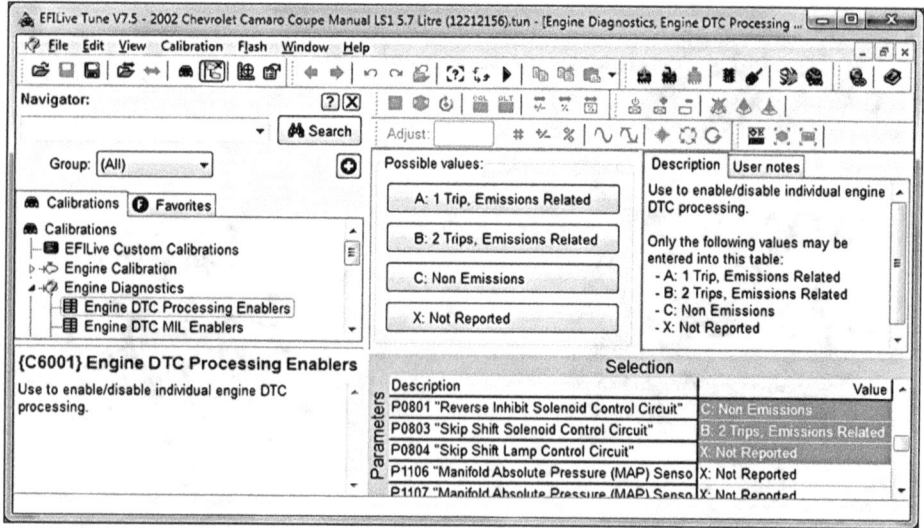

If disabling skip shift (and/or reverse lockout), also be sure to disable DTC processing in the engine diagnostics section of the PCM calibration. By setting DTCs P0801, P0803, and P0804 to "Not Reported" within the processing enablers, the PCM ignores the processing of these DTCs.

engine operating temperatures, the AIR system continues to serve the purpose of reducing carbon monoxide (CO) and hydrocarbons (HC) emissions.

The electronic AIR pump is controlled by the PCM through a relay. The AIR pump relay coil and switch receive 12V battery power through a fused source. When the PCM applies a ground to the relay coil, the relay routes 12V to the AIR pump and fresh air is then introduced into the exhaust manifolds.

Skip Shift Solenoid Control

Vehicles with 6-speed manual transmissions (T56 transmissions) have a feature called skip shift (or computer-aided ratio selection, CARS). It improves fuel economy by using a PCM-controlled solenoid to block out second and third gear during certain driving conditions. The PCM applies a ground to this control circuit to energize the solenoid. An increase in throttle angle or vehicle speed is required to deactivate the solenoid. Many conversions disable this feature. Devices to eliminate skip shift are available, but a simpler solution is to disable the feature in the calibration.

Reverse-Inhibit Solenoid Control

Vehicles with 6-speed manual transmissions contain a reverse-inhibit (or reverse lockout) feature that prevents the driver from (accidentally) shifting into reverse when the vehicle is in motion. The PCM energizes the reverse-inhibit solenoid by applying a ground. With the solenoid energized, the driver can shift the transmission into reverse. When the PCM removes ground from the solenoid, the solenoid is deactivated and the driver is prevented from shifting into reverse.

Transmission Control

All Gen III PCMs were used with 4L60-E transmissions. If your project includes a 4L60-E transmission, you can choose any Gen III PCM for 4L60-E control.)

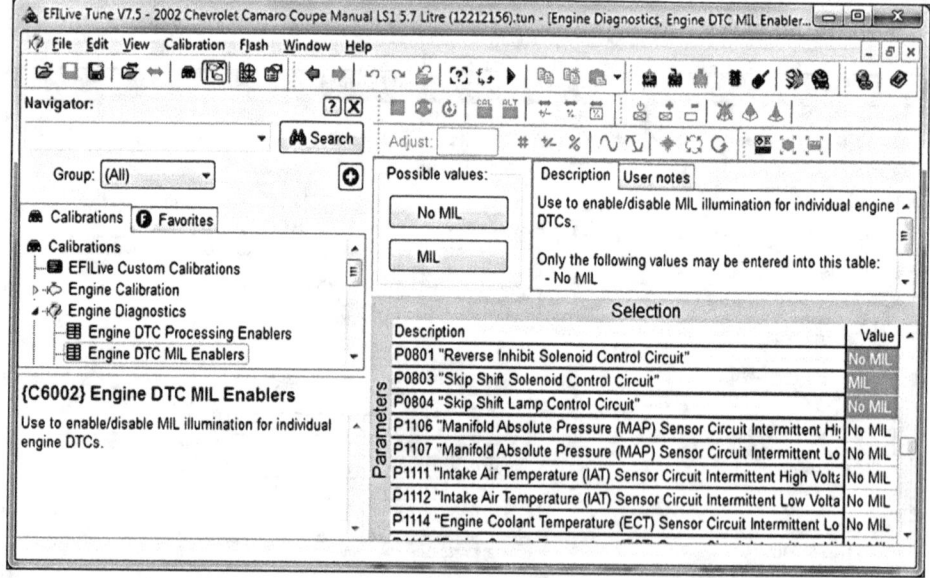

If disabling skip shift (and/or reverse lockout), also be sure to disable MIL illumination in the engine diagnostics section of the PCM calibration. By setting DTCs P0801, P0803, and P0804 to "No MIL" within the MIL enablers, the PCM does not apply ground to the MIL control circuit (the MIL does not illuminate).

PCM SIGNAL OUTPUTS

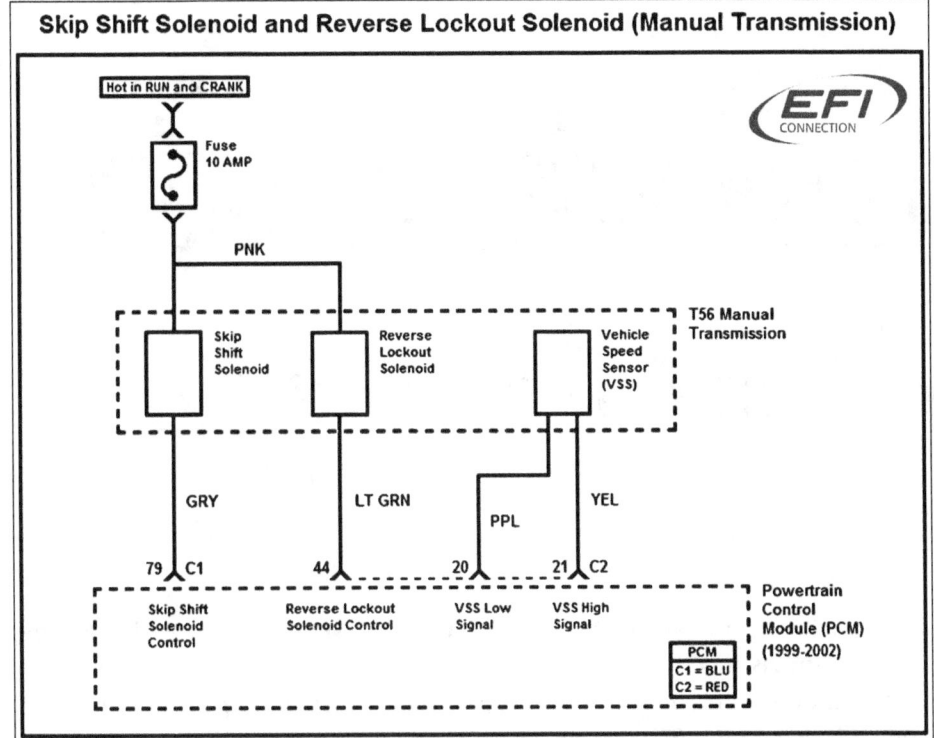

The Gen III PCMs are capable of controlling the skip shift and reverse-lockout solenoids found on the T56 6-speed manual transmission (Camaro, Firebird, and Corvette). PCM control of these solenoids can be enabled or disabled within the PCM calibration.

GM trucks and vans were the only vehicles to receive 4L80-E transmissions. Because the Gen III PCM was only used with 1999-newer trucks and vans, the 1997–1998 Gen III PCM does not directly support 4L80-E transmissions. If your project includes a 4L80-E transmission, choose any 1999-newer Gen III PCM for 4L80-E control. (See Chapter 10 for more information on transmissions.)

Serial Data Output

Gen III PCMs have two Class 2 serial data outputs. In most production vehicles with a Gen III PCM, pin 58 of the PCM's blue connector is used for Class 2 serial data communication. For conversions, this wire is used by the OBD-II DLC. (See Chapter 14 for more information about OBD-II.)

For use with electronic throttle systems only, the PCM has two discrete (meaning one source and one destination) universal asynchronous receiver-transmitter (UART) communication circuits for data transfer between the PCM and TAC module. (See Chapter 8 for more about electronic throttle systems.)

CHAPTER 7

Changing the Firing Order

Let's begin this chapter by agreeing that the "LS1 PCM" is just an ECU that has the designed purpose of controlling the sequencing of ignition and injector events based on a variety of sensor inputs. We can then agree that this ECU is uniquely programmed so that combustion results are favorable so that the stoichiometric ratio of air to fuel (approximately 14.7 to 1) is achieved during normal operating conditions (and so on). Simply put, the ECU can be calibrated for any V-6 or V-8 engine because General Motors designed it that way.

Injectors and Ignition Coils

A very common question goes something like this, "How can I use the LS1 PCM on my Gen I small-block engine when the firing order between the two engines is different?" To answer this question, let's take a look at how General Motors addressed this issue.

In model year 2001, General Motors released Gen I small-block and LS-series engines that all used the same PCM (GM# 12200411). The firing order for the Gen I small-block engine is 1-8-4-3-6-5-7-2. The firing order for the LS-series engines is 1-8-7-2-6-5-4-3. Notice that cylinders 4 and 7 have swapped, and cylinders 3 and 2 have swapped. When you compare this PCM's fuel injector wiring diagrams for the Gen I small-block with the LS-series engines, you see something interesting: General Motors simply swapped injector outputs 4 and 7, and 3 and 2 within the engine wire harness to address the firing order change.

Now compare this PCM's fuel injector calibration details for the Gen I small-block and LS-series engine. EFILive reveals that General Motors also changed the injection bank assignments table values to follow the wire harness fuel injector assignments. The PCM must be calibrated to know which injectors are assigned to bank 1 (cylinders 1, 3, 5, 7) and bank 2 (cylinders 2, 4, 6, 8) so that fuel trims are applied to the proper bank of cylinders. If the injection bank assignments are wrong, fuel trims are extreme and the engine runs poorly and may even stall.

GM V-8 Firing Order

Engine Type	Cylinder							
	A	B	C	D	E	F	G	H
Gen I Small-Block Chevy	1	8	4	3	6	5	7	2
Gen II LT1	1	8	4	3	6	5	7	2
Gen III LS-Series	1	8	7	2	6	5	4	3
Gen VI 454 and 502 Big-Block Chevy	1	8	4	3	6	5	7	2
Vortec 8100 8.1L Big-Block Chevy	1	8	7	2	6	5	4	3

Not all GM V-8 engines have the same firing order. This chart compares the order for five engine families. Notice that cylinders 4 and 7 and 3 and 2 are swapped for early small-/big-block engines and late small-/big-block engines.

CHANGING THE FIRING ORDER

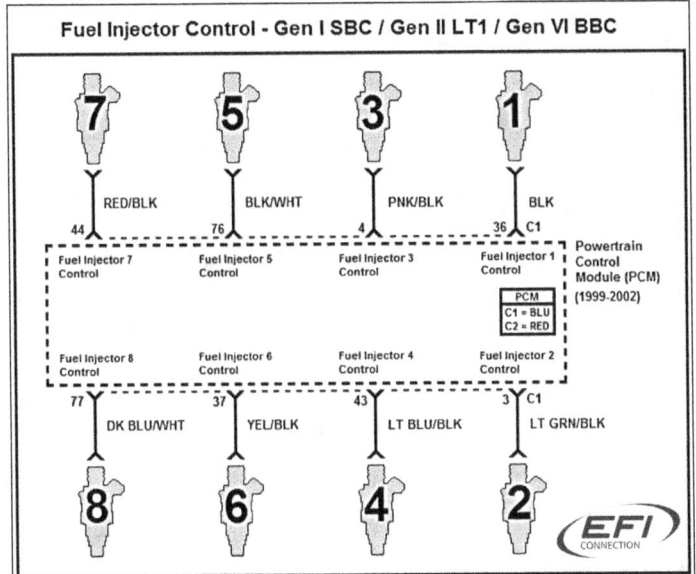

This schematic represents proper wiring of the eight fuel injectors for Gen I small-block, Gen II LT1, and Gen VI big-block engines with the firing order 1-8-4-3-6-5-7-2.

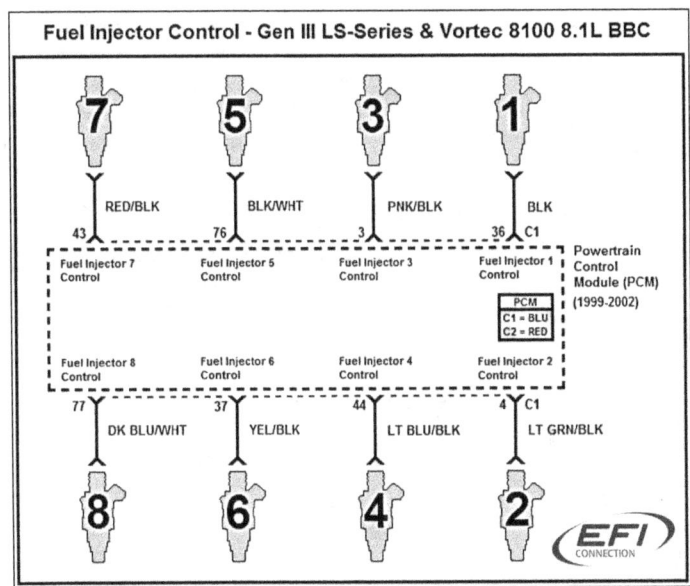

This schematic represents proper wiring of the eight fuel injectors for Gen III and Vortec 8100 8.1L big-block engines with the firing order 1-8-7-2-6-5-4-3.

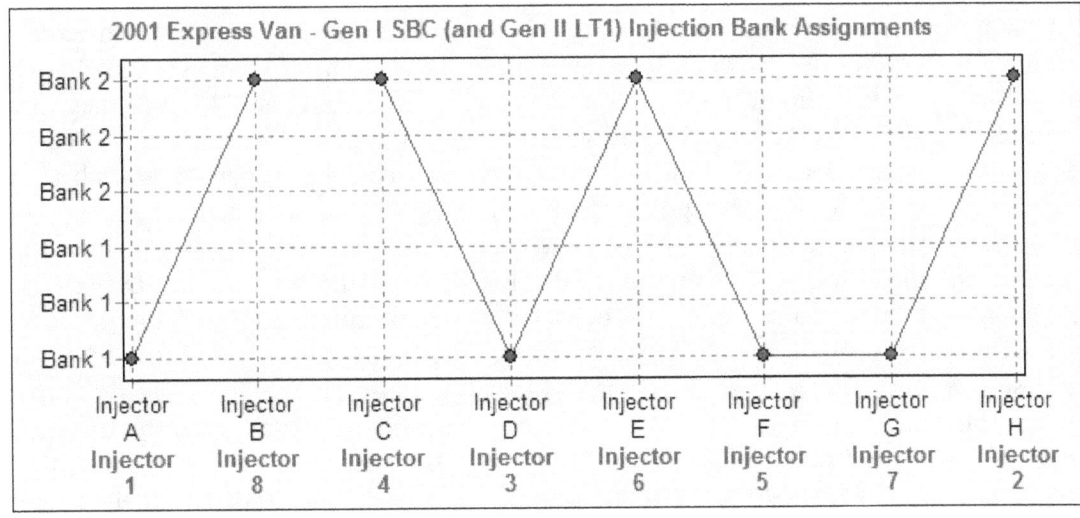

This EFILive table represents the assignment of fuel injectors to their proper cylinder in the engine firing order. These particular table values were taken from a 2001 5.7L Express Van.

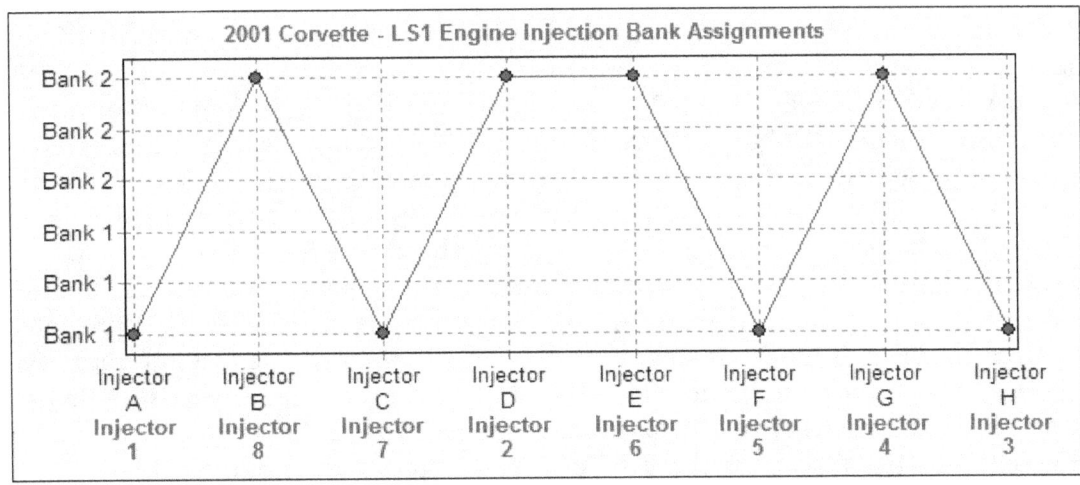

This EFILive table represents the assignment of fuel injectors to their proper cylinder in the engine firing order. These particular table values were taken from a 2001 LS1 Corvette.

CHAPTER 7

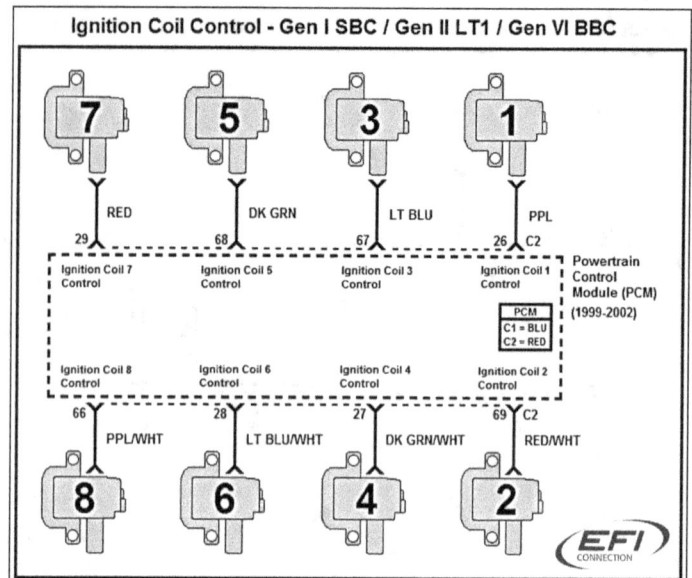

This schematic represents proper wiring of the eight ignition coils for Gen I small-block, Gen II LT1, and Gen VI big-block engines with the firing order 1-8-4-3-6-5-7-2.

This schematic represents proper wiring of the eight ignition coils for Gen III and Vortec 8100 8.1L big-block engines with the firing order 1-8-7-2-6-5-4-3.

Although the PCMs are the same, the ignition systems are different. Gen I Vortec V-8 engines use a four-pulse, low-resolution, crankshaft signal for single coil and distributor ignition. LS-series engines use a 24-pulse (24x), high-resolution, crankshaft signal for coil-per-cylinder ignition. However, the same logic applies here if using a Gen I small-block engine with the LS-series engine's 24x crankshaft signal. The wire harness requires that ignition coil assignments for cylinders 4 and 7, and 3 and 2 be swapped.

DTCs are assigned to ignition coil control circuits. The calibration table for the assignment of these DTCs is not available within most tuning software packages. A changed firing order may result in an incorrect DTC notification.

For instance, let's say you have a PCM from a 2001 Camaro with the LS1 engine. You installed a 24x conversion on the Gen I small-block and made the necessary wire harness and injection bank assignment updates. During engine operation, the PCM determines that the ignition coil 4 control circuit has shorted to a voltage. The DTC P0357 for cylinder 7 is set. Because the firing order has changed, and the ignition coil control circuit firing order diagnostics table has not been updated, this DTC actually represents cylinder 4 because of the firing order difference between a Gen I small-block and LS1 engine.

Modifying Calibration

To begin, open your previously saved calibration file or read the current calibration stored in your PCM (press Ctrl+PgUp). Once your calibration file is open in EFILive, access the Injection Bank Assignments table by expanding Engine Calibration, expanding Fuel, expanding Injectors, and then selecting the Injection Bank Assignments table.

For each fuel injector (labeled A through H in no particular order), the table indicates which bank of cylinders (bank 1 or 2) the fuel injector is located in. Bank 1 represents cylinders 1-3-5-7, and bank 2 represents cylinders 2-4-6-8. Notice all odd injectors are assigned to bank 1 and all even injectors are assigned to bank 2.

Let's first look at the injection bank assignments for an LS1 engine. (See Figure 7.1.) The firing order for Gen III engines is 1-8-7-2-6-5-4-3. Because the engine firing order begins with cylinder 1, the injection bank assignments table uses Injector A to represent the fuel injector located at cylinder 1.

Moving along with the firing order, the fuel injector located at cylinder 8 is represented as Injector B, the fuel injector at cylinder 7 is represented as Injector C, the fuel injector at cylinder 2 is represented as Injector D, the fuel injector at cylinder 6 is represented as Injector E, the fuel injector at cylinder 5 is represented as Injector F, the fuel injector at cylinder 4 is represented as Injector G, and the fuel injector at cylinder 3 is represented as Injector H.

CHANGING THE FIRING ORDER

Now let's look at an engine with a different firing order, the Gen I small-block. This firing order is 1-8-4-3-6-5-7-2. Just as with the LS1 example above, you see that the fuel injector at cylinder 1 is represented as Injector A and along the engine firing order through cylinder 8 represented by Injector H. Once again, all odd injectors are assigned to bank 1, and all even injectors are assigned to bank 2.

Six-cylinder engines do not use this entire table. If you were to open a calibration file from a 2001 S10 4.3L PCM (see Figure 7.1), you would see values for the last two injectors, G and H. (See Figure 7.2.) This is because the "LS1 PCM" is simply an ECM that is calibrated for the engine in which it is being used.

For the injection bank assignments table to exist in the PCM's memory space, it must be dimensioned. A programmer must define the size (memory space) that an object (such as a table or constant) requires. In this case, General Motors intended for this injection bank assignments table to be used with an engine that contains no more than

Diagnostic Trouble Codes (DTCs)

P Codes	Generic	Cylinder	LS-Series	Gen I SBC	Vortec V-6	Viper V-10	Ferrari V-12
P0351	A	1	A	A	A	A	A
P0352	B	2	D	H	F	J	I
P0353	C	3	H	D	E	E	E
P0354	D	4	G	C	D	D	K
P0355	E	5	F	F	C	G	C
P0356	F	6	E	E	B	F	G
P0357	G	7	C	G	—	I	B
P0358	H	8	B	B	—	H	J
P0359	I	9	—	—	—	C	F
P0360	J	10	—	—	—	B	L
P0361	K	11	—	—	—	—	D
P0362	L	12	—	—	—	—	H

This chart represents the assignment of cylinders (A through L) to DTCs (P0351 through P0362) for proper ignition coil control circuit malfunction detection. If an ignition coil control circuit is open or shorted, the PCM uses this table to assign the appropriate DTC.

Some OBD-II vehicles have engines with more than eight cylinders, so OBD-II systems have reserved DTCs P0351 through P0362 for ignition coil control circuit malfunction detection. The LS1 PCM never reports DTCs P0359 through P0362 because cylinders 9 through 12 are not supported.

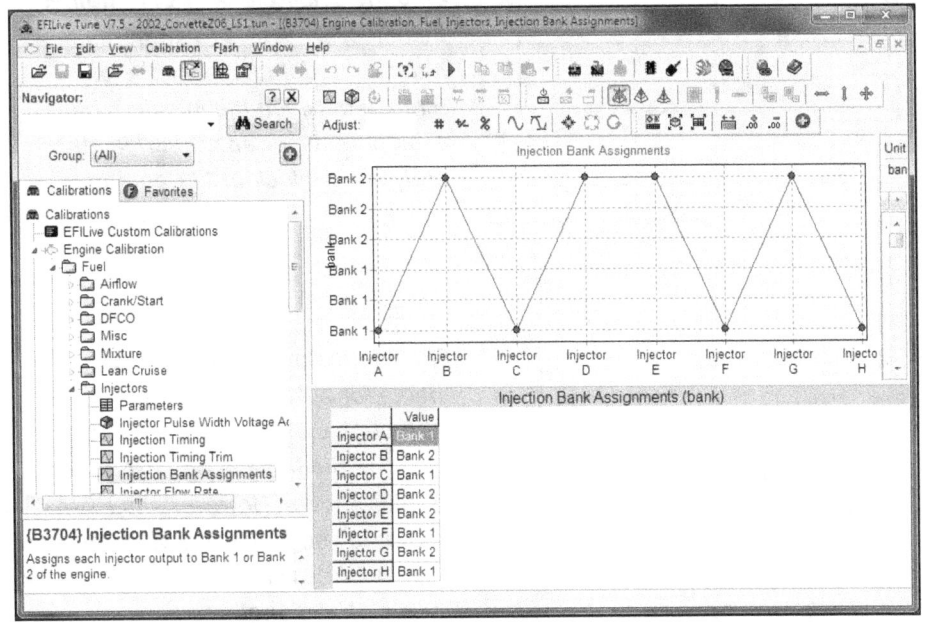

The injection bank assignments table must follow the wiring of the fuel injectors to the PCM. If the engine firing order changes and this table is not updated, fuel trims are extreme and eventually cause the engine to stall. The values represented here were taken from a 2001 LS1 Corvette.

CHAPTER 7

eight cylinders. This is why the table displays eight injectors for a calibration file written for an engine with only six cylinders. (Had General Motors written a calibration file for a PCM for an engine with four cylinders, the table would also display eight injectors.)

This is simply a lookup table as the PCM knows (from elsewhere) that this engine has six cylinders, is using a low-resolution 3x crankshaft signal to know engine position, and to fire injectors once every 60 degrees of crankshaft rotation. The last two injectors represented in this table are simply ignored when the PCM looks for injection bank assignments. The firing order for this 4.3L V-6 engine is 1-6-5-4-3-2.

Again, begin with the fuel injector at cylinder 1 being represented as Injector A and move along the engine firing order through cylinder 6 represented by Injector F. Here also, all odd injectors are assigned to bank 1, and all even injectors are assigned to bank 2. The value of Injector G and Injector H are ignored.

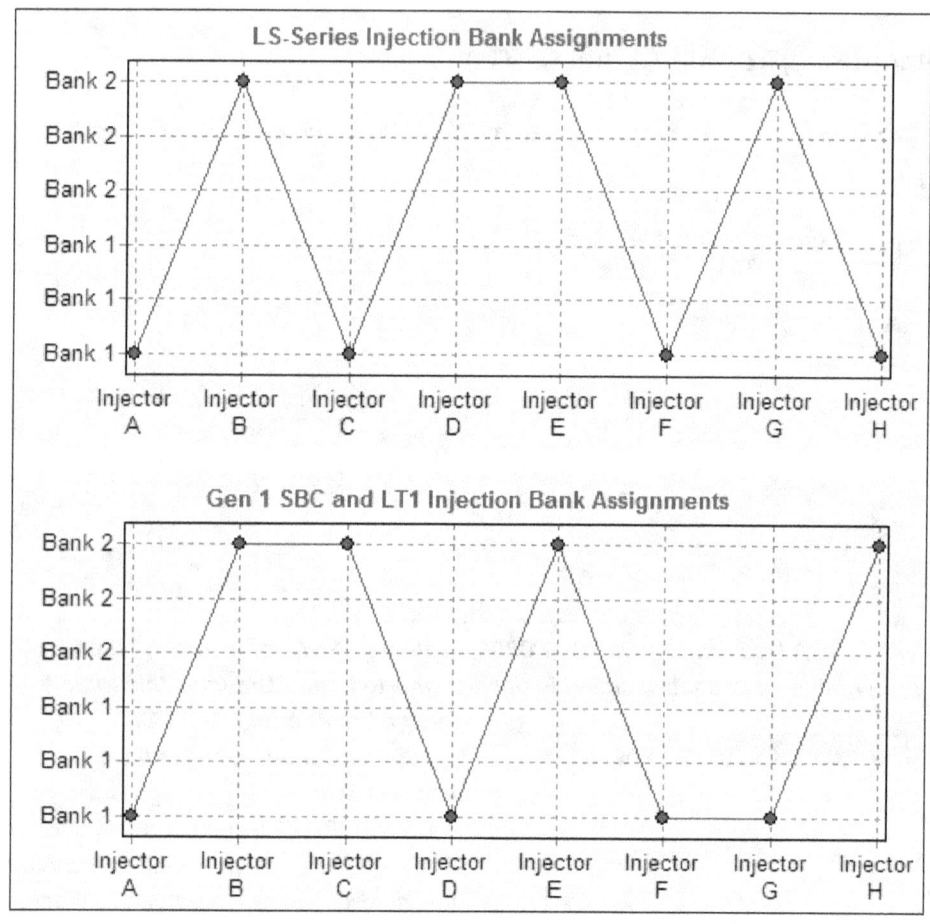

Fig. 7.1. The LS-series engines have a different firing order than the early small-block and LT1 engines. Cylinders 2 and 3 and 7 and 4 have been swapped in the engine firing order. When using an LS-series engine calibration (24x crank signal) with an early small-block or LT1 engine, the injection bank assignments table must be updated. Notice the difference between the injection bank assignments for an LS-series and early small-block or LT1 engine.

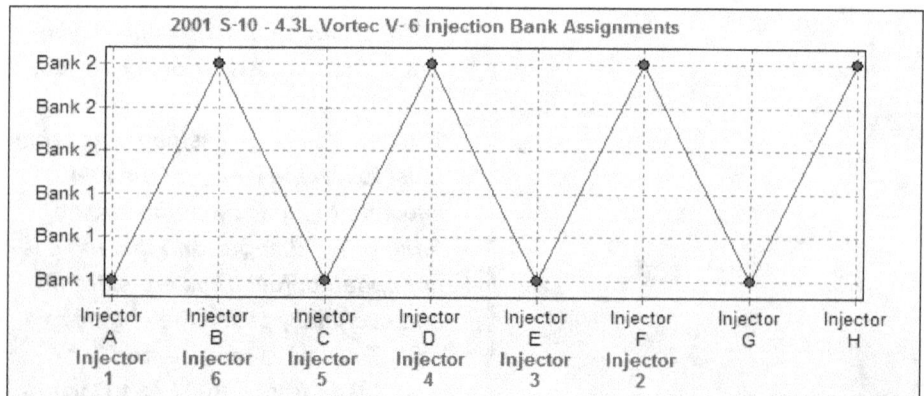

Fig. 7.2. The injection bank assignments for a 4.3L V-6 are displayed as though there are eight injectors because the table is provisioned for eight cylinders. However, the PCM knows to use only the first six injector assignments when using a calibration for a 4.3L V-6 engine.

CHAPTER 8

ELECTRONIC THROTTLE EQUIPMENT

General Motors introduced electronic throttle, or drive-by-wire, with the LS1 engine in the 1997 Corvette. Electronic throttle was released before cable throttle for the LS-series engine family. In 1998, the Camaro and Firebird received a cable throttle LS1 engine. The GM trucks received LS-series engines in 1999 and, depending on make/model, were available with either cable throttle or electronic throttle. Navigating through the various electronic throttle equipment may be intimidating, but look carefully at the components to ensure success.

1997–2004 Corvette

The Corvette received the same electronic throttle equipment from 1997–2004. Other than a few GM part number updates, the equipment remained the same and electronic throttle equipment can be interchanged. The LS1 and LS6 engines received the same equipment. Everything changed (throttle body, pedal assembly, and TAC) when the LS2 engine was introduced in 2005.

Throttle Body

The Corvette throttle body is fitted with a TPS to monitor throttle blade angle. It is also fitted with a motor, operated by the TAC module, to open and close the throttle blade. The TPS housing contains two individual sensors with separate signals, low reference, and 5V circuits. The two TPS signals are monitored by the TAC module. As the throttle blade is opened, TPS sensor 1 voltage sweeps toward 5V reference, and TPS sensor 2 voltage sweeps toward low reference. These opposing signals are used by the PCM to monitor and make one throttle angle PID available.

LS2/LS3 Throttle Body: The 2005–2008 LS2/LS3 throttle body is a popular upgrade for the 1997–2004 LS1/LS6 Corvette because it is electronically compatible with the 1997–2004 Corvette throttle control system. The larger 90-mm throttle opening and four-bolt pattern requires an intake manifold upgrade or an adapter plate. Aftermarket wire harness

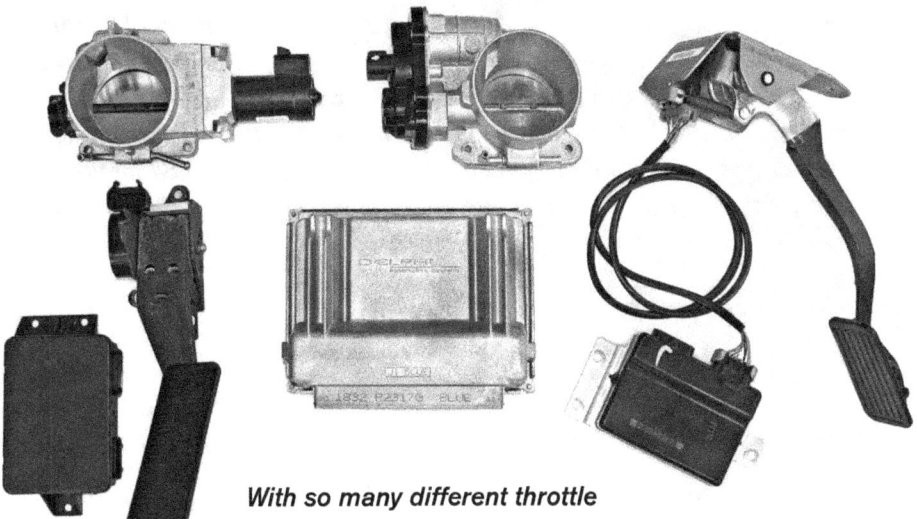

With so many different throttle bodies, pedals, and TAC modules, you must take caution to choose the correct combination of components. Choosing the wrong components could result in no throttle response and an illuminated MIL lamp.

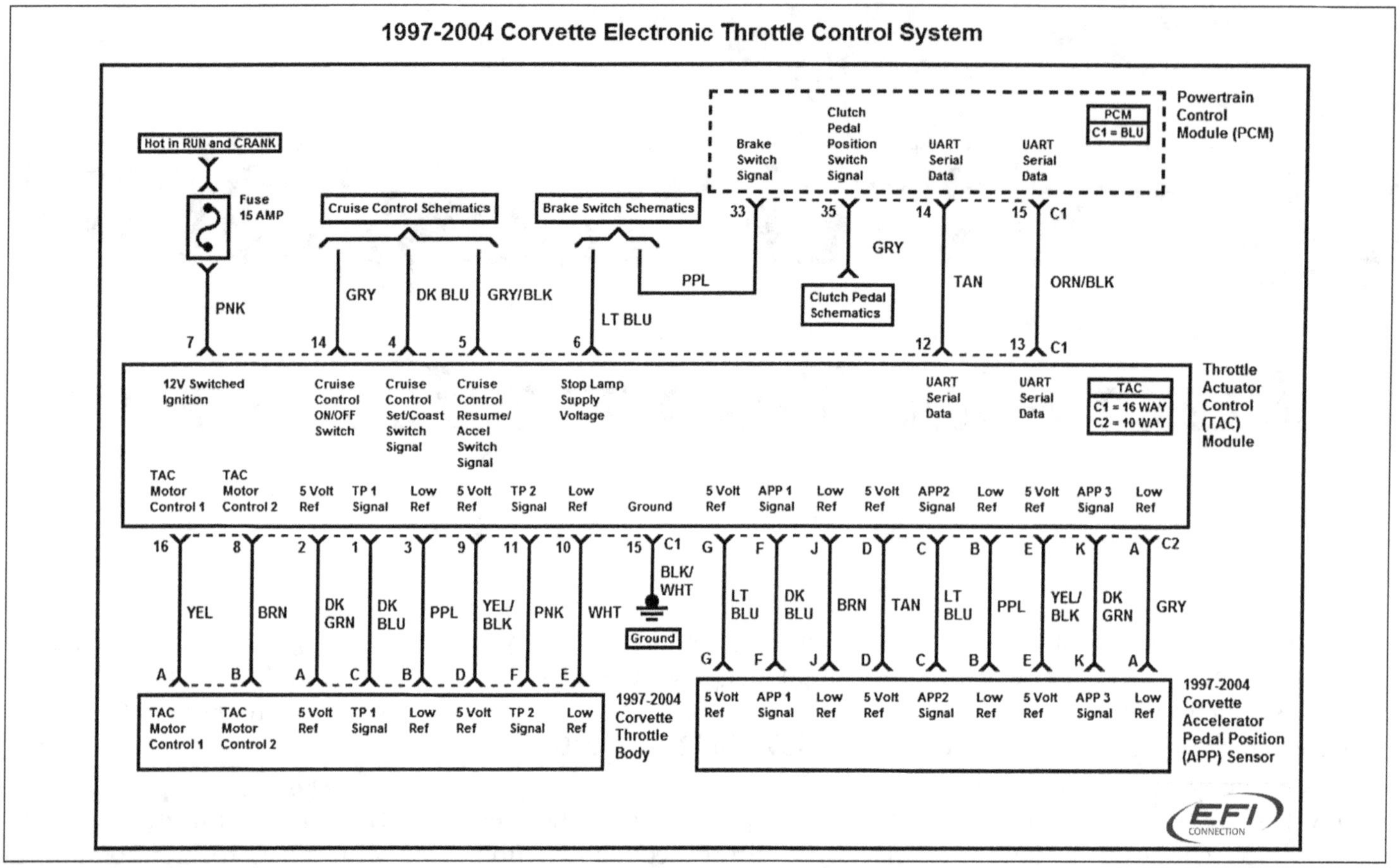

CHAPTER 8

![1997-2004 Corvette Electronic Throttle Control System wiring diagram]

This wiring diagram represents the 1997–2004 Corvette electronic throttle control system.

The LS1 Corvette throttle body was the first electronic throttle body used with Chevrolet V-8 engines. The throttle position sensor is mounted on the bank 2 side of the engine and the throttle shaft motor is mounted on the bank 1 side of the engine. The blade on this throttle body measures approximately 75 mm in diameter.

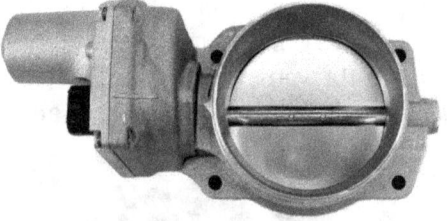

The LS2 and early LS3 Corvette throttle body is an electronically compatible alternative to the smaller LS1 throttle body. The blade on this throttle body measures approximately 90 mm in diameter. Because the bore is larger and the four-bolt pattern is different than the three-bolt pattern of the LS1 intake manifold, the use of this throttle body requires a different intake manifold or adapter plate.

LS1/LS6 Corvette TPS DTC Processing Limits

DTC	Description	TPS Failure	0% TPS Range	100% TPS Range
P1120	Throttle Position (TP) Sensor 1 Circuit	else 0.13 - 4.87 V	0.13 - 0.67 V	4.09 - 4.87 V
P1220	Throttle Position (TP) Sensor 2 Circuit	else 0.13 - 4.87 V	4.30 - 4.80 V	0.13 - 1.0 V

The Corvette PCM and TAC monitor values from the two throttle position signals to identify proper operation of the throttle body. A DTC sets if a TPS value exceeds one of GM's predetermined threshold values. This chart reviews the allowable operating ranges for each TP sensor (see "TPS Failure") and the expected 0-percent and 100-percent voltage ranges for each TP sensor.

ELECTRONIC THROTTLE EQUIPMENT

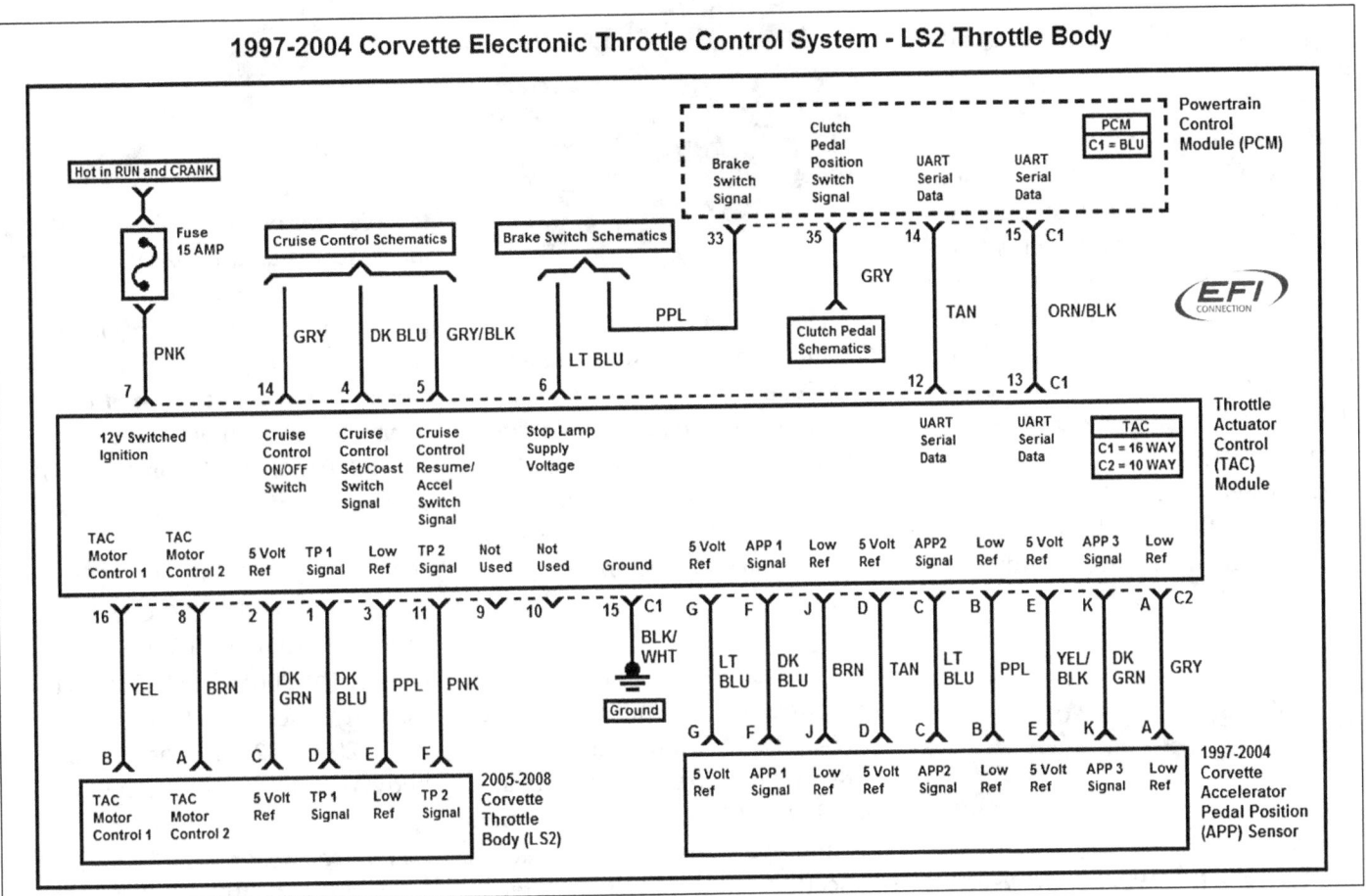

This wiring diagram represents the 1997–2004 Corvette electronic throttle control system with LS2 throttle body. Notice the 5V reference and low reference for TP sensor 2 is not used because TP signal 1 and TP signal 2 share the same 5V reference and low reference from the TAC module.

LS2 Throttle Body TPS Limits

	Sensor 1 (limits)	Sensor 2 (limits)
Blade Closed (0% Throttle Angle)	0.56 V (0.13 to 0.67 V)	4.38 V (4.30 to 4.80 V)
Wide Open Throttle (WOT)	4.33 V (4.09 to 4.87 V)	0.57 V (0.13 to 1.0 V)

This bench test of the LS2 throttle body demonstrates the electronic compatibility with the 1997–2004 Corvette electronic throttle system.

LS1/LS6 Corvette APP DTC Processing Limits

DTC	Description	APP Failure	0% APP Range (expected)	100% APP Range (expected)
P1275	Accelerator Pedal Position (APP) Sensor 1 Circuit	else 0.24 to 4.49 V	0.25 to 2.2 V (below 1 volt)	2.24 to 4.2 V (above 2 volts)
P1280	Accelerator Pedal Position (APP) Sensor 2 Circuit	else 0.83 to 4.81 V	3.90 to 4.81 V (above 4 volts)	0.83 to 2.9 V (below 2.9 volts)
P1285	Accelerator Pedal Position (APP) Sensor 3 Circuit	else 1.63 to 4.28 V	3.29 to 4.28 V (above 3.8 volts)	1.63 to 3.1 V (below 3.1 volts)

The Corvette PCM and TAC monitor values from the three accelerator position signals to identify proper operation of the accelerator pedal assembly. A DTC sets if an APP value exceeds one of GM's predetermined threshold values. This chart reviews the allowable operating ranges for each APP sensor (see "APP Failure") and the expected 0- and 100-percent voltage ranges for each APP sensor.

CHAPTER 8

adapters are available for a plug-and-play installation.

Pedal Assembly

The LS1/LS6 Corvette accelerator pedal assembly has an APP sensor that contains three APP signals. The TAC module uses the three APP signals to determine absolute pedal position. APP sensor 1 signals voltage increases as the pedal is depressed. APP sensor 2 and sensor 3 signal voltage decreases as the pedal is depressed. The APP sensor signals are used by the PCM to monitor and make available one accelerator pedal percent PID.

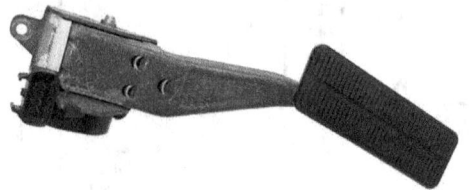

The C5 Corvette (1997–2004) used only one accelerator pedal assembly. It is very popular because of its size and mounting configuration.

Throttle Actuator Control Module

There have been a few part number changes for the 1997–2004 Corvette TAC module but the Corvette TAC modules are interchangeable

The 1997–2004 Corvette and 2004–2005 Cadillac CTS-V use the same TAC module. Although these vehicles use a different accelerator pedal assembly and TAC-to-pedal wire harness, electronic throttle equipment can be used interchangeably among these vehicles.

and General Motors maintains only one current part number for all 1997–2004 TAC modules. The Corvette TAC module looks identical to the 1999–2002 GM Truck TAC module, and even has the same harness connections, but carries a different GM part number and is not interchangeable with GM trucks.

2004–2005 Cadillac CTS-V

The 2004–2005 Cadillac CTS-V has much in common with the LS6 Corvette. General Motors used the Corvette TAC module, 2004 PCM

The 2004–2005 Cadillac CTS-V accelerator pedal assembly is unique. What is worth noting for Gen IV systems is that this pedal assembly uses the same housing (but a different harness connector) as some of the common LS-series applications (such as LS2 Trailblazer SS and Chevrolet Performance LS2/LS3/LS7 kits).

(GM# 12586243), and LS1/LS6 throttle body with the LS6 CTS-V. In the same way that the LS1/LS6 Corvette can use the 2005–2008 LS2/LS3 throttle body, the LS6 CTS-V can use the 2005–2008 LS2/LS3 Corvette throttle body as a performance upgrade.

Pedal Assembly

Even though a different accelerator pedal assembly was used with the 2004–2005 CTS-V, its APP sensor functions in similar ways to the 1997–2004 Corvette APP sensor. APP sensor 1 signals voltage increases as the pedal is depressed. APP sensor 2 and APP sensor 3 signal voltage decreases as the pedal is depressed. The APP sensor signals are used

2004-2005 Cadillac CTS-V APP DTC Processing Limits

DTC	Description	APP Failure	0% APP Range (expected)	100% APP Range (expected)
P2120	Accelerator Pedal Position (APP) Sensor 1 Circuit	else 0.24 to 4.49 V	0.25 to 2.2 V (below 1 volt)	2.24 to 4.2 V (above 2 volts)
P2125	Accelerator Pedal Position (APP) Sensor 2 Circuit	else 0.83 to 4.81 V	3.90 to 4.81 V (above 4 volts)	0.83 to 2.9 V (below 2.9 volts)
P2130	Accelerator Pedal Position (APP) Sensor 3 Circuit	else 1.63 to 4.28 V	3.29 to 4.28 V (above 3.8 volts)	1.63 to 3.1 V (below 3.1 volts)

The CTS-V PCM and TAC monitor values from the three accelerator position signals to identify proper operation of the accelerator pedal assembly. A DTC sets if an APP value exceeds one of GM's predetermined threshold values. This chart reviews the allowable operating ranges for each APP sensor (see "APP Failure") and the expected 0- and 100-percent voltage ranges for each APP sensor.

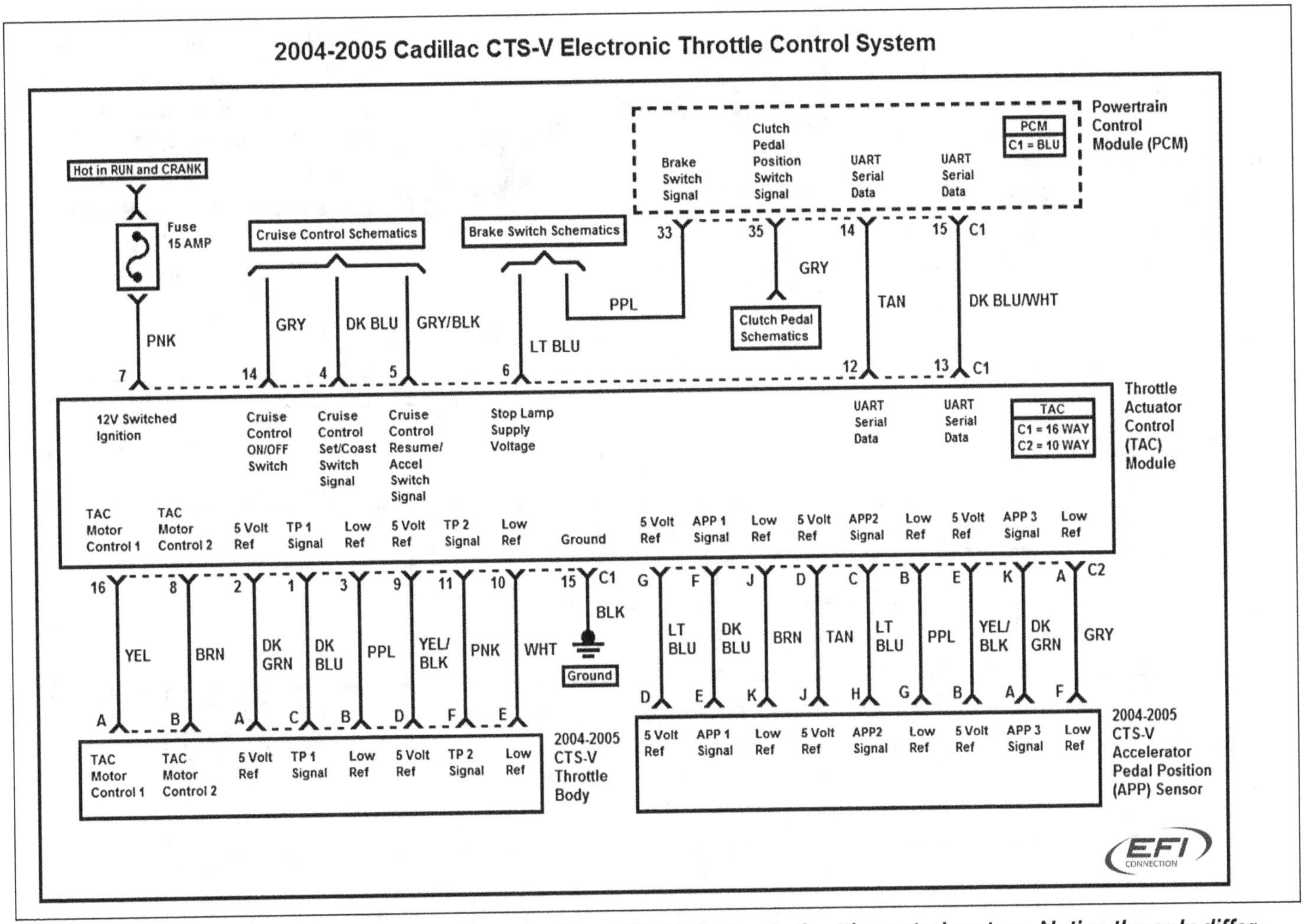

ELECTRONIC THROTTLE EQUIPMENT

This wiring diagram represents the 2004–2005 Cadillac CTS-V electronic throttle control system. Notice the only difference between the CTS-V and 1997–2004 Corvette is the accelerator pedal assembly and TAC-to-pedal wire harness.

by the PCM to monitor and make available one accelerator pedal percent PID. Be careful to use a matching accelerator pedal and TAC-to-pedal wire harness. The Corvette harness does not work with the CTS-V accelerator pedal.

GM Truck

In general, trucks with a Gen III engine have two different electronic throttle configurations: 1999–2002 and 2003–2007. However, a careful look at the Gen III electronic throttle systems used in GM trucks from 1999–2007 reveals four specific configurations.

1999–2002

Throttle Body: The truck throttle body is fitted with a TPS to monitor throttle blade angle and a motor, operated by the TAC module, to open and close the throttle blade. The TPS housing contains two individual sensors with separate signal, low reference, and 5V circuits. The two TPS signals are monitored by the TAC module. As the throttle blade is opened, TPS sensor 1 voltage sweeps toward 5V reference and TPS sensor 2 voltage sweeps toward low reference. These opposing signals are used by the PCM to monitor and make available one throttle angle PID.

The GM truck throttle body looks much like the 1997–2004 Corvette throttle body but with the TPS and throttle shaft motor on opposite sides. The truck and Corvette share the same throttle shaft motor (which is not serviceable separately) but with opposing polarity. The blade on this throttle body measures approximately 75 mm in diameter.

CHAPTER 8

Pedal Assembly: The 1999–2002 truck accelerator pedal assembly contains an APP sensor that contains three APP signals. The TAC module uses the three APP signals to determine absolute pedal position. APP sensor 1 signals voltage increases as the pedal is depressed. APP sensor 2 and sensor 3

The GM truck pedal introduced in 1999 was used through 2005. There is an adjustable pedal assembly but the APP sensor is the same. The 1999–2002 systems use all three of the APP signals while the 2003–2005 systems use only two of the three APP signals.

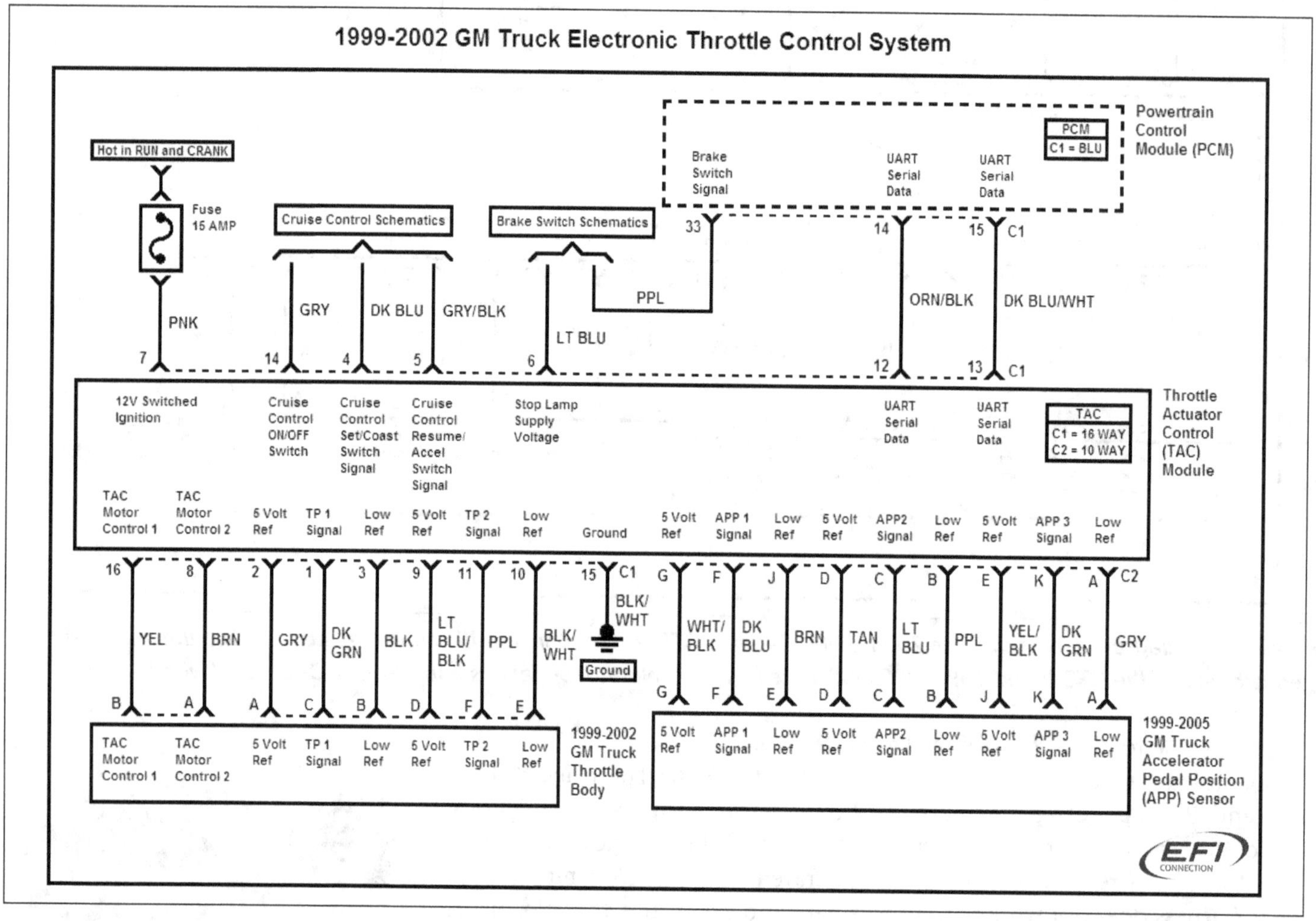

This wiring diagram represents the 1999–2002 GM truck electronic throttle control system. This is the only GM truck system that uses the three APP sensors in the accelerator pedal. Later systems use two APP sensors.

1999–2002 Truck TPS DTC Processing Limits

DTC	Description	TPS Failure	0% TPS Range	100% TPS Range
P1120	Throttle Position (TP) Sensor 1 Circuit	else 0.13 to 4.87 V	0.13 to 0.67 V	4.09 to 4.87 V
P1220	Throttle Position (TP) Sensor 2 Circuit	else 0.13 to 4.87 V	4.30 to 4.80 V	0.13 to 1.0 V

The GM truck PCM and TAC monitor values from the two throttle position signals to identify proper operation of the throttle body. A DTC sets if a TPS value exceeds one of GM's predetermined threshold values. This chart reviews the allowable operating ranges for each TP sensor (see "TPS Failure") and the expected 0- and 100-percent voltage ranges for each TP sensor.

ELECTRONIC THROTTLE EQUIPMENT

signal voltage decreases as the pedal is depressed. The APP sensor signals are used by the PCM to monitor and make available one accelerator pedal percent PID.

Throttle Actuator Control Module: The 1999–2002 truck TAC module is specific to 1999–2002 trucks and must use a 1999–2002 truck PCM. The truck TAC module looks identical to the 1997–2004 Corvette TAC module, and even has the same harness connections, but carries a different GM part number and is not interchangeable with the Corvette.

2003–2004

In 2003, General Motors introduced a new Gen III truck throttle body, TAC module, and PCM. This new throttle body is not backward compatible with the 1999–2002 trucks. Always use matching equipment to ensure compatibility.

Throttle Body: The 2003 throttle body was used with Gen III trucks from 2003 to 2007. The truck throttle body is fitted with an internal TPS to

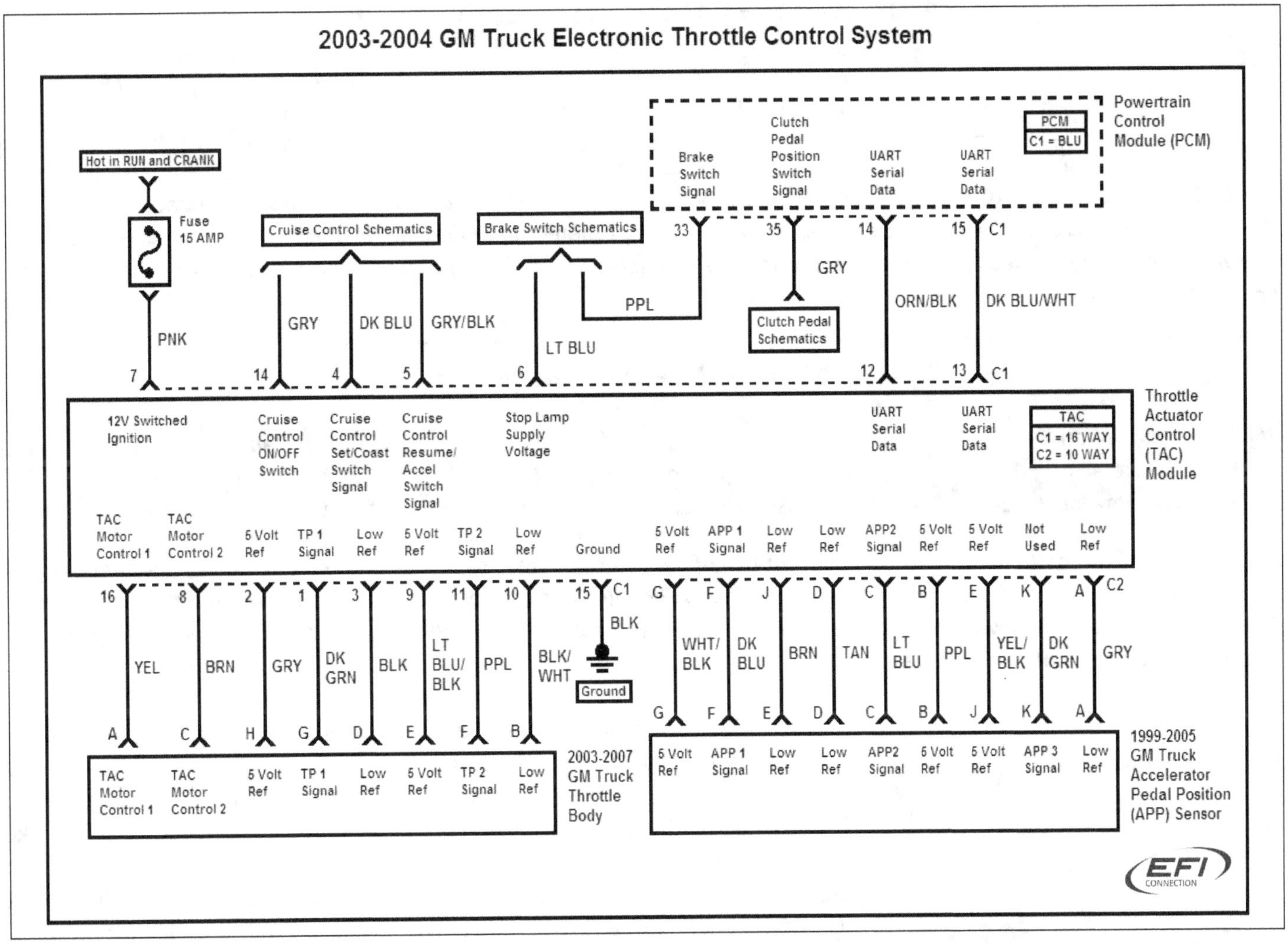

This is the 1999–2002 GM truck TAC module. It looks identical to the 1997–2004 Corvette TAC module but it is not interchangeable with other electronic throttle systems.

This wiring diagram represents the 2003–2004 GM Truck electronic throttle control system. This system uses only two of the three APP sensors. As compared to the 1999–2002 GM truck TAC module, the 5V reference and low reference for APP sensor 2 have been swapped. Although 2003–2004 GM trucks use only two of the three APP sensors, the 2003–2004 TAC-to-pedal wire harness contains the three wires for APP sensor 3. This is probably a carry-over from 1999–2002 GM stock.

CHAPTER 8

1999–2002 Truck APP DTC Processing Limits

DTC	Description	APP Failure	0% APP Range (expected)	100% APP Range (expected)
P1275	Accelerator Pedal Position (APP) Sensor 1 Circuit	else 0.25 to 4.22 V	0.25 to 2.24 V (below 1 volt)	2.24 to 4.23 V (above 2 volts)
P1280	Accelerator Pedal Position (APP) Sensor 2 Circuit	else 0.83 to 4.81 V	3.90 to 4.81 V (above 4 volts)	0.83 to 2.9 V (below 2.9 volts)
P1285	Accelerator Pedal Position (APP) Sensor 3 Circuit	else 1.63 to 4.28 V	3.29 to 4.28 V (above 3.8 volts)	1.63 to 3.1 V (below 3.1 volts)

The GM truck PCM and TAC monitor values from the three accelerator position signals to identify proper operation of the accelerator pedal assembly. A DTC sets if an APP value exceeds one of GM's predetermined threshold values. This chart reviews the allowable operating ranges for each APP sensor (see "APP Failure") and the expected 0- and 100-percent voltage ranges for each APP sensor.

2003–2007 Truck TPS DTC Processing Limits

DTC	Description	TPS Failure	0% TPS Range	100% TPS Limit
P0120	Throttle Position (TP) Sensor 1 Circuit	else 0.37 to 4.51 V	0.37 to 0.71 V	4.51 V
P0220	Throttle Position (TP) Sensor 2 Circuit	else 0.28 to 4.60 V	0.28 to 0.81 V	4.60 V

The GM truck PCM and TAC monitor values from the two throttle position signals to identify proper operation of the throttle body. A DTC sets if a TPS value exceeds one of GM's predetermined threshold values. This chart reviews the allowable operating ranges for each TP sensor (see "TPS Failure") and the expected 0-percent range and 100-percent limit voltages for each TP sensor.

2003–2005 Truck APP DTC Processing Limits

DTC	Description	APP Failure	0% APP Range	100% APP Limit
P2120	Accelerator Pedal Position (APP) Sensor 1 Circuit	else 0.24 to 4.49 V	0.24 to 2.24 V	4.49 V
P2125	Accelerator Pedal Position (APP) Sensor 2 Circuit	else 0.24 to 4.49 V	0.24 to 2.24 V	4.49 V

The GM truck PCM and TAC monitor values from two of the three accelerator position signals to identify proper operation of the accelerator pedal assembly. A DTC sets if an APP value exceeds one of GM's predetermined threshold values. This chart reviews the allowable operating ranges for each APP sensor (see "APP Failure") and the expected 0-percent range and 100-percent limit voltages for each APP sensor.

monitor throttle blade angle and an internal motor, operated by the TAC module, to open and close the throttle blade. The throttle body contains two individual TP sensors with separate signal, low reference, and 5V circuits. The two TP signals are monitored by the TAC module. As the throttle blade is opened, both TP sensor 1 and TP sensor 2 signal voltages sweep toward 5V reference. These signals are used by the PCM to monitor and make available one throttle angle PID.

Pedal Assembly: The 2003–2004 truck accelerator pedal assembly is the same as used with 1999–2002

The 2003–2007 truck TAC modules are interchangeable. This TAC module uses the same wire harness connectors as 1999–2002 GM trucks, with an aluminum back plate and smooth plastic cover, but the housing looks very different.

ELECTRONIC THROTTLE EQUIPMENT

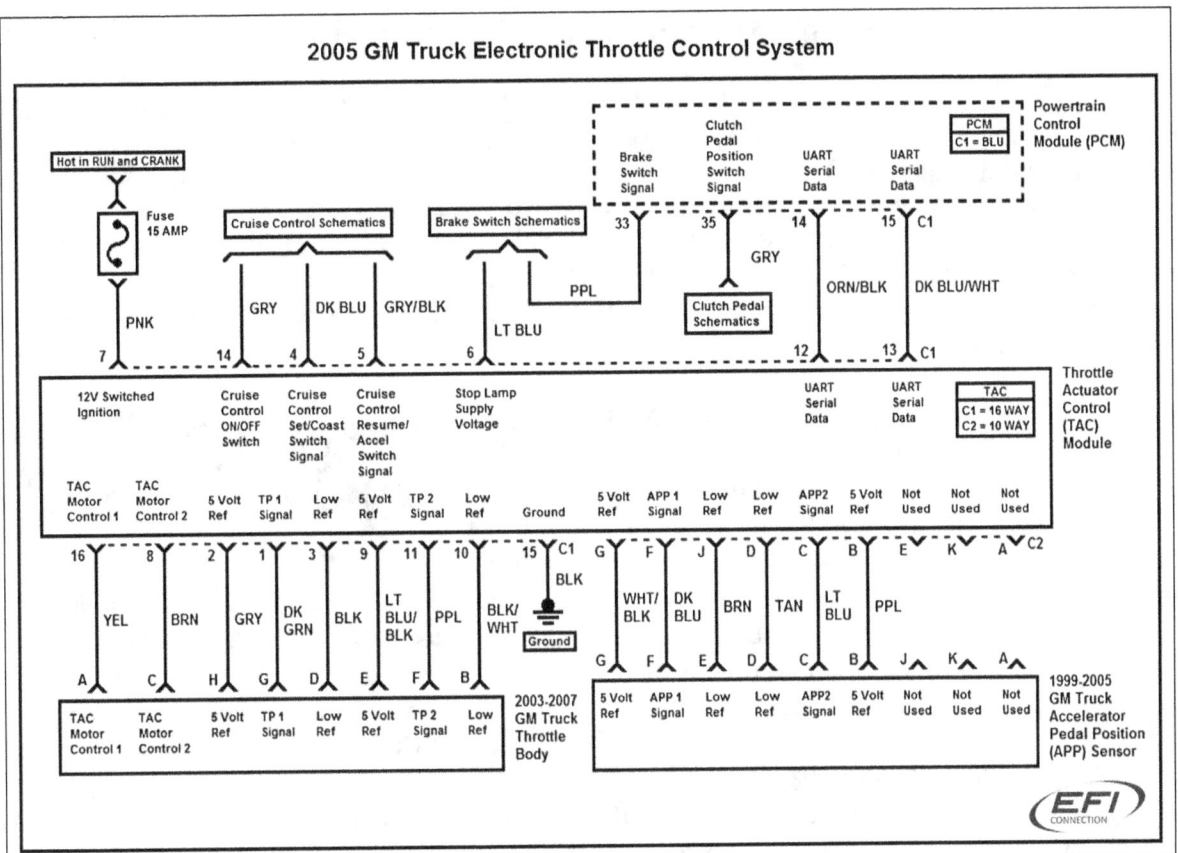

This wiring diagram represents the 2005 GM truck electronic throttle control system. Just like the 2003–2004 GM truck system, only two of the three APP sensors are used. By 2005 you should not expect to see the unused three wires for APP sensor 3.

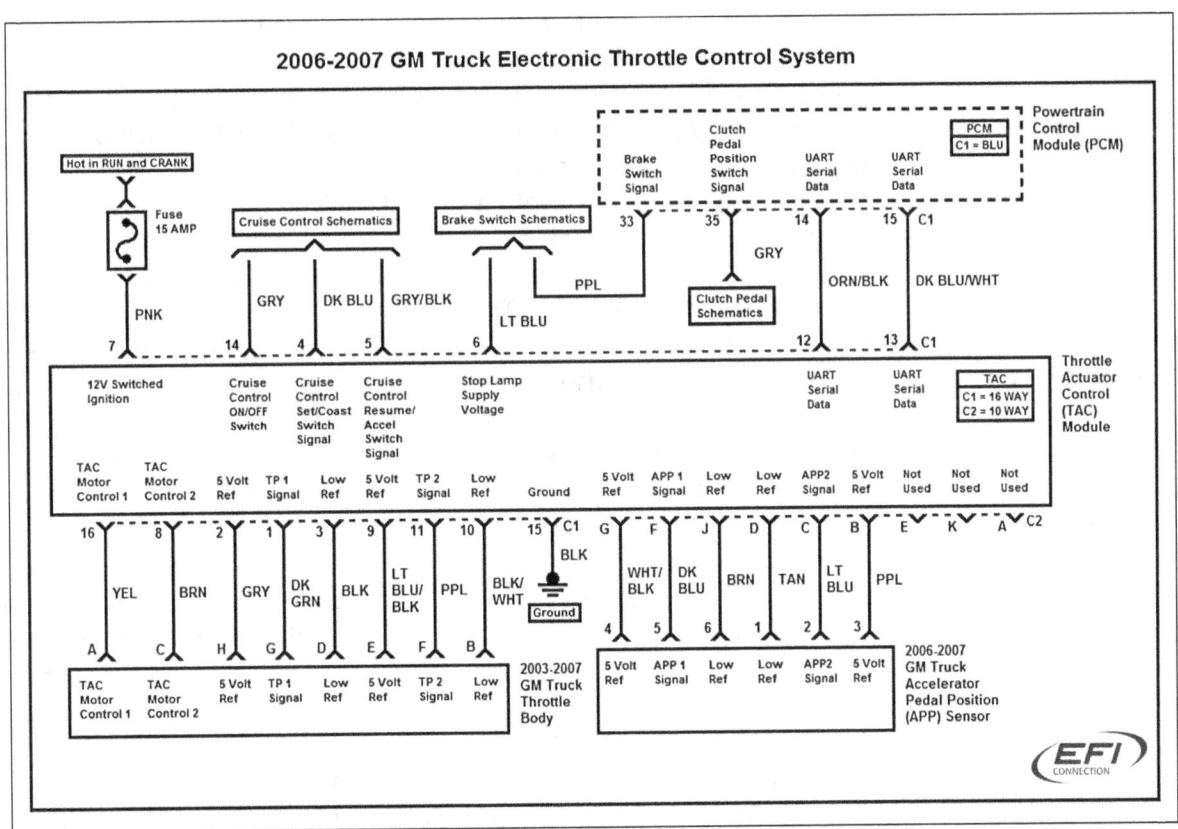

This wiring diagram represents the 2006–2007 GM truck electronic throttle control system. As shown in this schematic, the introduction of a new accelerator pedal assembly means a different TAC-to-pedal wire harness.

GM GEN III LS-SERIES POWERTRAIN CONTROL SYSTEMS

CHAPTER 8

2006–2007 Truck APP DTC Processing Limits

DTC	Description	APP Failure	0% APP Range	100% APP Limit
P2120	Accelerator Pedal Position (APP) Sensor 1 Circuit	else 0.24 to 4.49 V	0.24 to 2.24 V	4.49 V
P2125	Accelerator Pedal Position (APP) Sensor 2 Circuit	else 0.24 to 4.49 V	0.24 to 2.24 V	4.49 V

The GM truck PCM and TAC monitor values from two accelerator position signals to identify proper operation of the accelerator pedal assembly. A DTC sets if an APP value exceeds one of GM's predetermined threshold values. This chart reviews the allowable operating ranges for each APP sensor (see "APP Failure") and the expected 0-percent range and 100-percent limit voltages for each APP sensor.

trucks. With an option for an adjustable pedal assembly, the APP sensor is the same. The TAC module uses only two of the three APP signals to determine absolute pedal position. A change from the 1999–2002 truck TAC system is that both APP sensor 1 and APP sensor 2 signal voltage increases as the pedal is depressed. APP sensor 3 is no longer used by the 2003–2007 truck TAC modules, but the 2003–2004 TAC-to-pedal harnesses contain the three wires once used for APP sensor 3 (as found in 1999–2002 truck TAC-to-pedal harnesses). The APP sensor signals are used by the PCM to monitor and make available one accelerator pedal percent PID.

Throttle Actuator Control Module: The 2003–2004 truck TAC modules are interchangeable with 2005–2007 truck TAC modules. With an aluminum back plate and smooth plastic housing, this truck TAC module has an appearance different from the 1999–2002 truck TAC modules. The harness connections at the TAC module are the same, but the 1999–2002 truck engine wiring harnesses are not directly compatible with the 2003–2007 Gen III trucks.

2005

The 2005 truck electronic throttle system uses the same throttle body, TAC module, PCM, and accelerator pedal as the 2003–2004 trucks, but the non-use of APP sensor 3 shows itself with the removal of the three APP sensor 3 wires in the TAC-to-pedal harness. The 2003–2005 TAC-to-pedal harnesses can be used interchangeably because APP sensor 3 is not used by the 2003–2007 truck TAC module.

2006–2007

The 2006–2007 Gen III truck electronic throttle system uses the same throttle body, TAC module, and PCM as the 2003–2005 trucks. The only change in 2006 was a new accelerator pedal assembly. All other electronic throttle system components are interchangeable with 2003–2005 trucks.

Pedal Assembly: Although smaller in size, the 2006–2007 truck accelerator pedal assembly is functionally the same as the 2003–2005 assembly. Containing only the required two APP sensors, the harness connection on this pedal assembly uses only six wires. The 2003–2005 accelerator pedal assembly contains three APP sensors, but only two are used, leaving three connector cavities unused (as is found in 2005 truck TAC-to-pedal harnesses). The TAC module uses the two APP signals to determine absolute pedal position. Both APP sensor 1 and APP sensor 2 signal voltage increases as the pedal is depressed. The APP sensor signals are used by the PCM to monitor and make available one accelerator pedal percent PID.

This accelerator pedal assembly is used with 2006–2007 GM trucks and is functionally interchangeable with the 2002–2005 system. A matching TAC-to-pedal wire harness is required.

EFI Connection 24x Throttle Body Assemblies

Bringing LS fuel management to early small- and big-block Chevrolet engines requires an electronic throttle body assembly that fits the early fuel injection intake manifolds. EFI Connection's solution was to use the 1997–2004 LS1/LS6 Corvette throttle body, but within a new housing designed for TPI and LT1 intake manifolds.

Offered with twin 52-mm blades, twin 58-mm blades, or an oval mono blade, an electronic throttle body solution is available for any intake manifold using the popular TPI/LT1-type four-bolt pattern. All three throttle bodies are machined from a solid block of 6061 T6 heat-treated

ELECTRONIC THROTTLE EQUIPMENT

aluminum. The throttle blade shaft is supported by sealed ball bearings for longevity and the throttle blades are CNC machined, rather than being stamped, for a precise fit. These CNC-manufactured throttle bodies are among the highest quality from the aftermarket.

This EFI Connection 58-mm electronic throttle body flows approximately 1,100 cfm, making it appropriate for engines making 480 to 600 hp.

52-mm TPI/LT1 Throttle Body

EFI Connection's 52-mm electronic throttle body is intended to be used on stock to mild small-block engines. With nearly 920 cfm of airflow, this throttle body is good for engines making 325 to 480 hp. Most intake manifolds with the dual-bore, TPI-type throttle openings require minor port matching for smooth airflow transition from the throttle body into the intake plenum.

This 52-mm electronic throttle body is installed on a TPI engine. The TPI plenum was slightly ported to line up with the 52-mm throttle bore openings. Flowing approximately 920 cfm, this throttle body is adequate for engines making 325 to 480 hp.

58-mm TPI/LT1 Throttle Body

EFI Connection's 58-mm electronic throttle body is intended to be used on mild to aggressive small- and big-block engines. With nearly 1,100 cfm of airflow, this throttle body is good for engines making 480 to 600 hp. This throttle body requires port matching for smooth airflow transition and throttle blade clearance into the intake plenum.

Mono Blade TPI/LT1 Throttle Body

EFI Connection's mono blade electronic throttle body is intended to be used on maximum-effort small- and big-block engines. With nearly 1,250 cfm of airflow, this throttle body is good for engines making more than 600 hp. This throttle body requires port matching for smooth airflow transition and throttle blade clearance into the intake plenum.

EFI Connection's lineup of electronic throttle bodies for TPI, LT1, and Ram Jet 502 are available in common sizes: 52 mm, 58 mm, and oval mono blade.

This Ram Jet 502 engine receives much more air with this mono blade electronic throttle body. With an LS1 Corvette-based electronic throttle system and PCM, this engine has much more to offer than it did with the bundled MEFI (marine electronic fuel injection) ECU and 48-mm cable throttle body. This mono-blade throttle body flows approximately 1,250 cfm and is a good choice for engines making more than 600 hp.

CHAPTER 9

ELECTRIC FAN OPERATION

Gen III PCMs are powerful control modules but they are of little use without tuning software to change engine (and transmission) operating parameters.

Before getting too far into a discussion of electric fans and PCM calibrations, it is important to first consider air conditioning control.

Air Conditioning Considerations

Prior to buying a custom wire harness or doing PCM calibration work, determine if the vehicle will have air conditioning, if electric fan(s) are required when the A/C compressor is on, and if the PCM will be used to control the electric fan(s). (See Chapter 12 for more detail.)

Will the Vehicle Have Air Conditioning?

If the vehicle is fitted with air conditioning, the engine experiences additional load when the A/C compressor clutch is engaged (A/C is on). For engine retrofits, many PCMs (excluding 2003- newer) have an A/C on input that allows the PCM to adjust for the additional engine load, avoiding low-RPM stumble. Wired properly, and if using an LS1 Camaro, Firebird, or Corvette PCM calibration, the electric fan(s) turn on when the A/C is on to pull air through the A/C condenser.

Will the Electric Fan(s) be Required when the A/C Compressor is On?

When the A/C system is turned on, low-pressure refrigerant gases are drawn into the A/C compressor and transferred to the A/C condenser (located in front of the engine radiator) as high-pressure gas. The A/C condenser is essentially a radiator that cools the high-pressure refrigerant gases into a liquid again, in order to cool the interior of the car. To cool the A/C condenser, air must pass through it. One method of cooling the condenser is to install a permanent mechanical fan in front of the engine (as on many GM trucks). A more common method of drawing air through the condenser (and engine radiator) is through electric fan(s).

Will the PCM be Required to Control the Electric Fan(s)?

Many owners operate electric fan(s) independently of the PCM by triggering a relay through either the A/C compressor clutch circuit or through a trinary pressure switch. One drawback to these methods when using Gen III PCMs is that unwanted DTCs set as the PCM detects the fan(s) have turned on during conditions that the PCM has determined the fan(s) should be off. One solution is to simply disable these DTCs, which also disables the intended function of the DTC processing. A better solution is to use the PCM's A/C control functions to gain improved A/C system control and A/C system diagnostics. (See Chapter 11 for more about A/C control.)

PCM Calibration

Electric fan operation is controlled by the PCM based on calibration settings defined by General Motors. To gain access to the calibration parameters, tuners must rely on aftermarket tuning software

ELECTRIC FAN OPERATION

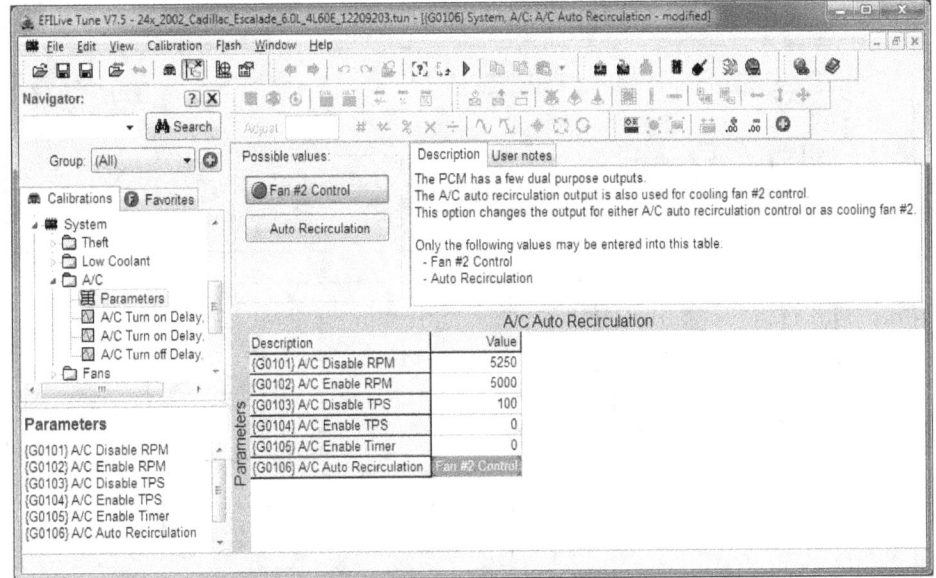

Many GM trucks equipped with a Gen III PCM use a mechanical fan. They use the typical high-speed-fan control output (red PCM connector, pin 33) as A/C automatic recirculation. When using a PCM with truck calibration, change calibration {G0106} from Auto Recirculation to Fan #2 Control.

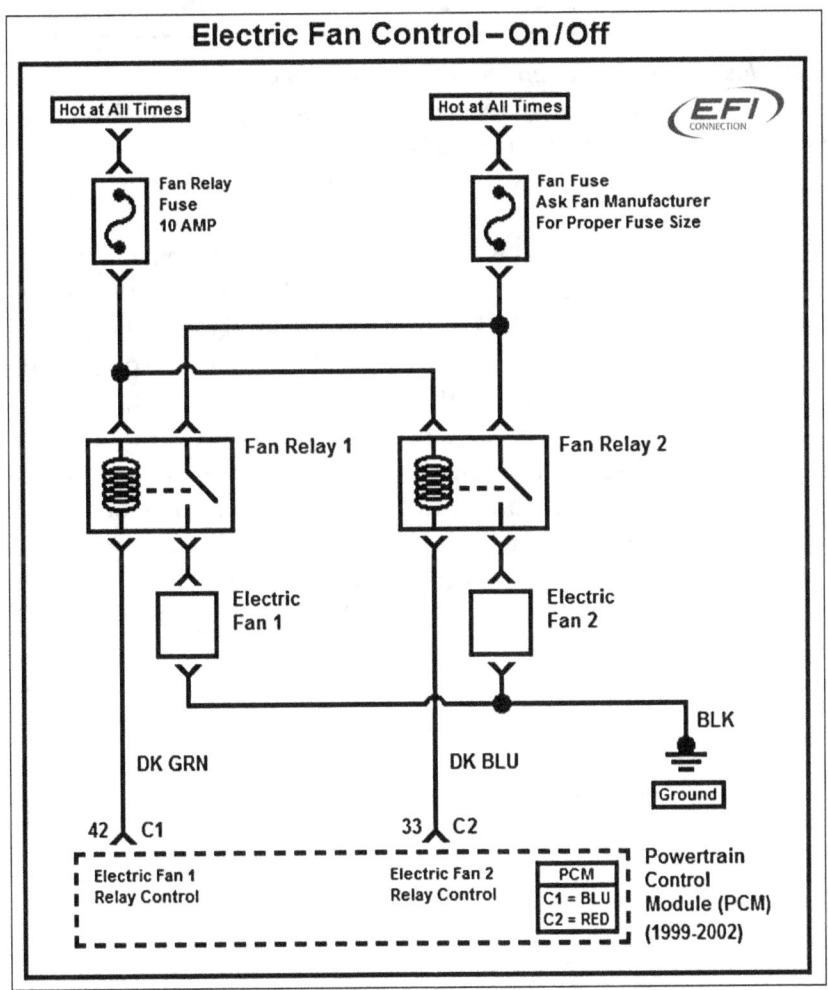

(such as EFILive, HP Tuners, etc.) to expose the electric fan settings and make desired changes. Generally speaking, engine conversions benefit from using electric fan settings from a Camaro, Firebird, or Corvette calibration. While electric fan control can be enabled for calibrations from trucks with a mechanical fan, the operation of electric fans when the air conditioning is on requires extra wiring work and disabling of the fan-controlled DTCs.

Camaro, Firebird and Corvette

The LS1 Camaro and Firebird are fitted with two electric fans and manual A/C controls. The PCM is responsible for controlling both A/C operation and electric fan operation. When the A/C controls are turned on, the PCM receives a 12V on signal, and validates A/C operation through a pressure sensor and 12V A/C compressor clutch status circuit. When the PCM is satisfied that the A/C is truly on, the PCM activates low-speed electric fan operation (for series/parallel operation), or only turns on electric fan 1 relay (on/off operation).

Because the Camaro and Firebird were only available with a cable throttle body, PCMs loaded with the LS1 Camaro or Firebird calibration are the best choice for cable throttle engine retrofits where the PCM controls both A/C and electric fans.

GM vehicles equipped with an LS-series PCM and electric fans operate both fans in low-speed and high-speed mode only. This requires two PCM outputs and three relays. By using the two PCM outputs and only two relays, two electric fans can be controlled independently.

CHAPTER 9

The LS1 Corvette was available with either automatic or manual A/C controls. Those fitted with automatic A/C controls use a Class 2 data signal from the A/C controls to the PCM to indicate A/C control status. A PCM loaded with a Corvette calibration using automatic A/C controls does not provide the necessary A/C on signal to the PCM for electric fan operation. Owners using Corvette electronic throttle equipment on their engine retrofit should use a PCM calibration from a Corvette with manual A/C controls to satisfy the PCMs A/C on input for electric fan control.

Trucks

GM trucks were fitted with a mechanical fan until 2005 so those PCM calibrations do not have provision for electric fan control with A/C on. In 2005, when electric fans were introduced in GM trucks, both manual and automatic A/C controls communicated with the PCM using the Class 2 data stream, a signal not available in early retrofit vehicles. The best solution for retrofits using the PCM for electric fan control is a 1999–2002 Camaro, Firebird, or Corvette calibration.

PCM Operation

All Gen III PCMs are capable of controlling one or two electric fans.

On/Off

Production vehicles operate two fans with low- and high-speed capability using three relays to switch between series and parallel opera-

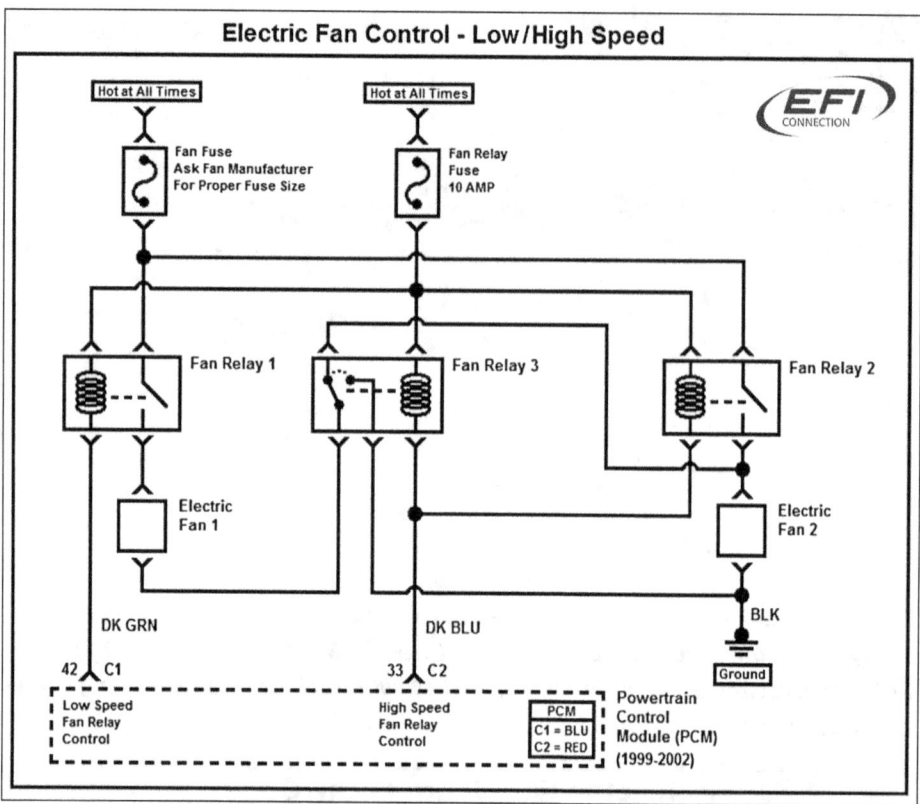

GM vehicles equipped with an LS-series PCM and electric fans operate both fans in low-speed and high-speed mode only. This requires two PCM outputs and three relays. By using the two PCM outputs and three relays, two electric fans can be controlled in low-speed and high-speed modes.

tion. However, since the PCM is only applying a ground to each fan relay signal circuit, two fans can be controlled through two relays for on/off operation. In this way the electric fans are always wired in parallel so that each fan receives system voltage.

PCMs with a truck calibration, depending on the year, require the fan outputs to be turned on and on/off temperatures to be set.

Low/High Speed

Production vehicles operate two fans with low- and high-speed capability by using three relays to switch between series and parallel opera-

tion. The third relay is responsible for switching from series (low-speed) to parallel (high-speed) operation.

When the PCM triggers only the low-speed fan output, current flows through both electric fan motors. In this way the electric fan motors are wired in a series and voltage is reduced, causing the fan motors to spin at low speed.

When the PCM triggers the two additional relays, the same voltage flows through each electric fan motor. In this way the electric fan motors are wired in parallel, causing the fan motors to spin at high speed.

CHAPTER 10

TRANSMISSION

Gen III PCM control goes beyond the engine to be one of best solutions for electronically controlled 4-speed automatic transmissions. Owners not using the LS1 PCM for engine control must look to the aftermarket for a standalone transmission controller that may cost in excess of $1,000. While many who desire an automatic transmission choose either a 4L60-E or 4L80-E transmission when using the LS-series PCM, others may simply disregard the PCM's transmission functions and use a non-electronically controlled automatic or manual transmission.

Automatic Transmissions

In general, any automatic transmission can be used in a vehicle where the engine is controlled by a Gen III PCM. For early transmissions, the aftermarket offers simple solutions for an electronic vehicle speed signal and standalone torque converter lockup. Most late-model, electronically controlled transmissions can be fully controlled with the LS-series PCM. For electronically controlled transmissions not compatible with the LS-series PCMs (1993–1995 4L60-E transmissions), the aftermarket offers standalone transmission controllers.

Regardless of automatic transmission choice, tuners usually begin with an LS-series calibration from an automatic transmission vehicle to retain proper engine idle characteristics.

It is wise to consult a professional transmission builder for actual fitment details. With the wide variety of engines, transmissions, flexplates, and torque converters, a mismatch of components can easily be avoided with help from someone with experience.

Non-Electronic Control

Transmissions with no electronic control should be fitted with a VSS to satisfy the PCM's vehicle speed input requirement. Although early transmissions are typically equipped to accept a mechanical speedometer cable, the aftermarket offers electronic VSS adapters that continue to allow the use of the speedometer cable while satisfying the PCM's VSS input.

Electronic Torque Converter Lockup

The electronic torque converter lockup function for non-electronically shifted transmissions (200-4R and 700-R4) is not compatible with the Gen III PCMs. These transmissions use an ON/OFF solenoid to apply torque converter lockup while the LS-series PCMs provide PWM control to a torque converter lockup solenoid. Fortunately, the aftermarket offers standalone torque

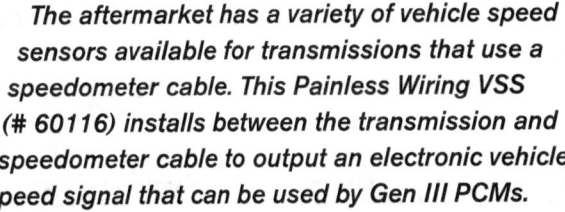

The aftermarket has a variety of vehicle speed sensors available for transmissions that use a speedometer cable. This Painless Wiring VSS (# 60116) installs between the transmission and speedometer cable to output an electronic vehicle speed signal that can be used by Gen III PCMs.

CHAPTER 10

4L60-E Changes

The early 4L60-E transmissions went through a few internal electronic control changes. These changes include the addition of a TCC PWM solenoid in 1995 and 3-2 downshift solenoid control in 1996. To understand these differences, look to the circuit descriptions as explained in transmission DTC processing.

1994

- TAN/BLK, CKT 422, cavity T, TCC solenoid is ON/OFF controlled by a ground path from the PCM
- BRN, cavity U is not used
- WHT, CKT 687, cavity S, 3-2 downshift solenoid is controlled PWM from the PCM

DTC 90 Transmission Converter Clutch Circuit

The TCC solenoid is an electrical device used to control fluid acting on the TCC converter clutch valve, which then controls TCC apply and release. The PCM monitors TP voltage, vehicle speed, and other inputs to determine when to energize the TCC solenoid. Ignition voltage is supplied directly to the TCC solenoid. The PCM controls the solenoid by providing the ground path through CKT 422.

DTC 85 Transmission Converter Clutch Stuck "ON"

The PCM energizes the TCC solenoid by grounding CKT 422. The TCC solenoid allows converter release fluid to exhaust past the #9 check ball, applying the TCC. The TCC solenoid de-energizes when the PCM no longer provides a ground. When the TCC solenoid is de-energized, this blocks exhaust fluid and releases the TCC.

DTC 84 Automatic Transmission 3-2 Control Solenoid Circuit

Hydraulically, the 3-2 control solenoid coordinates the apply rate of the 2-4 band with the hydraulic release of the 3-4 clutch during a 3-2 downshift. The PCM continually monitors the 3-2 circuit duty cycle depending on the commanded state of circuit terminal B13. When the transmission is in first gear the duty cycle of the solenoid is equal to 0 (OFF). When the transmission is in second gear or higher the duty cycle of the solenoid is about 90 percent (ON). When the transmission downshifts, 3-2, the duty cycle of the solenoid drops.

1995

- TAN/BLK, CKT 422, cavity T, TCC solenoid control is ON/OFF controlled by a ground path from the PCM
- BRN, CKT 418, cavity U, TCC PWM solenoid control is controlled PWM from the PCM
- WHT, CKT 687, cavity S, 3-2 downshift solenoid is controlled PWM from the PCM

DTC 90 Transmission Converter Clutch Circuit

The TCC solenoid is an electrical device used to control fluid acting on the TCC converter clutch valve, which then controls TCC apply and release. The PCM monitors TP voltage, vehicle speed, and other inputs to determine when to energize the TCC solenoid. Ignition voltage is supplied directly to the TCC solenoid. The PCM controls the solenoid by providing the ground path through CKT 422.

DTC 85 Transmission Converter Clutch Stuck "ON"

The PCM energizes the TCC solenoid by grounding CKT 422. The TCC solenoid allows converter release fluid to exhaust past the # 9 check ball, applying the TCC. The TCC solenoid de-energizes when the PCM no longer provides a ground. When the TCC solenoid is de-energized, this blocks exhaust fluid and releases the TCC.

DTC 84 Automatic Transmission 3-2 Control Solenoid Circuit

Hydraulically, the 3-2 control solenoid coordinates the apply rate of the 2-4 band with the hydraulic release of the 3-4 clutch during a 3-2 downshift.

The PCM continually monitors the 3-2 circuit duty cycle depending on the commanded state of circuit terminal B13. When the transmission is in first gear the duty cycle of the solenoid is equal to 0 (OFF). When the transmission is in second gear or higher the duty cycle of the solenoid is about 90 percent (ON). When the transmission downshifts, 3-2, the duty cycle of the solenoid drops.

TRANSMISSION

DTC 83 TCC/PWM Solenoid Circuit

The TCC PWM solenoid is used in combination with the TCC solenoid to regulate fluid to the torque converter and is attached to the control valve body within the transmission.

The PCM supplies a ground-allowing current to flow through the solenoid coil according to the duty cycle (percentage of ON and OFF time). This current flow through the solenoid coil creates a magnetic field that magnetizes the solenoid core. The magnetized core attracts the check ball to seat against spring pressure. This blocks the exhaust for the TCC signal fluid and allows 2-3 drive fluid to feed the TCC signal circuit. The TCC signal fluid pressure acts on the TCC regulator valve to regulate line pressure and to apply fluid pressure to the TCC shaft valve[is it a "shaft" or "shift" valve?]. When the TCC shift valve is in the apply position, regulated apply fluid pressure is directed through the TCC valve to apply the torque converter clutch.

1996

- TAN/BLK, CKT 422, cavity T, TCC solenoid control is ON/OFF and controlled by a ground path from the PCM
- BRN, CKT 418, cavity U, TCC PWM solenoid control is controlled PWM from the PCM
- WHT, CKT 687, cavity S, 3-2 downshift solenoid is ON/OFF and controlled by a ground path from the PCM

Compatible with LS1 PCM
- P1860, TCC PWM solenoid circuit
- P0785, 3-2 downshift solenoid circuit
- P0742, TCC system stuck on
- P0740, TCC enable solenoid circuit

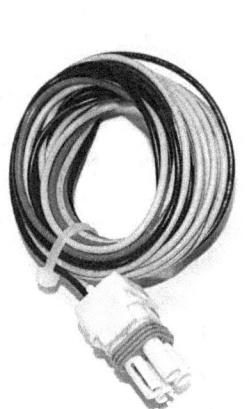

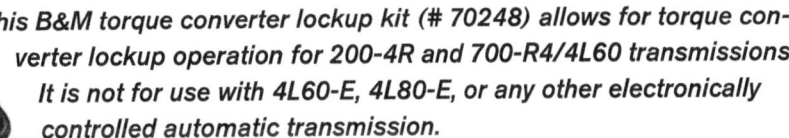

This B&M torque converter lockup kit (# 70248) allows for torque converter lockup operation for 200-4R and 700-R4/4L60 transmissions. It is not for use with 4L60-E, 4L80-E, or any other electronically controlled automatic transmission.

converter lockup kits for applications where the ECM/PCM cannot control torque converter lockup.

1993–1994 4L60-E Transmissions

The 1993–1994 4L60-E transmissions are not compatible with Gen III PCMs. General Motors introduced the 4L60-E transmission in 1993. In design, this transmission is unique in that the PCM is used to control shift solenoids. Drivability is a seat-of-the-pants noticeable improvement compared to the 700-R4; the 700-R4 shifts through the gears by means of a detent cable attached to the throttle linkage and weights and springs in the governor.

These early 4L60-E transmissions do not have a TCC PWM solenoid, which was added to the 4L60-E transmission in 1995 to assist in applying torque converter lockup.

1995 4L60-E Transmission

The 1995 4L60-E transmission is not compatible with the Gen III PCM. In 1995, General Motors added a TCC PWM solenoid that was used in combination with the TCC lockup solenoid to assist in smoothly applying torque converter lockup. This update is visually noticeable in the 1995 wire harness as a brown wire that was added to connector cavity U of the 4L60-E harness connector.

1996-Newer 4L60-E Transmissions

The 1996-newer 4L60-E transmissions are compatible with Gen III PCMs. In fact, they are compatible with 1996-newer GM PCMs. In 1996, General Motors changed the operation of the 3-2 downshift

4L80-E Transmission Calibration Segment Swap

EFILive supports swapping calibration segments when the OS numbers between two calibration files are a match. Not all tuning software allows for calibration segment swaps.

Here, an original 4L60-E transmission calibration is receiving a 4L80-E transmission segment swap.

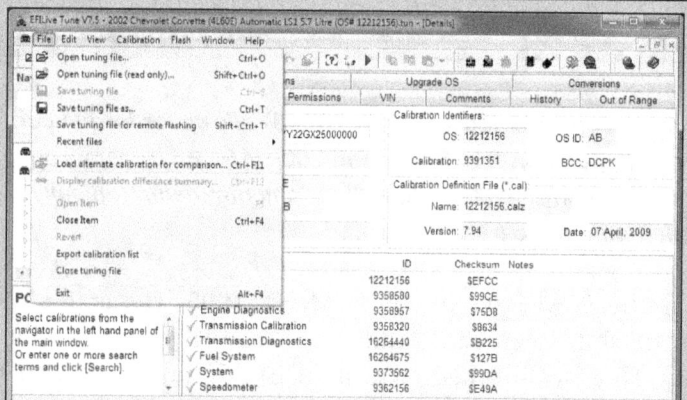

1 To begin a transmission segment swap using EFILive tuning software, first open the PCM calibration file for your engine application.

For this example, open a calibration file for a 5.7L LS1 engine with 4L60-E transmission. This is a calibration file that expects a 24x crankshaft signal and the use of an electronic throttle body. Because the Corvette was never offered with a 4L80-E transmission, you will need to later identify a calibration that has 4L80-E to swap the transmission segment into the LS1/4L60-E calibration file.

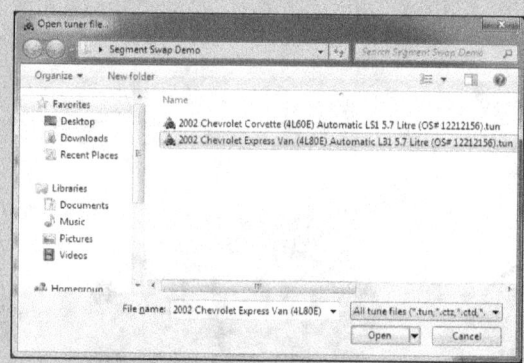

3 Next choose a vehicle calibration file that contains the same OS number as the original LS1/4L60-E calibration file. A 4L80-E calibration from a 2002 Express Van with 5.7L Gen I small-block and 4L80-E transmission works here. While this engine calibration requires a 4x crankshaft signal, uses single coil and distributor, and requires a cable-driven throttle body, only the 4L80-E transmission segment is needed. Crankshaft signal type and throttle type are irrelevant.

2 Next load an alternate calibration file from a vehicle equipped with a 4L80-E transmission. Choose File > Load alternate calibration for comparison, or simply press the Ctrl+F11 keys on the keyboard.

solenoid from PWM to ON/OFF operation through a ground path provided by the PCM. The 1995 and 1996 wire harnesses are identical, using 13 cavities of the transmission harness connector.

Other compatible 4L60-E type transmissions include the 4L65-E and 4L70-E. But don't let the 4L65-E name fool you; this transmission is electronically equivalent to the 4L60-E transmission, receiving little more than one additional planetary gear (five gears total) and several stronger internals for improved strength.

The 4L70-E is used with Gen IV ECM/TCM systems and can be found in the Chevrolet Trailblazer. This transmission adds an ISS but it is electronically compatible with Gen III PCMs. Very simply, the ISS output signal is not used (or required) by Gen III PCMs.

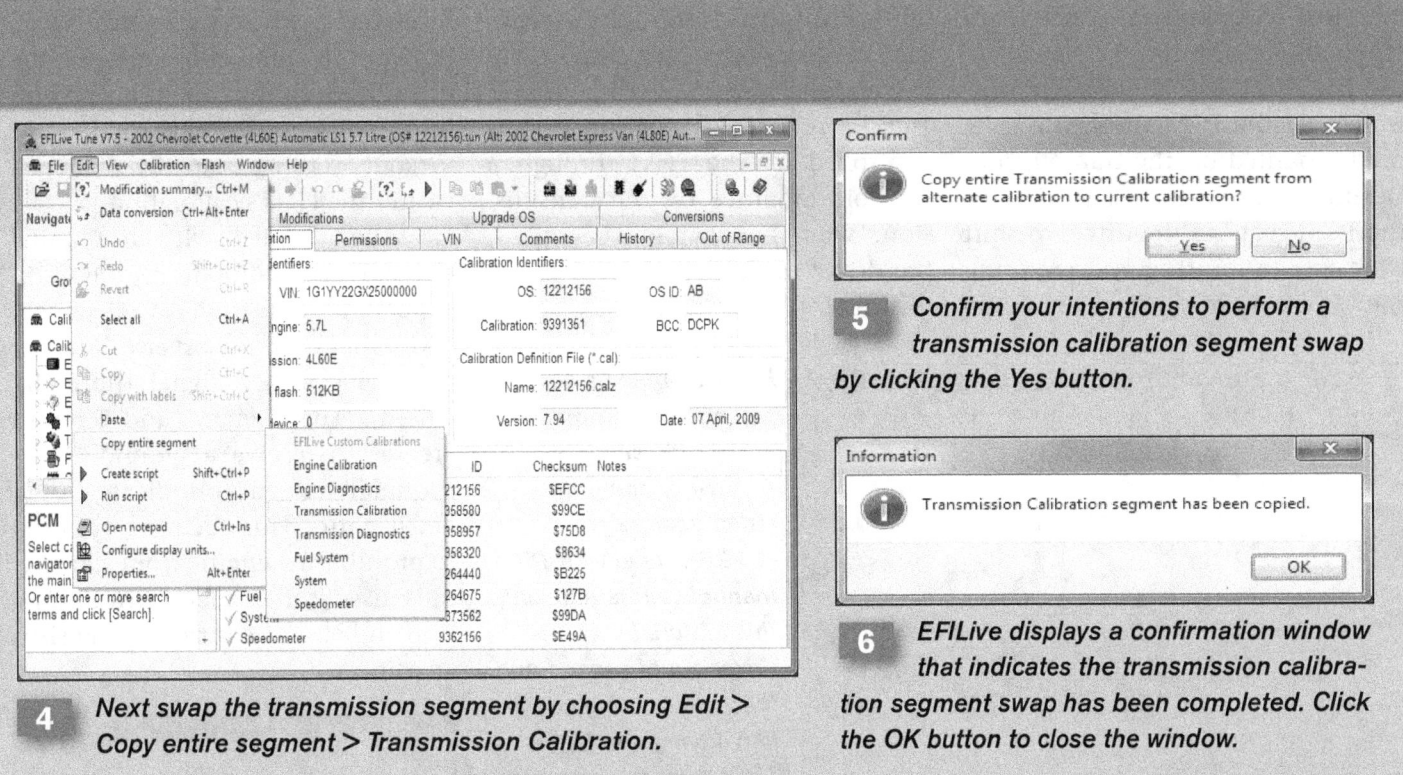

5 Confirm your intentions to perform a transmission calibration segment swap by clicking the Yes button.

6 EFILive displays a confirmation window that indicates the transmission calibration segment swap has been completed. Click the OK button to close the window.

4 Next swap the transmission segment by choosing Edit > Copy entire segment > Transmission Calibration.

4L80-E Transmissions

Enthusiasts requiring a stronger, electronically controlled automatic transmission may consider the 4L80-E transmission. These were installed in many 2500-series GM trucks and can be controlled with Gen III PCMs. The 4L60-E and 4L80-E transmissions use the same harness connector, but are wired a little differently. Tuners must use either a calibration from a truck that has a 4L80-E or perform a transmission segment swap within the PCM calibration.

6L80 and 6L90 Transmissions

General Motors introduced 6-speed automatic transmissions in certain 2006 performance vehicles (Corvette and Pontiac G8). These transmissions feature a built-in TCM identified as a T43 TCM. It communicates with the ECM through CAN messaging. Without the proper CAN messaging (to and from a Gen IV ECM), these transmissions cannot be used.

At the time of this writing, the aftermarket has not made a stand-alone controller available for the 6L80 and 6L90 transmissions. With no

The 6L80 and 6L90 (shown) transmissions are used with Gen IV vehicles. These transmissions require a TCM mounted internally on the valve body. These T43 TCMs require CAN bus communication with a Gen IV ECM for operation. The 6L80 and 6L90 transmissions cannot be used in a Gen III PCM conversion.

CAN support, the Gen III PCM cannot be used to control the T43 TCM.

Manual Transmissions

In general, any manual transmission can be used in a vehicle where the engine is controlled by a Gen III PCM. Regardless of manual transmission choice, tuners usually begin with an LS-series calibration from a manual transmission vehicle. It is wise to consult a professional transmission builder for actual fitment details. With the wide variety of engines, transmissions, flywheels, and clutches, a mismatch of components can easily be avoided with help from someone with experience.

The 1999–2002 PCM has been used in the Camaro and Firebird to control two T56 manual transmission functions: skip shift and reverse lockout. The PCM may also receive an input from the CPP switch. These

CHAPTER 10

functions are optional and most owners choose to eliminate skip shift.

The skip shift function is controlled by the PCM through a solenoid mounted on the transmission. During certain operating conditions, the PCM requires the driver to shift from first to fourth gear, preventing the driver from shifting into second or third gear. Skip shift settings can be changed within the PCM's calibration.

The reverse lockout function is controlled by the PCM through a solenoid mounted on the transmission. When the solenoid is energized, the driver can easily shift the transmission into reverse. The PCM allows reverse gear whenever vehicle speed is below 5 mph and prevents the driver from shifting the transmission into reverse above 5 mph. Reverse lockout settings can be changed within the PCM's calibration.

When loaded with a manual transmission calibration, the PCM expects a signal from a CPP switch. GM trucks and Corvette are set to receive a 12V signal (normally closed). The Camaro and Firebird are set to receive a ground signal (normally closed) to indicate clutch pedal status. This circuit is not used to prohibit the engine from starting; it is used for cruise control function and engine control during shift transitions.

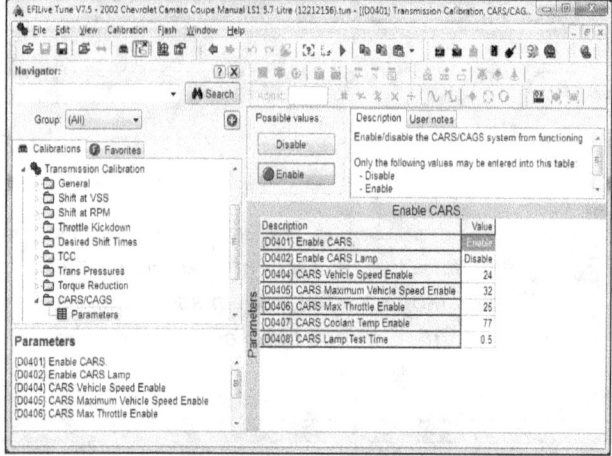

EFILive presents several settings for computer-aided ratio select (CARS) or computer-aided gear select (CAGS). Used with T56 manual calibrations only, this feature locks the driver out of second and third gear during city-like driving conditions. Most owners choose to disable this feature.

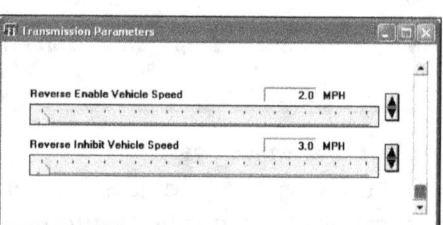

C.A.T.S OBD-II tuner software presents settings for the reverse lockout feature used with T56 manual transmission calibrations. This feature assists the driver by making it difficult to enter reverse gear while the vehicle is in motion.

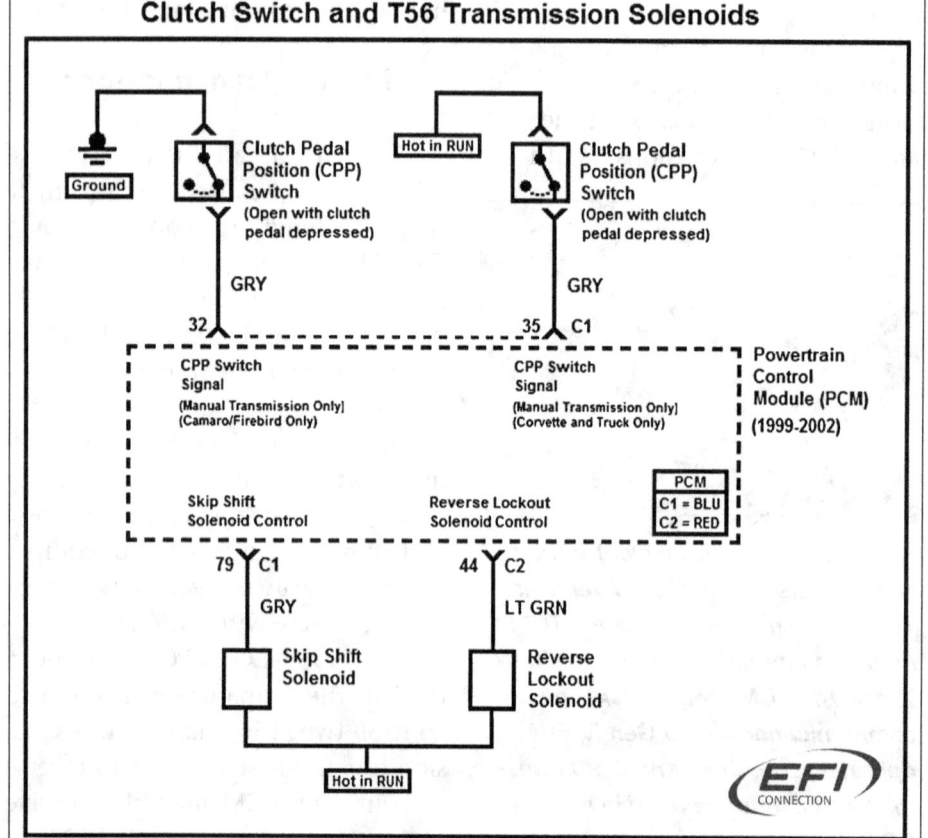

Corvettes and GM trucks use a 12V CPP signal; Camaro and Firebirds use a ground CPP signal. The type of CPP signal is set within the PCM calibration, but requires an advanced tuner to make the change.

CHAPTER 11

AIR CONDITIONING

All too often PCM-controlled (or monitored) air conditioning is overlooked after the engine has been swapped, the new wire harness has been installed, and custom calibrated PCM has been received from the tuner. The A/C system is commonly one of the many "I'll think about that later..." tasks as the excitement builds for the first engine startup.

I recall an LS1 engine conversion in an early Corvette that followed this scenario. I discussed the project with the shop owner before building the engine harness so that nothing would be missed. He wanted to keep the wiring "clean" and not have A/C wiring related to the PCM. He neglected to think through the aftermarket A/C system wiring and did not realize, until the car was days from scheduled delivery, that there was no way to turn the electric fans on when the A/C system was on.

Being pressed for time to meet the deadline and out of money to make further changes to the car, he compromised with an undesirable workaround, by turning the fans on at 30 degrees F through the PCM. Now he had a $100,000 Corvette with an electric fan solution that General Motors never would have implemented, even in a $10,000 car!

Base Calibration

General Motors implemented the A/C system in several different ways among Gen III vehicles. The PCM calibration is specific to each of these implementations. Of most importance is the consideration of electric fan control.

If your project uses electric fans, begin with a PCM calibration from a vehicle that has electric fans.

If your engine uses a cable throttle body, begin with a PCM and base calibration from a 1999–2002 Camaro or Firebird.

If your engine uses an electronic throttle body, begin with a PCM and base calibration from a 1999–2002 Corvette. (See Chapter 8 for more about Corvette electronic throttle equipment.)

If your project uses electric fans and the PCM and calibration is based on a truck, the PCM does not turn on the electric fans when the A/C is on. Truck PCMs older than 2003 can be reflashed with 1999–2002 Camaro, Firebird, or Corvette calibrations for proper electric fan operations.

Operation Overview

In the 1990s, General Motors introduced PCM control of the A/C compressor clutch. While the

Engine DTC Processing Enablers	
Description	Value
P0530 "Air Conditioning (A/C) Refrigerant Pressure Sensor Circuit"	C: Non Emissions
P0531 "Air Conditioning (A/C) Refrigerant Pressure Sensor Performance"	X: Not Reported
P0645 "Air Conditioning (A/C) Clutch Relay Control Circuit"	C: Non Emissions
P1539 "Air Conditioning (A/C) Clutch Feedback Circuit High Voltage"	C: Non Emissions
P1546 "Air Conditioning (A/C) Clutch Feedback Circuit Open"	C: Non Emissions

The Gen III PCM supports DTC processing for the A/C system. The DTCs shown here may be enabled to report a fault in the A/C pressure sensor or A/C compressor clutch (or related wiring). Notification of a fault is presented to the driver through the MIL or a scan of the OBD-II diagnostic port.

operation of the A/C system hasn't changed significantly, there's been a few improvements. Fuel injection enthusiasts should consider several things such as the diagnostic feedback, functional benefits, and safety of PCM-controlled A/C.

OBD-II diagnostics can be helpful in troubleshooting your vehicle's A/C system. With a handful of A/C-related DTCs, the first step in identifying a problem may be a quick look through the OBD-II diagnostic port at DTCs that have been set. A brief description of a logged DTC malfunction may point you directly to the source of the problem. Depending on your PCM's calibration settings, your scan tool may display very useful information about A/C faults.

It is not always appropriate to engage the A/C compressor clutch when the driver commands the A/C compressor to turn on. The PCM monitors the pressure of the A/C system to determine if the A/C compressor clutch should engage with the driver's turn of the A/C control knob. More than that, the PCM also considers other engine operating data such as RPM, throttle position, and intake air temperature.

To prevent damage to the A/C system, it is crucial that air passes through the A/C condenser when the A/C compressor clutch is engaged. Because the PCM controls the operation of the electric fan(s), it is capable of turning on the fan(s) when the A/C is on to pass air through the A/C condenser. The PCM applies coolant temperature and A/C pressure logic to the operation of the electric fan(s).

Request Input

A 12V signal wire is monitored at pin 17 of the red PCM connector. With no voltage applied, the circuit is open and the PCM does not attempt to turn on the A/C compressor clutch. When 12V is applied to the circuit and based on the pressure in the system, the PCM commands the A/C compressor to turn on.

Pressure Sensor

Common among Camaros, Firebirds, and Corvettes, the A/C pressure sensor provides a 0 to 5V signal to pin 14 of the red PCM connector. Based on this signal, the PCM does or does not command the A/C compressor to

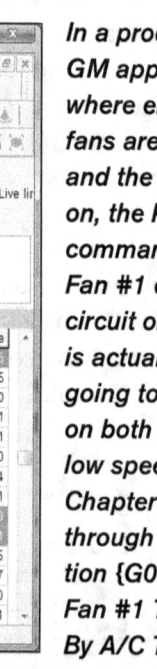

EFILive tuning software presents calibration details for the operation of the A/C compressor clutch. Notice that the A/C compressor is disabled above 4,895 rpm or a TPS value of 100 percent (also known as WOT).

In a production GM application where electric fans are used and the A/C is on, the PCM commands the Fan #1 control circuit on (which is actually going to turn on both fans at low speed; see Chapter 10) through calibration {G0903} Fan #1 Turn-on By A/C Temp.

With the electric fans on above the specified coolant temperature, the PCM monitors the A/C pressure signal and uses calibration {G0911} Fan #1 A/C Pressure Enable to allow electric fan operation, and calibration {G0912} Fan #1 A/C Pressure Disable to prohibit electric fan operation.

AIR CONDITIONING

This sensor is in a 1997 Trans Am. In this vehicle, the LT1 PCM also uses the same 0 to 5V A/C pressure signal as part of the logic that determines whether the A/C compressor clutch is engaged.

This switch is in a 2003 Silverado A/C accumulator/drier. Be sure to check the wiring schematics for the vehicle type your PCM calibration is based on because this switch is not used with all LS-series vehicles.

In the 1997 Trans Am, General Motors located the A/C compressor clutch relay within the fuse and relay box in the front driver's side of the engine bay.

turn on when the driver requests A/C operation. A common location for the A/C pressure sensor is the passenger's side of the engine compartment ahead of the A/C accumulator/drier.

Low-Pressure Switch

Common among trucks and vans, the A/C low-pressure switch is used as an input to the PCM (up to 2002) or HVAC control module (2003-newer) as part of the logic that determines whether the A/C compressor clutch is engaged. This switch provides a ground signal to the PCM or HVAC control module when the A/C pressure is not low. When the A/C pressure is low, the circuit is open and the A/C does not turn on.

Clutch Relay

When the driver commands the A/C on from the control unit and the system pressure criteria is met, the PCM grounds the A/C compressor clutch relay coil to turn on the A/C. This relay is most often found within a fuse block assembly.

On Input

As a secondary check, the PCM looks for A/C compressor clutch voltage on pin 18 of the red PCM connector. If the PCM has commanded the A/C on and 12V is not found on this input, the PCM sets DTC P1546 to indicate that the circuit is unexpectedly open. A likely cause for this DTC is a faulty A/C compressor clutch relay.

Compressor Clutch Solenoid

Located within the A/C compressor, this solenoid is responsible for engaging the A/C compressor clutch. A diode is installed either in the wire harness or within a fuse block assembly to block a high-voltage spike as the A/C compressor is cycled on and off.

While there is a variety of A/C compressors, they all use a solenoid to engage the compressor clutch to pressurize the system. This A/C compressor is included with the Chevrolet Performance small- and big-block Chevy front accessory drive kits. Notice the wire harness connection for the clutch solenoid at the top of the compressor just behind the pulley.

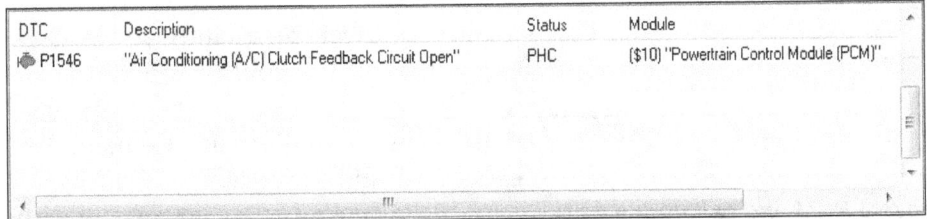

DTC	Description	Status	Module
P1546	"Air Conditioning (A/C) Clutch Feedback Circuit Open"	PHC	($10) "Powertrain Control Module (PCM)"

When the driver turns on the A/C system and the PCM determines the system is ready for A/C operation, the PCM activates the A/C compressor clutch relay. If the relay does not supply 12V to the A/C compressor clutch, then the PCM sets DTC P1546. This indicates a problem with the A/C compressor clutch relay or related wiring.

CHAPTER 11

Electric Fan Wiring

For proper electric fan control when the A/C is on, the best PCM and calibration choice is 1999–2002 Camaro/Firebird/Corvette. In these vehicles, the PCM receives a 12V request from the control head, checks the refrigerant pressure, activates the compressor clutch relay, and monitors the voltage on the compressor clutch to verify that the compressor has been turned on.

When the A/C system is on, the PCM activates low-speed electric fan operation for series/parallel operation. It turns on only the electric fan 1 relay for on/off operation. (See Chapter 9 for electric fan schematics.)

Eliminating the Pressure Sensor

The A/C pressure sensor can be difficult to install in early vehicles because there may be no provision for it. An alternative to using this pressure sensor is to fake the refrigerant pressure signal by replacing the sensor with an 80,000-ohm, 1/4-watt resistor. The resistor can be installed between the 5V reference (pin 45, blue PCM connector) and signal (pin 14, red PCM connector). The compressor clutch engages regardless of refrigerant pressure.

An alternate method of logic should be applied to the 12V A/C Request Signal on pin 17 of the red PCM connector. Install some type of safety pressure switch(es) between the A/C control head and the PCM. An existing or aftermarket system may already include logic to the 12V A/C compressor clutch supply circuit. This circuit can be used to supply the 12V A/C request signal on pin 17 of the red PCM connector.

Compressor Clutch Control

Early LS-series trucks and 2001–2002 vans were not equipped with electric fans. These vehicles use one or more switches as part of the logic that determines if the compressor clutch should turn on when the driver commands the A/C on through the control head. This system does not use the 0 to 5V pressure sensor found in the Camaro, Firebird, and Corvette.

There are variations on the implementation of this A/C system, so refer to the GM schematics when necessary.

A benefit of implementing this wiring in your non-electric fan

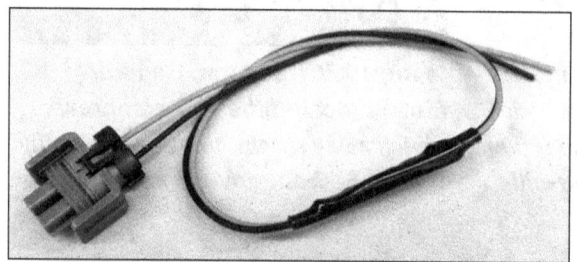

Because the A/C compressor cycles on and off, a diode is found in GM wire harnesses to block a high-voltage spike. This diode is sometimes found within a fuse block assembly.

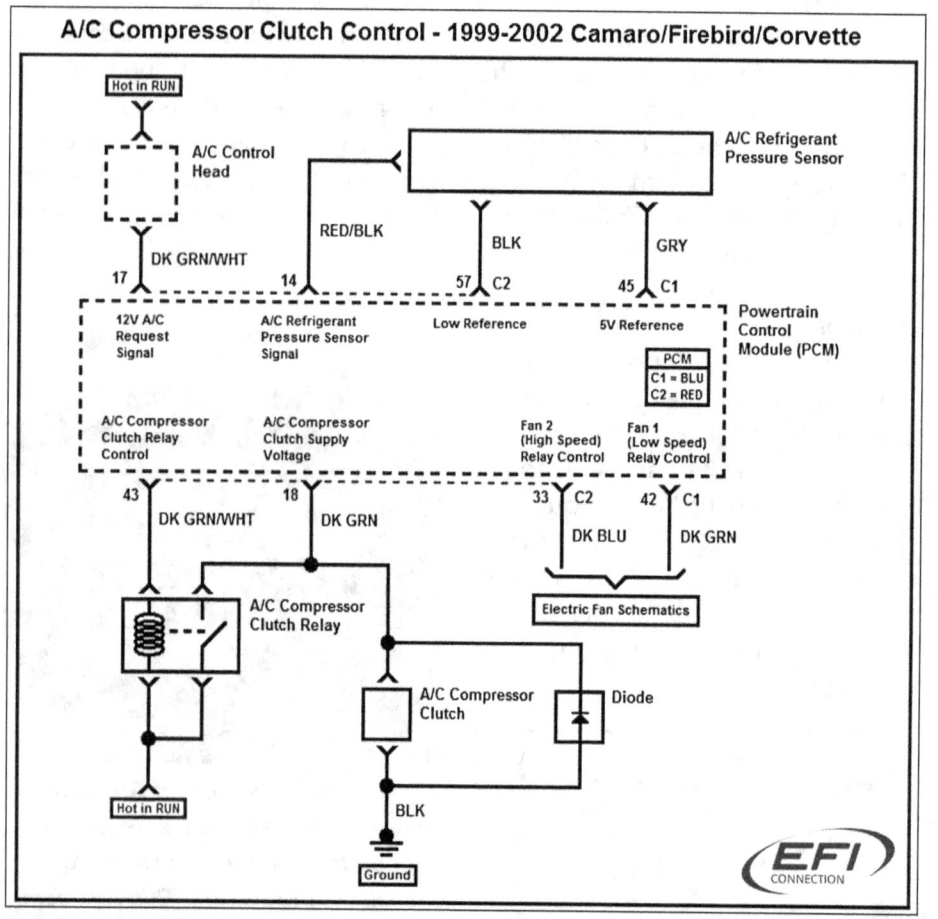

When using electric fans, it is best to choose a PCM and calibration from a 1999–2002 Camaro, Firebird, or Corvette. General Motors fitted these vehicles with electric fans and made a provision within the PCM for A/C operation that relies on the use of the electric fans for keeping the condenser cool. This wiring schematic represents the A/C system in the 1999–2002 Camaro, Firebird, and Corvette.

AIR CONDITIONING

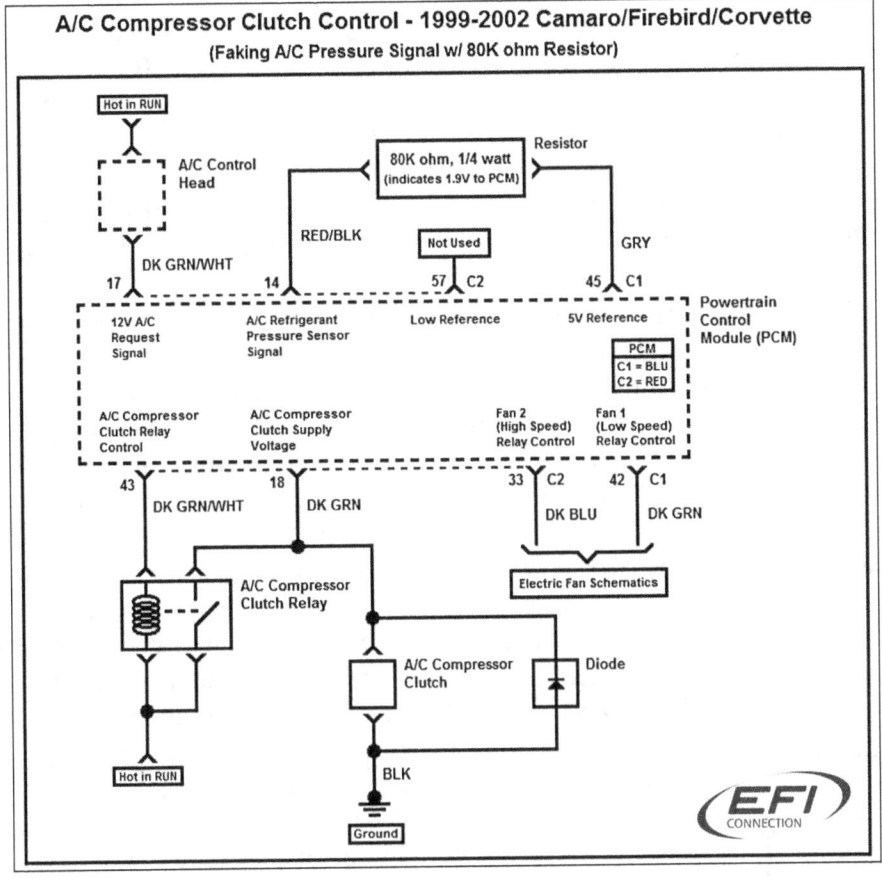

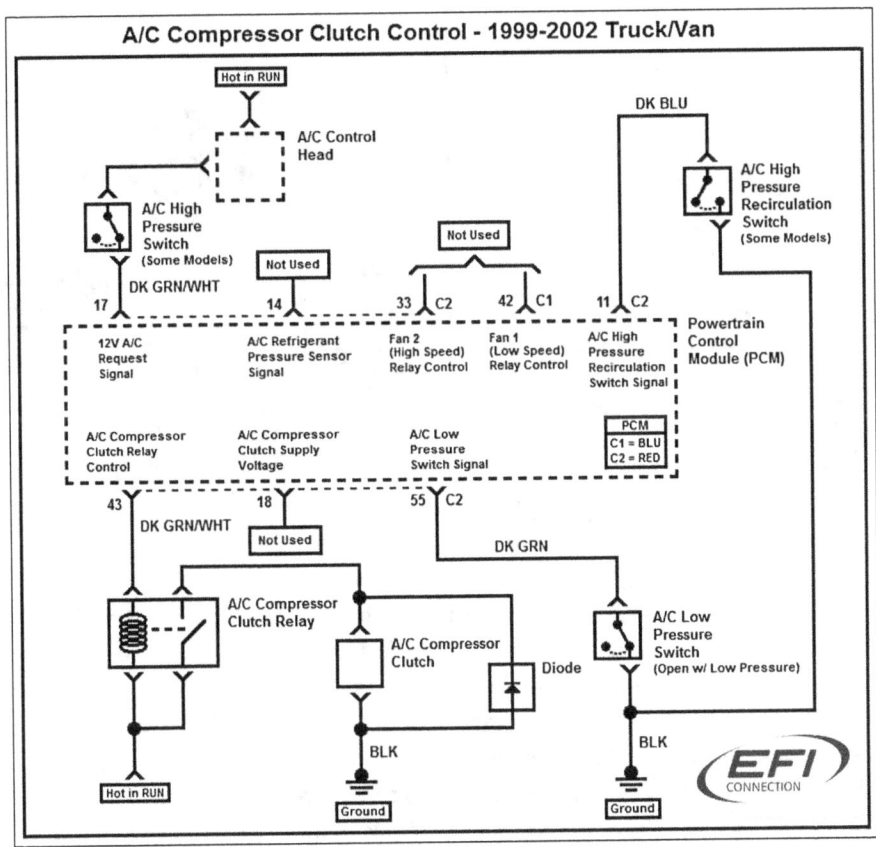

For vehicle installations where the A/C pressure sensor cannot be installed, the voltage necessary to indicate proper line pressure can be created through the installation of a resistor. By installing an 80,000-ohm, 1/4 watt resistor across the A/C pressure sensor, 5V reference, and signal circuits, the PCM thinks the A/C pressure is always adequate for A/C compressor clutch operation. This workaround should be used with extreme caution as it eliminates the safeguards General Motors has implemented through the use of an A/C pressure sensor.

project is that you can make use of PCM control of the A/C compressor clutch based on engine RPM, throttle position, and so on.

A big problem with PCM-controlled A/C was introduced in 2003. In an effort to reduce the amount of wire in newer automobiles, serial communication lines were established for modules to communicate across the vehicle. Most 2003-newer PCMs receive Class 2 serial data messaging from the HVAC control module. The early 12V A/C request from the A/C control unit is no longer used and has not been used in a GM vehicle since.

LS PCM conversions using the 2003-and-newer PCMs must disable

The A/C system wiring for the 1999–2002 trucks and vans is represented here. This system does not use the 0 to 5V A/C pressure sensor found in the Camaro, Firebird, and Corvette. These trucks and vans were not fitted with electric fans. If you plan to use electric fans, consider using the wiring and PCM calibration from a 1999–2002 Camaro, Firebird, or Corvette.

the DTCs related to A/C and not bother with wiring in the A/C pressure sensor.

If the vehicle is equipped with electric fan(s), they must be turned on when the compressor clutch is engaged. A trigger wire from the A/C wiring must be wired into the electric fan relay(s) to pass air through the condenser when the A/C is on. If the PCM has not commanded the electric fan(s) on based on high coolant temperature and a ground is applied to the fan relay signal wire(s), DTC(s) set to indicate that the fan(s) have been turned on unexpectedly. The DTC(s) can be disabled through tuning software.

PCM Conversion Recommendations

For LS PCM conversions with cable throttle, the most desirable PCM and base calibration is the 1999–2002 Camaro/Firebird. Those calibrations support A/C compressor control and electric fan control. The Camaro/Firebird calibrations allow you to choose between manual transmission and 4L60-E automatic transmission. Should your LS PCM project require control of a 4L80-E transmission, a segment swap does the trick. Not all tuning software packages allow segment swaps but those that do, such as EFILive, provide necessary details.

For LS PCM conversions with Corvette electronic throttle equipment, a Corvette base PCM calibration must be used. The Corvette calibrations allow you to choose between manual transmission and 4L60-E automatic transmission. Should your LS PCM project require control of a 4L80-E transmission, a segment swap does the trick.

For LS PCM conversions with truck electronic throttle equipment, the corresponding truck PCM and base calibration must be used. The early truck calibrations support A/C control, but not electric fan control. The 2003-newer truck calibrations do not support A/C control without the enormous task of integrating the HVAC control module for Class 2 communications with the PCM. For these types of LS PCM conversions, when the A/C system is on, electric fan operation has to be implemented without control from the PCM.

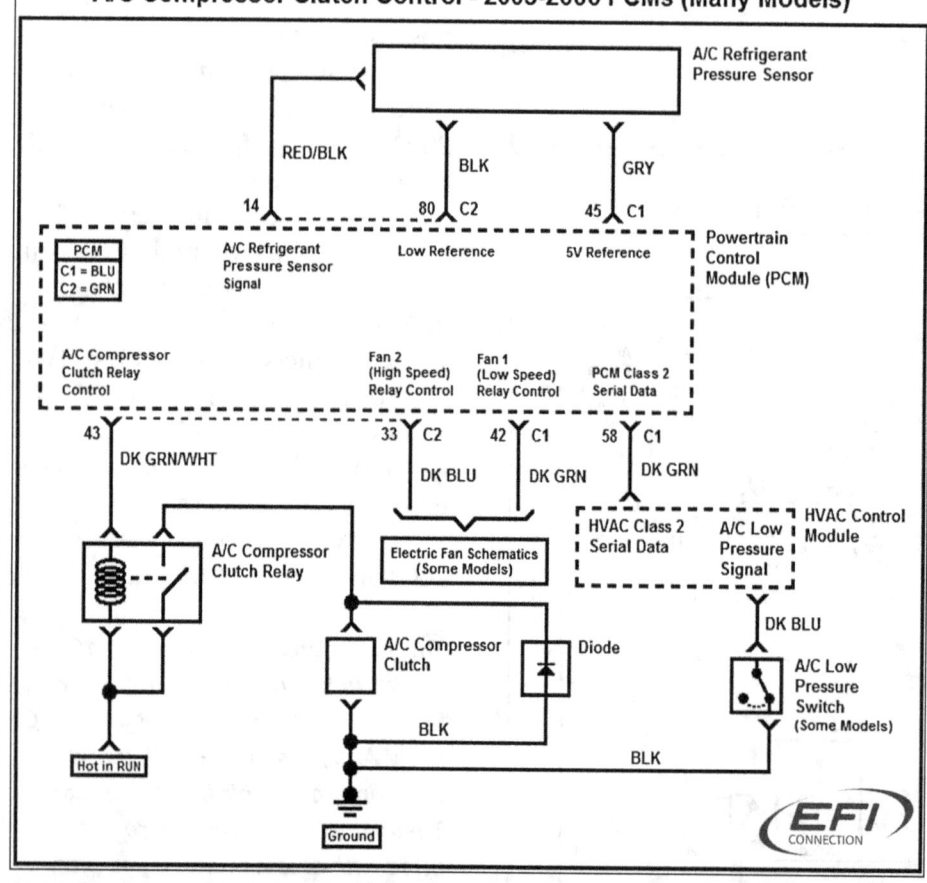

In 2003, General Motors introduced HVAC control modules in trucks and vans that replaced the traditional 12V A/C on signal with Class 2 serial data messaging. For conversions requiring a 2003-newer Gen III PCM, the A/C system has to be wired independent of the PCM.

The A/C pressure sensor (left) reports a 0 to 5V signal to pin 14 of the red PCM connector that represents the pressure of the A/C system. The A/C low-pressure switch (right) indicates whether the A/C pressure is low by applying a ground to pin 55 of the red PCM connector.

CHAPTER 12

CRUISE CONTROL

All Gen III vehicles were available with cruise control. Engines with a cable-actuated throttle body require an electronic cruise control module with an internal stepper motor to pull and release a throttle cable to maintain vehicle speed. Engines with an electronic throttle body rely on the TAC module to increase and decrease throttle blade angle to maintain vehicle speed.

Cable Throttle Systems

Early cruise control systems took control of the throttle blade angle through a vacuum-operated actuator that pulled and released a throttle cable. The actuator relied on engine vacuum for operation. Early cruise control systems have a lag response to driver commands. Making cruise control performance worse is an aged diaphragm that has developed a leak and no longer operates properly.

Newer cruise control systems abandoned the vacuum actuator for an electronic module with an internal stepper motor to pull and release a throttle cable to maintain vehicle speed. These systems have a better performance feel than the old vacuum-type systems. The required components of the cruise control system, however, have not changed much.

Required Components

To install a GM cruise control module for your cable throttle system, several components are required. Most of them, such as cruise control switches, clutch switch, and brake switches, may already be in your car. Any missing components can either be sourced from a salvaged GM vehicle or through the aftermarket.

Cruise Control Module: The cruise control module for cable throttle vehicles is a relevant discussion for Gen III PCMs because of the PCM's availability of primary and secondary VSS outputs that may be used to satisfy the cruise control module's 4,000-pulse-per-mile input requirement. Also, the 1999–2002 Camaro/Firebird cruise control modules require cruise inhibit and cruise enabled status communication signals with the PCM.

Cruise control modules compatible with Gen III conversions are plentiful. You may choose from cruise

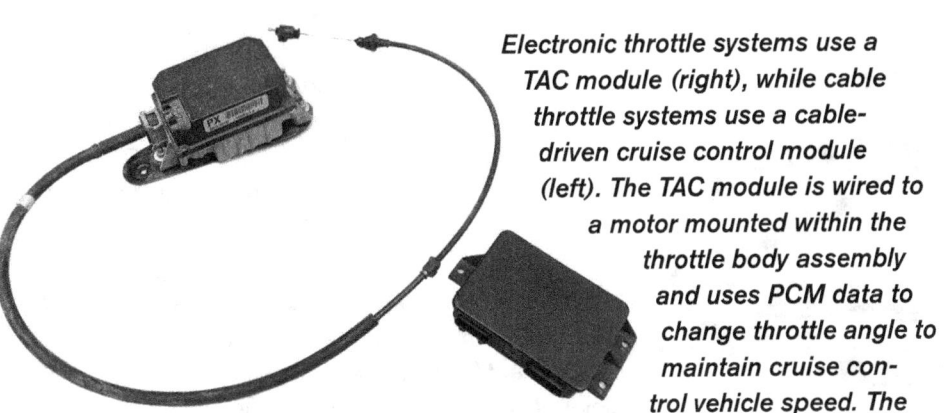

Electronic throttle systems use a TAC module (right), while cable throttle systems use a cable-driven cruise control module (left). The TAC module is wired to a motor mounted within the throttle body assembly and uses PCM data to change throttle angle to maintain cruise control vehicle speed. The cable throttle cruise control module shown here also uses PCM data to maintain cruise control vehicle speed, but must manually pull the throttle linkage to change throttle angle.

CHAPTER 12

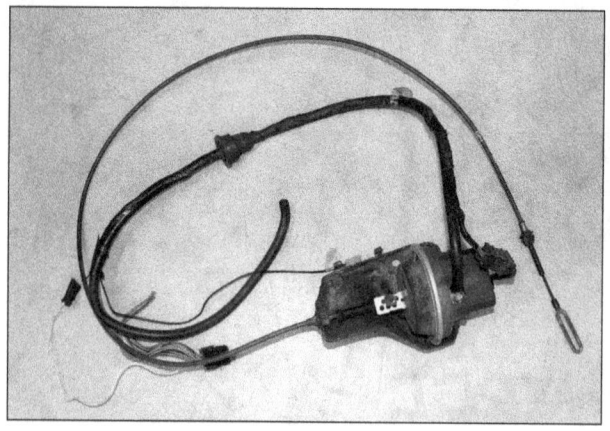

Early GM systems used a vacuum-controlled actuator to pull a throttle cable. These systems require a VSS (most commonly a 2,000-pulse-per-mile signal) to maintain cruise control vehicle speed. Rather than using an internal motor like the newer cable-driven cruise control modules, these early units use engine vacuum to control a diaphragm that pulls a throttle cable. The result is a lazy response to the driver's cruise control commands.

control modules found in 1996-newer Vortec trucks and LS-series vehicles. The cruise control module receives signals from several switches and, when necessary, takes control of throttle blade angle through a cable attached to the engine's throttle body. Installation is rather simple. The most difficult part may be adapting the cruise control throttle cable to your throttle body's linkage if the cable end does not match.

PCM: In production vehicles, the PCM is used to output a 4,000-pulse-per-mile VSS signal to the cruise control module. This is a common pulse count used with many early GM ECMs and VSS buffer boxes. An optional cruise engaged status signal is available for communication between the PCM and cruise control module. For retrofits using a 1999–2002 Camaro/Firebird cruise control module, the cruise engaged status and cruise inhibit signal wires must be used.

VSS Signal: The 4,000-pulse-per-mile VSS input to the cruise control module is required, but the PCM is not required to provide it. Retrofit projects sometimes introduce VSS buffer modules to receive a VSS signal that is not compatible with the Gen III PCM and to provide several VSS outputs for devices such as the speedometer or PCM.

A VSS buffer module may also be used to provide a 4,000-pulse-per-mile VSS signal to the cruise control module. Remember, however, the Gen III PCM has two configurable VSS outputs to choose from that provide a 4,000-pulse-per-mile signal dedicated to the cruise control module. (See Chapter 15, Project 1, on page 112 for setting the 4,000-pulse-per-mile VSS signal with EFILive.)

Cruise Control Switches: The required cruise control switch signals

This 1996-newer GM cruise module assembly contains a circuit board for processing cruise control logic, an internal motor to operate a worm-driven gear, and a short braided strap to pull the throttle cable. This cruise control module uses PCM data to control the movement of the throttle cable when cruise control is active.

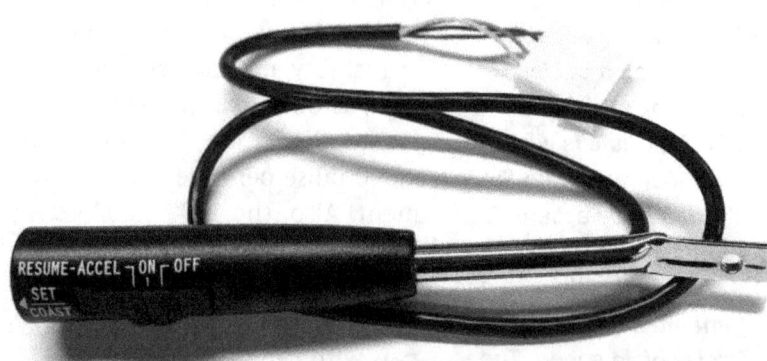

This Rostra cruise control switch (# 250-3020) may be used in a GM application for on/off and set/coast signals. The aftermarket offers several types of cruise control switches for different steering column configurations. If you cannot identify one to suit your application, you could make your own set of dash or center console mounted switches. With an on/off switch, two momentary switches, and little creativity, you can create an inexpensive cruise control switch solution.

CRUISE CONTROL

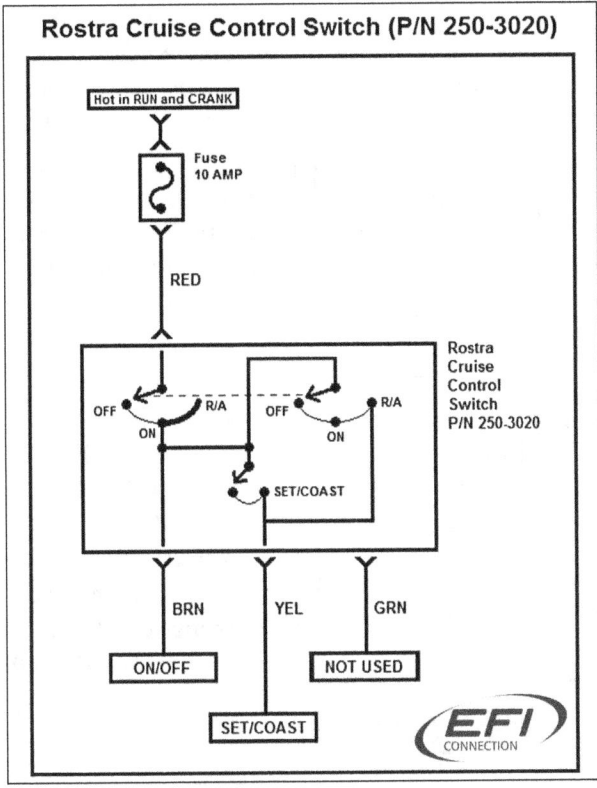

Not all aftermarket cruise control switches provide the signals required by the GM systems. This Rostra switch does not provide an independently pulsed 12V signal for the resume/accel function. In such cases, only the on/off and set/coast switches may be used.

are common to the switches found in the multifunction lever of GM steering columns. The on/off signal is normally open switched 12V, the set/coast signal is momentary 12V, and the resume/accel signal is momentary 12V.

Rostra Precision Controls offers a variety of cruise control switches that may be used if your steering column's multifunction lever does not have the necessary cruise control switches. (See Chapter 15, Project 1, on page 112 to see an early GM steering column with only a set/coast cruise control switch.)

Brake Switch: The cruise control module requires two brake switch signals. A normally closed 12V switch applies power to the clutch/brake switch input (pin D) and a normally open 12V switch applies stop lamp

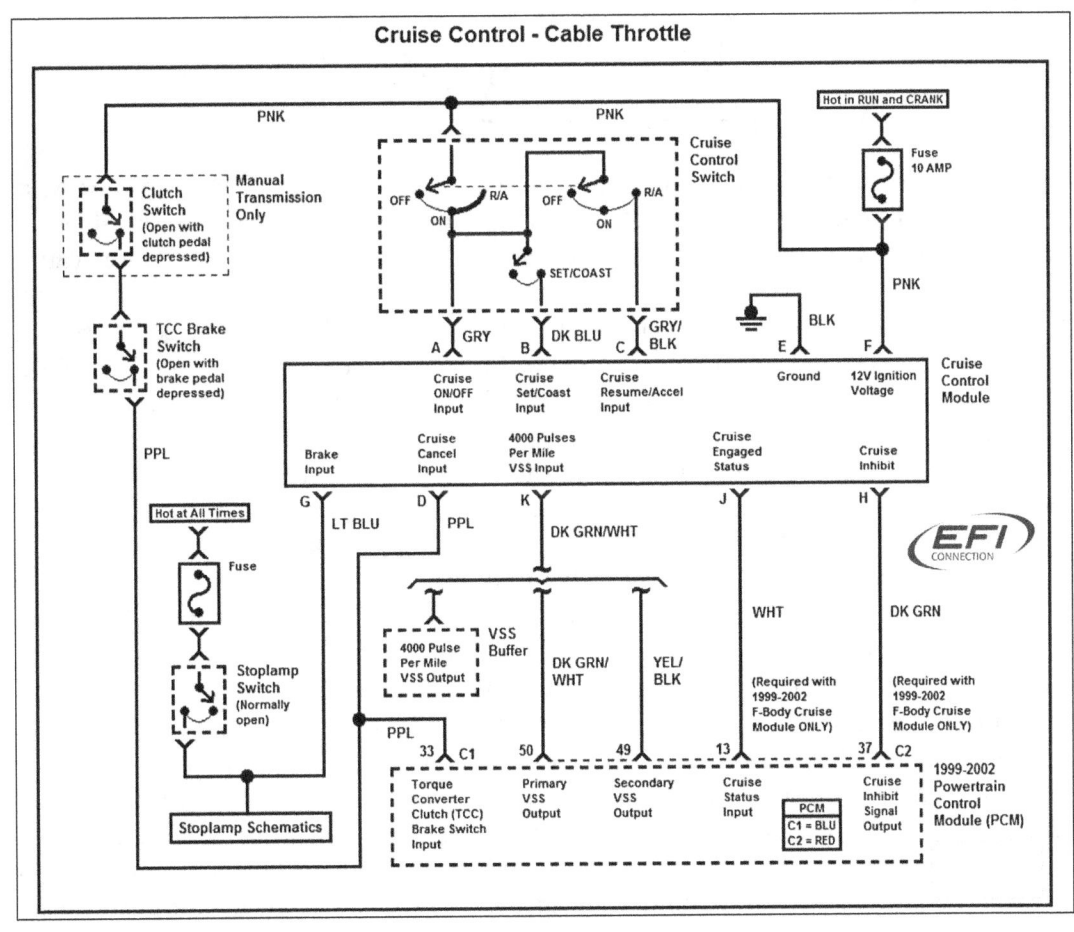

A typical 1996-newer GM cruise control module schematic looks like this. Notice the PCM cruise status and cruise inhibit signals are only required for 1999–2002 Camaro and Firebird cruise control modules. In general, the cruise control module requires 12V switched ignition, ground, VSS, cruise control switches, normally open brake switch (stop lamp switch), normally closed brake switch (commonly a torque converter clutch switch), and a manual transmission clutch switch (if so equipped).

GM GEN III LS-SERIES POWERTRAIN CONTROL SYSTEMS

CHAPTER 12

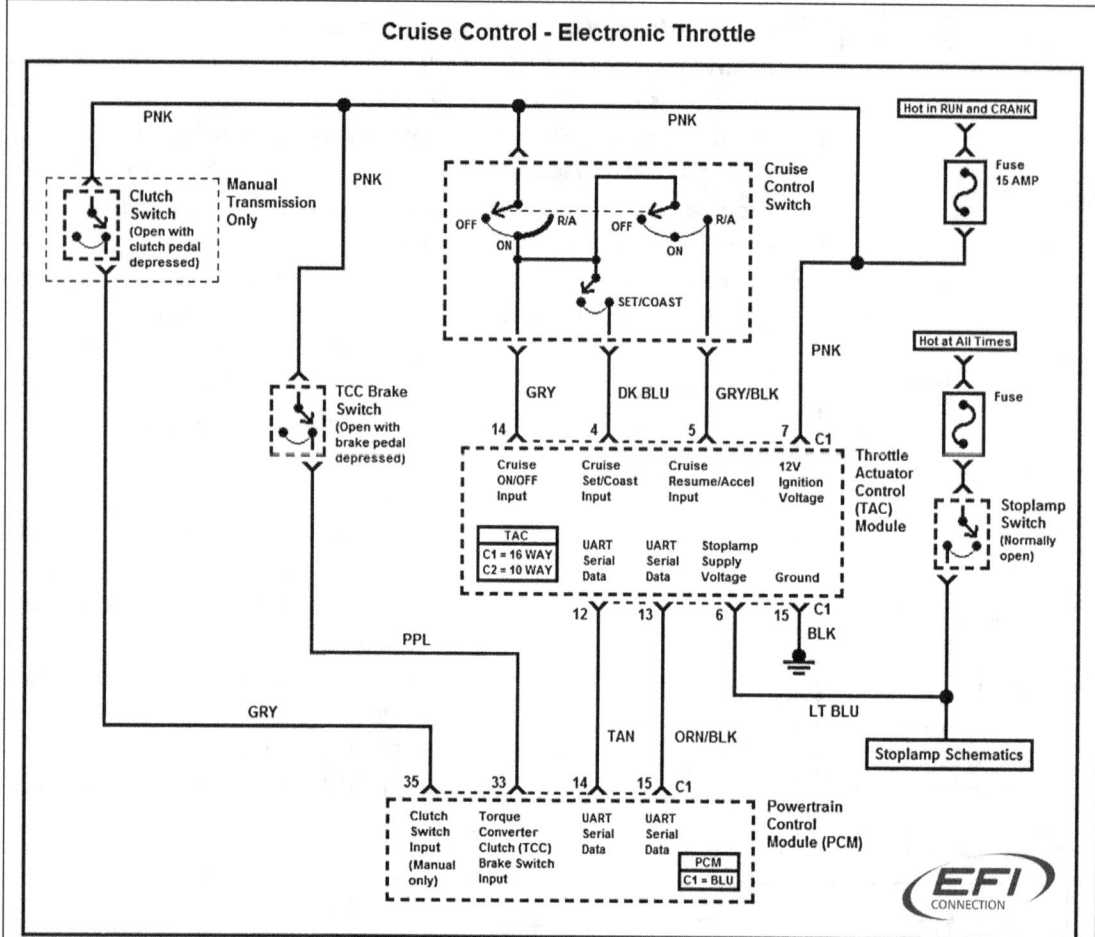

This schematic represents a typical GM cruise control switch wired to a TAC module. The TAC module generally requires 12V switched ignition, ground, PCM serial data circuits, cruise control switches, normally open brake switch (stop lamp switch), normally closed brake switch (commonly a torque converter clutch switch), and a manual transmission clutch switch (if so equipped).

voltage to the brake input (pin G). These signals are used to disengage cruise control when the brake pedal is depressed.

Clutch Switch: If using a manual transmission, a normally closed clutch switch should be wired on the same circuit as the normally closed brake switch. Depressing the clutch switch removes 12V from the cruise control module (pin D) to disengage cruise control.

Operation Overview

With the exception of the 1999–2002 Camaro/Firebird cruise control modules, the 1996-newer truck and 1998 Camaro/Firebird cruise control modules can be used as stand-alone units. These modules require 12V ignition, ground, cruise control switch signals, brake switch signal, clutch switch signal, stop lamp switch signal, and a 4,000-pulse-per-mile vehicle speed signal. Once installed in a retrofit vehicle, the performance is improved compared to early cruise control systems operated by engine vacuum.

Set/Coast: To set cruise control, the cruise control module requires a 12V switched-on signal and a 12V momentary set signal from the multifunction lever. With the 12V on signal present at the cruise control module and the vehicle at a desired speed, pushing the set button adds the vehicle's current speed to the cruise control module's memory.

The driver may remove his or her foot from the accelerator pedal and the cruise control module overrides the throttle blade angle to increase or decrease vehicle speed. Pressing and holding the set/coast button causes the vehicle to coast to a reduced speed. Releasing the set/coast button stores the new reduced vehicle speed in the cruise control module's memory. Quickly pressing and releasing the set/coast button subtracts 1 mph from the cruise control module's memory.

Resume/Accelerate: Once cruise control is active and the driver depresses the clutch or brake pedal, the cruise control module no longer controls throttle blade angle. The previously set vehicle speed remains stored in the cruise control module's memory. Sliding the resume/accel switch requests the cruise control module to take over throttle blade

CRUISE CONTROL

angle and accelerate the vehicle to the previously set vehicle speed.

Sliding and holding the resume/accel switch increases vehicle speed until the switch is released. The new vehicle speed is stored in the cruise control module's memory. Quickly sliding and releasing the resume/accel switch adds 1 mph to the cruise control module's memory.

If the cruise control on/off switch is set to off or the vehicle is shut off, the cruise control module's memory is erased and sliding the resume/accel switch does not return the vehicle to a previously set speed.

Erasing Cruise Speed Memory: When the driver disengages cruise control by depressing the clutch or brake pedal, the cruise control module retains its memory and allows the driver to use the resume/accel switch to resume the vehicle speed stored in memory. To clear the cruise control module's memory of vehicle speed, turn off the on/off switch or shut off the vehicle's ignition switch. This removes 12V power from the cruise control module and clear its memory.

Disengaging Cruise Control: The cruise control module retains the set vehicle speed in its memory until it loses 12V power through the cruise control on/off switch or the vehicle's ignition switch. To disengage (but not disable) the cruise control module's control of throttle blade angle, gently apply the clutch or brake pedal to momentarily remove 12V

Gen IV Systems

Although Gen IV LS systems are not covered in this book, it is worth noting that most Gen IV LS engine conversions never have a practical option of cruise control. Most vehicles with a Gen IV ECM require a BCM to receive cruise control switch signals and then broadcast CAN communication signals to the ECM for cruise control operation.

There are a few Gen IV exceptions where cruise control signals are received at the ECM from 12V switches, but the majority of conversions would require a CAN interface module capable of performing the cruise control functions of the BCM for cruise control operation; this is a module that has not been created at the time of this writing.

Those who strongly prefer cruise control for their retrofit project should consider using a Gen III PCM and an engine with a 24x crankshaft reluctor.

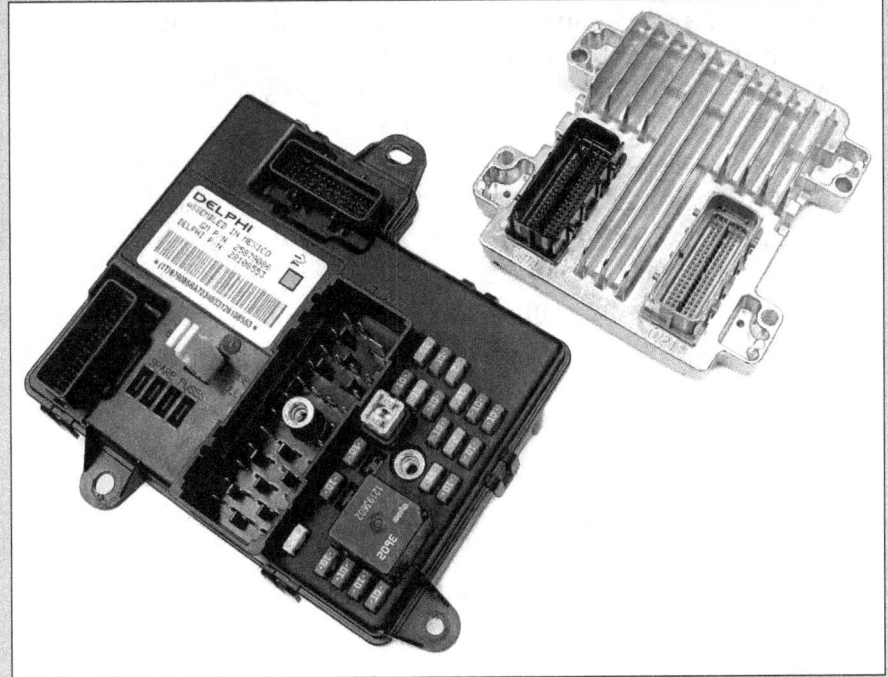

Most Gen IV vehicles require a BCM for cruise control operation. In newer vehicles, the BCM sends packets of data (or messages) through the CAN bus. The ECM monitors the CAN bus (a twisted pair of wires) to look for messages sent from the BCM for cruise control operation. The ECM responds to cruise control messages by changing throttle angle through the built-in TAC system when cruise control is active. This 2008 Corvette ECM and BCM work together for cruise control operation.

CHAPTER 12

power from the cruise control module's brake/clutch signal input.

To disable cruise control, slide the cruise control on/off switch to the off position.

Inhibit Signal

Be cautious of cruise control modules from 1999–2002 Camaros/Firebirds. These cruise control modules are "more intelligent" than truck modules. In the 1999–2002 Camaro/Firebird, the PCM may inhibit (prevent) cruise control operation based on vehicle speed, park/neutral switch signal, engine RPM, or battery voltage. If the PCM commands the cruise inhibit signal to the cruise control module and the cruise control module returns an active cruise engaged status signal, the PCM sets a DTC related to the cruise control system.

Most people find this extra layer of protection unnecessary and prefer a cruise control module from a 1996-newer truck or 1998 Camaro/Firebird. The 1998 Camaro/Firebird PCM cannot output a cruise inhibit signal, so the 1998 Camaro/Firebird cruise module functions the same as the 1996-newer truck modules.

Identifying a 1999–2002 Camaro/Firebird cruise control module is rather easy. All ten harness connector cavities are used. Vehicles with the cruise inhibit signal require its use when installing the cruise control module in a retrofit vehicle. While you likely do not see a wire in connector cavity H for any other vehicle, a quick visual inspection of the wire harness shows whether the cruise inhibit signal is required.

Electronic Throttle Systems

All Gen III vehicles with an electronic throttle body rely on the TAC module for cruise control operation. During normal engine operation, the TAC module is used to increase and decrease the throttle blade angle. By using the available cruise control switch inputs, the TAC module can respond to the driver's cruise control commands to maintain vehicle speed.

Being fully integrated into the electronic throttle system, the driver's cruise control commands are instantaneously applied to the throttle and the feel of acceleration and deceleration is smooth and seamless.

The switches and inputs are very similar to those of cable-operated cruise control modules.

Required Components

It's likely that after an electronic throttle installation your vehicle will have all of the components necessary for integrated cruise control. By using the TAC module's cruise control switch inputs and brake/clutch switches, any retrofit vehicle can be ready for cruise control. The following switch signals are required by the electronic throttle system for cruise control operation.

Cruise Control Switch: The required cruise control switch signals are no different than those for Gen III vehicles with cable throttle body and cruise control module. The on/off signal is normally open switched 12V, the set/coast signal is momentary 12V, and the resume/accel signal is momentary 12V. If your retrofit vehicle does not have a multifunction lever on the steering column with cruise control switches, you can find them in the aftermarket.

Brake Switch: The cruise control system requires two brake switch signals. A normally closed 12V switch applies power to the TCC brake switch input of the PCM and a normally open 12V switch applies stop lamp voltage to the stop lamp input of the TAC module. These signals are used to disengage cruise control when the brake pedal is depressed.

Clutch Switch: If using a manual transmission, a normally closed 12V clutch switch must be wired to the PCM (blue connector, pin 35). Depressing the clutch switch removes 12V from the PCM's clutch switch input to disengage cruise control.

CHAPTER 13

WIRE HARNESS SELECTION

As the owner of EFI Connection, engine wire harness manufacturing is my specialty. In the early days of my career, I took on used harness rework for 1985–1992 Camaro and Firebird owners who wanted to add a TPI system to their car. I've also revised newer LS harnesses for customers who have relocated components in the engine bay. Today, however, I decline nearly all used harness rework. With few exceptions, I recommend new engine wire harness builds whenever possible.

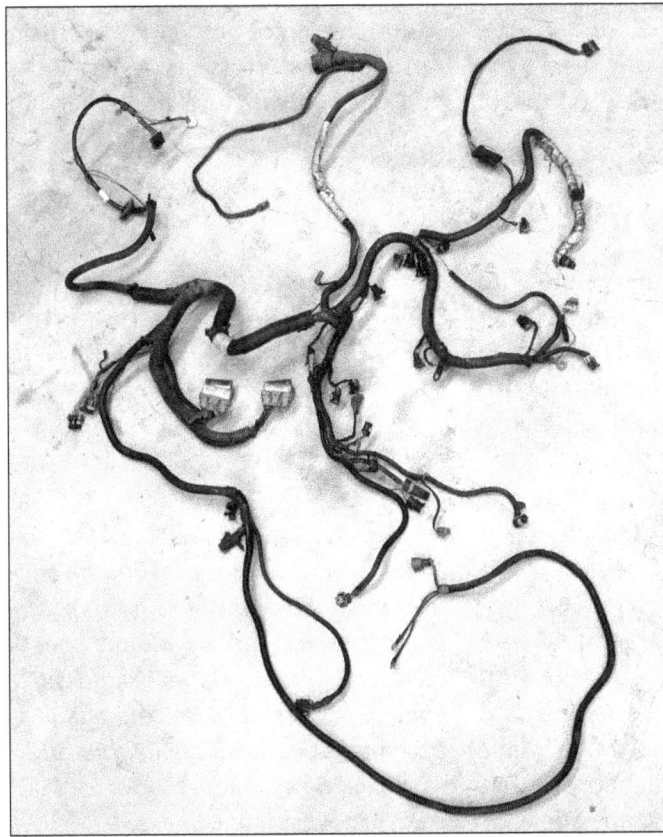

This engine wire harness was pulled from a 1997 Trans Am before an LS1 PCM conversion (see Chapter 15, Project 3, on page 122). Through a transmission swap, ignition controller, and nitrous installation, this engine wire harness has been modified. The longevity of an engine wire harness may decrease depending on the quality of the modifications.

Used Wire Harnesses

The reality of any used engine wire harness is that it was removed from an old, and likely salvaged, vehicle. These harnesses may have damage due to heat, chaffing, or improper repair. Proceed with caution before reusing an old wire harness for your high-dollar retrofit.

"Let sleeping dogs lie."

You know that old adage. If it works, leave it alone. If you start messing around, things may get ugly. Some engine bays are left untouched except for oil changes and adding washer fluid; other engine bays have additional wiring for car stereo, alarm, nitrous solenoids, fuel pump relay upgrade, electric water pump, and the list goes on. These add-ons require power, ground, and maybe even sensor signals.

Have you seen the uninsulated butt splice in a vehicle's wire harness? You know, the red, blue, or yellow plastic barrel that has been crimped on each end? Or maybe you've seen an uninsulated blue wire tap? Yes, it's the handiwork of someone who

CHAPTER 13

Hardware store electrical tape (top) is not the same as harness tape (bottom). Engine wire harness repairs should be completed with quality shrink tube and not wrapped in electrical tape. The electrical tape found at local hardware store contains a lot of adhesive and may not hold up well to engine bay heat. Many auto manufacturers use high-quality Tesa harness tape.

was in a rush to tie into or repair the vehicle's wire harness.

Alternations to a vehicle's harness often create future points of failure. Even the improper handling of a used wire harness from time of removal to your garage floor may have introduced points of failure that may make you wish you had a custom-built new harness for your project.

Let me pause here to tell you about a local street rod project. The early Ford pickup was fitted with an LT1 engine and 4L60-E transmission.

The shop that took on the restoration received the project with a used, reworked engine wire harness. Part of the rework service had included the addition of gear select switch wiring to interface with the LT1 PCM and a custom gear indicator panel mounted on the dash.

I was called after the vehicle was finished because the electric fan did not turn on when the A/C system was on. I also found the used gear select switch connectors were damaged and a previous repair attempt involved forcing wire too large into the connector cavity using a terminal not designed to accept such a large wire size.

Had I been involved with this restoration from the start, the vehicle would have had a brand-new wire harness with all necessary provisions for the vehicle. There would have been no need for a mechanic to add the gear select switch and A/C wiring using the wrong type of insulated wire, butt splice connectors, and generic crimp tool.

This restoration project exceeded $100,000 and, sadly, still has a used engine wire harness with surprises yet to be seen under the black electrical tape.

I've heard stories of used engine harness reworks where unused sensor connectors were cut and taped, causing a short as the PCM reference voltage circuit made contact with the PCM low-reference circuit. The methods used to rework used wire harnesses often introduce points of failure.

"Beauty is only skin deep, but ugly goes clear to the bone."

Going back to that LT1 Ford street rod restoration, I found other surprises as I made repairs. The used harness rework was completed with the application of black electrical tape, which oozes adhesive when the wire harness experiences engine bay heat and leaves a sticky residue as it is removed.

As I unwrapped the sticky electrical tape, I found segments of wire spliced and/or crimped to the harness so that the desired length was achieved. Some "professionals" take the completed engine harness that was designed to fit a specific GM application and shorten or lengthen it by splicing wires to fit the layout of another vehicle. It looks pretty all wrapped up in black tape and split loom. The quality of work within? You roll the dice.

"An ounce of prevention is worth a pound of cure."

Building a plug-and-play wire harness for any production vehicle requires sourcing connectors and related components (associated secondary locks, dress covers, retaining clips, etc.) that are often specific to the vehicle. These items, if serviceable, are often only available in very large quantities. A harness builder would have to purchase the thousands of connectors, secondary locks, and dress covers and then mark up

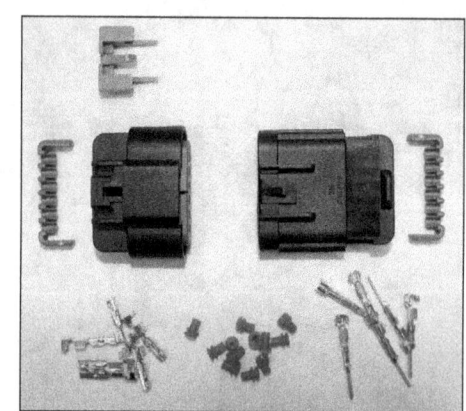

Delphi manufactures most of the connectors found in GM wire harnesses. In most cases, General Motors uses all available secondary locks during connector assembly. Be cautious of aftermarket harness manufacturers who exclude secondary locks for the sake of saving a few bucks.

WIRE HARNESS SELECTION

All production vehicles pass wires through the firewall somehow. Many have a two-part connection at the firewall called a bulkhead connection. This connection passes through power, ground, and other circuits not carrying sensor signal voltage. Sensor circuits passing through the firewall are typically sealed with a grommet and never cut.

the price of wire harness builds to reflect these costs.

A vehicle that is not appropriate for a standalone, street rod type of wire harness is the 1985–1992 Camaro and Firebird. Unfortunately, General Motors merged much of the engine bay wiring together in 1989, making a new plug-and-play harness a bit more involved than a typical new LS conversion engine wire harness build.

When a customer requests an LS-series PCM conversion wire harness for a 1989–1992 Camaro or Firebird, my typical approach is to build a brand-new wire harness segment for the LS-series PCM with added length at the sensor ends.

The customer sends me the original engine bay harness. It is carefully disassembled to remove the TPI ECM-related wiring and then inspected for damage. Rather than splice in repair segment(s) for a damaged circuit, such as a cut ring terminal at the starter, I place a brand-new length of 10-gauge purple wire in the wire harness, which is terminated at the starter and at the bulkhead connector for the firewall.

I remove the original damaged circuit. After the repairs, I set the remaining original engine bay harness on top of the new harness and finish it on a vehicle-specific template.

The end result is an OEM-quality engine harness that would have been built by General Motors had it used the LS-series PCM in that car.

A wire harness shop should have the proper terminals for GM engine harnesses, be tooled up to make proper crimps using production tooling, and apply proper techniques for reworking an original engine harness. You typically do get what you pay for as many side businesses offering only used harness rework have not invested in the proper supplies (TXL wire and replacement terminals) or crimp tooling to provide you with a product that matches the quality of a new engine harness.

This equipment is expensive and, as a result, causes the repair costs and new construction costs to exceed any low-price deal you find on eBay.

New Wire Harnesses

A brand-new custom wire harness (using the same production tooling and quality components as an OEM harness) is always superior to a reworked, used engine harness. Wire lengths are appropriate for your

A connector may be used for several different applications. Depending on the circuit requirements, a larger or smaller wire size may be required. Connectors accept a variety of wire sizes but require an appropriately sized terminal.

This connector accepts two types of terminals. The 18- to 16-gauge Metri-Pack 150 terminals (the two on the left) allow for 18- and 16-gauge wire. The 22- to 20-gauge terminals (the two on the right) allow for 22- and 20-gauge wire.

Each of these terminals was designed to be used with two sizes of wire. What makes this possible is the production crimp die that is used to crimp the terminal to the wire. Cheap, inexpensive, wire harnesses are often built with improper terminal sizes and wrong crimp tooling.

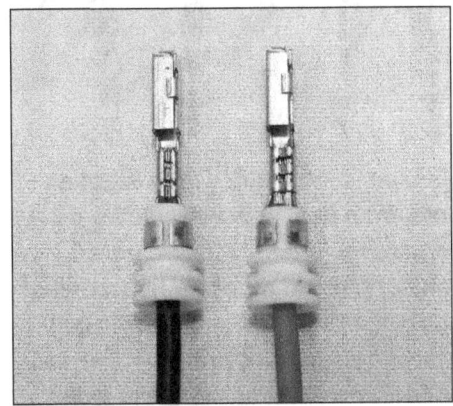

The 18-gauge black wire (left) was crimped with a proper production crimp tool and die set. The 18-gauge red wire (right) was crimped with a general repair tool. You can see that, even with the correct general repair tool, the crimp quality of the red wire is poor compared to the crimp on the terminal with black wire.

GM GEN III LS-SERIES POWERTRAIN CONTROL SYSTEMS 105

CHAPTER 13

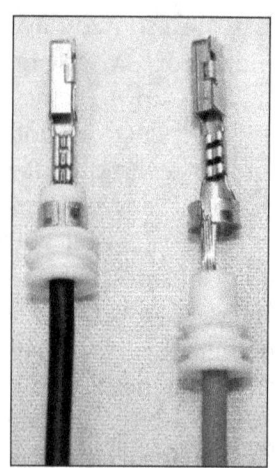

The 18-gauge black wire (left) was crimped with a proper production crimp tool and die set. The 18-gauge red wire (right) was crimped with a general repair tool. With a tug of the black wire, the terminal remains firmly attached. However, with a tug of the red wire, the terminal separates from the wire. Be cautious of harness builders who are able to sell products for less by using inexpensive, general repair, tooling.

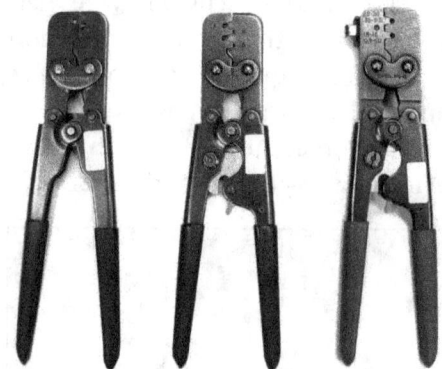

Inexpensive Gen III wire harnesses are often built with inexpensive general repair crimp tools. Delphi offers a line of general repair crimp tools that do not provide the same crimp quality as with pneumatic press and die sets. Kent-Moore issues the same tools (branded Delphi/Rostra/Kent-Moore/Sargent) to GM service technicians and clearly explains in terminal repair guides that solder is required for all terminations made with hand tooling.

Some wire harness manufacturers may boast they use Delphi tooling. Don't let that fool you into thinking their wire harnesses are properly assembled.

application, connectors are new (not dirty, brittle, or broken), and the wire does not suffer from oxidation due to years of use in temperature and moisture extremes.

The recipe for a quality engine harness is rather simple: Use the same components and production tooling as General Motors did. Only a few harness shops stand out from the rest because of the high cost involved in material and tooling.

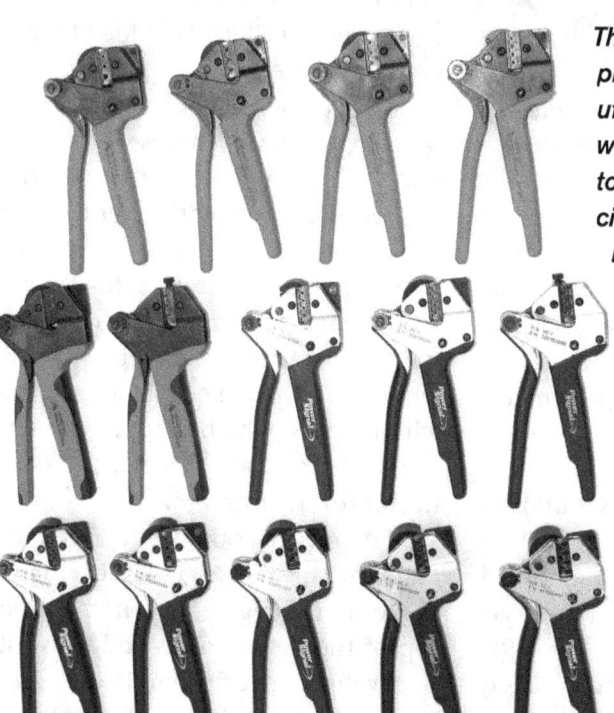

These hand tools represent production tooling for manufacturing Gen III engine wire harnesses. Each crimp tool contains a die set specific to a type of terminal. In some cases, several die sets are required for a family of terminals. For example, Delphi Metri-Pack 150 sealed terminals require three different die sets to cover 22- to 16-gauge wire. These tools use a parallel crimp (not scissor-like) strategy to accomplish the same quality crimp used with production GM harnesses.

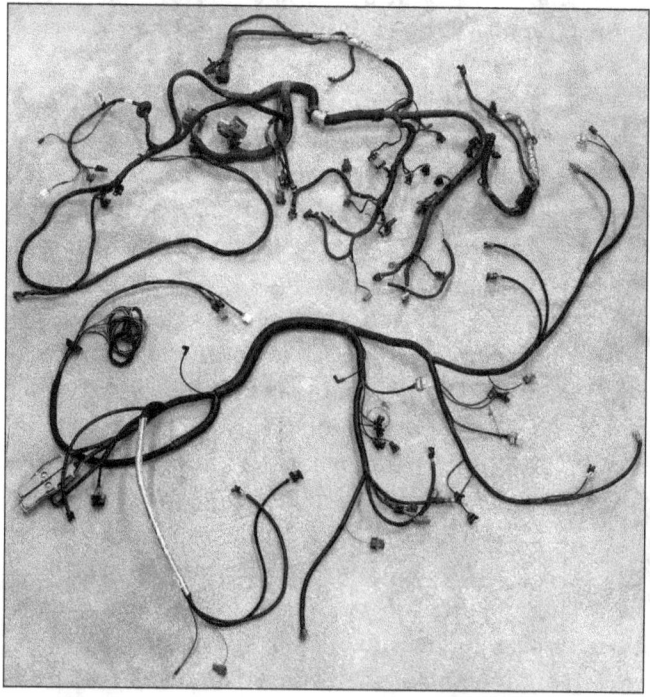

This brand-new, plug-and-play Camaro/Firebird engine wire harness was assembled using all proper TXL wire, Delphi connectors/terminals/seals, and production tooling. Quality wire harness manufacturers are out there, but be sure to ask the right questions about quality before you choose a manufacturer.

CHAPTER 14

ON-BOARD DIAGNOSTICS AND TROUBLESHOOTING

Modern fuel injection systems have many sensors and switches installed at key locations on the engine and transmission to allow the engine (and transmission) computer to operate in the ways they are intended. These sensors and switches are used to deliver the proper amount of fuel, the correct amount of spark timing, the most appropriate transmission gear, and so on. They also provide important information that is valuable for problem diagnosis. The process by which the engine and transmission controller(s) process sensor data and report errors is called on-board diagnostics (OBD). OBD has been used with GM engine controllers since the 1980s. Since that time, OBD has improved to a robust diagnostic system.

Assembly Line Diagnostic Link

The OBD system of the first multi-port V-8 electronic fuel injection system, or Tuned Port Injection, was implemented into the 1985 ECM found in the Corvette, Camaro, and Firebird. This basic system uses sensor data to determine if unusual operating behavior exists. When the ECM determines a malfunction, it applies a ground to the service engine soon (SES) lamp in the instrument cluster to indicate the need for service. SAE recommendations have since renamed the SES lamp to the MIL for standardization among vehicle manufacturers.

When the MIL has illuminated, the repair technician must be able to see what the ECM has detected as a malfunction. The malfunction is logged in the ECM as a trouble code. A physical method for retrieving a trouble code is to connect a scan tool to the assembly line diagnostic link (ALDL) connector beneath the dashboard near the steering column. The scan tool displays the trouble code number and the repair technician can then look up the diagnostic procedure to troubleshoot through the problem.

For example, the ECM may log a "Code 33." The GM service manual diagnostic description informs the repair technician that the MAF sensor signal voltage was too high during an engine operating condition that should not produce such high voltage. In other words, the MAF sensor reported an amount of incoming air that General Motors preconfigured the ECM to determine as improbable for the engine speed and throttle angle at which the trouble code was set.

The GM service manual diagnostic procedure leads the repair technician through a series of tests to determine why this occurred and may point to a faulty MAF sensor. This early OBD system offers a way to flash (illuminate) the MIL to represent the numerically named trouble codes that are set.

OBD-I System

In the 1980s, automotive manufacturers had widely implemented

CHAPTER 14

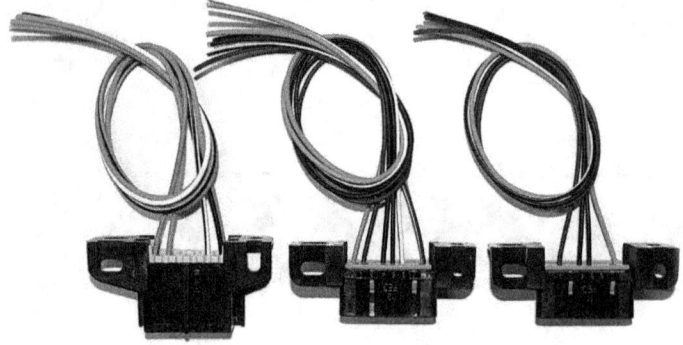

The OBD-I diagnostic connector (left) is easily identifiable because it is dimensionally different than the OBD-1.5 connector (middle) and the OBD-II connector (right), which are dimensionally the same.

OBD-I, OBD-1.5, and OBD-II diagnostic connectors are not wired the same. Provision was made with the OBD-1.5 connector to allow for the OBD-II wiring standard. Compared to the OBD-II connector wiring, the OBD-1.5 adds wires for OBD-I diagnostic test and serial data communication. A look at 1995 GM wiring schematics reveals that the Class 2 serial data wire in connector cavity 2 was not used, but terminated in the dash harness for use in 1996. An OBD-II scan tool is not appropriate for use with an OBD-1.5 vehicle because it cannot read the OBD-I serial data stream.

Diagnostic Connectors

OBD-I Diagnostic Connector

Cavity	Color	Function
A	Black/White	Ground
B	White/Black	Diagnostic Test
E	Orange	Serial Data (160 Baud)
F	Tan/Black	Torque Converter Lockup
M	Orange	Serial Data (8192 Baud)

OBD-1.5 Diagnostic Connector

Cavity	Color	Function
2	Purple	Class 2 Serial Data (Not Used)
4	Black	Ground
5	Black/White	Ground
6	White/Black	Diagnostic Test
9	Tan	Serial Data
16	Orange	12V Battery

OBD-II Diagnostic Connector

Cavity	Color	Function
2	Purple	Class 2 Serial Data
4	Black	Ground
5	Black/White	Ground
16	Orange	12V Battery

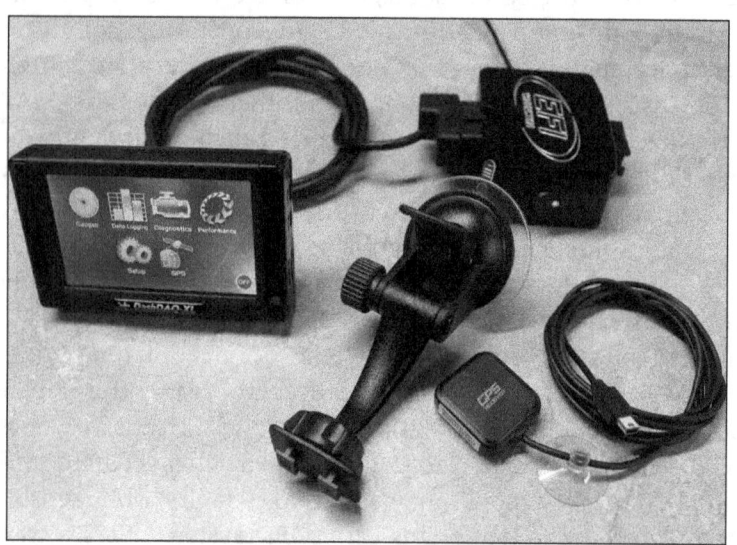

OBD-II standardization has been an incentive for manufacturers to offer OBD-II scan tools. A brief Internet search reveals hundreds of available OBD-II scan tools. This is Drew Technologies' DashDAQ-XL, a high-end, feature-packed scan tool. This model has windshield mount (standard), GPS receiver (optional), and bench-top OBD-II power assembly (an EFI Connection product used here as a power source).

The DashDAQ-XL touch-screen user interface is used to retrieve and clear DTCs, display both generic and enhanced OBD-II PIDs for monitoring real-time data, and accept aftermarket analog and serial input devices (such as wide-band O_2 sensors, thermocouple, and accelerometer). Because of OBD-II standardization, the DashDAQ-XL is compatible with all vehicles since 1996.

OBD into ECMs. The OBD-I systems were used with annual California emissions testing, but without OBD standardization, the emissions testing program was not as effective as it is today.

OBD-1.5 System

The precursor to the standardized OBD-II system was implemented in select 1994 and 1995 GM vehicles. Although not an official name, this OBD system is now referred to as OBD-1.5 because it introduced elements of the OBD-II system. Enthusiasts recognize the 1994–1995 LT1-equipped vehicles as OBD-1.5.

This OBD hybrid continues to use some of the same naming conventions as the early OBD systems, but also implements some of the newer OBD-II naming conventions. For

ON-BOARD DIAGNOSTICS AND TROUBLESHOOTING

example, with OBD-I, a "Code 15" indicates that the ECT sensor signal is too high. With OBD-II, a "P0118" indicates that the ECT sensor signal is too high.

Trouble code retrieval from OBD-1.5 systems requires a scan tool.

OBD-II System

In 1996, OBD-II was largely standardized and became a requirement for production automobiles. Benefits include improved diagnostics with many more parameters, ECU programming through the vehicle's diagnostic connector, and bi-directional control of certain on-board modules.

OBD-II Data Link Connector

The SAE J1962 OBD-II standard calls for a standardized DLC that is typically located beneath the dashboard and near the steering column. The DLC is used to retrieve DTCs, retrieve real-time data from all networked ECUs, bi-directional diagnostic communication, and ECU programming. For the purposes of Gen III fuel management discussion, the DLC is pinned as follows. Unused connector cavities may be used for vehicle specific functions.

Diagnostic Trouble Code Retrieval

The standardization of OBD-II allows for DTC retrieval with any off-the-shelf OBD-II scanner. DTCs may be present within multiple on-board ECUs and are distinguished by a prefix character followed by four digits. The PCM processes and may set engine- and transmission-related DTCs. Other modules, such as the BCM, are responsible for processing non-powertrain–related DTCs.

All off-the-shelf OBD-II scan tools have the capability to retrieve DTCs and clear DTCs from memory. In some cases, and through certain scan tools, freeze-frame data can be retrieved to see operating parameters that occurred when a DTC was set.

Real-Time Data Monitoring

OBD-II scan tools display real-time data by querying (request and response) on-board ECUs. Although scan tool interfaces vary, a repair technician specifies a parameter ID (PID) and the scan tool sends a request through the DLC for that PID (or list of PIDs). The on-board ECU containing that PID responds with the data values for the requested PID. While PIDs are technically codes, scan tools identify PIDs by their representative name, such as "Engine Speed."

Most off-the-shelf scan tools are universal in that they only retrieve the list of PIDs that automobile manufacturers are required to display. The

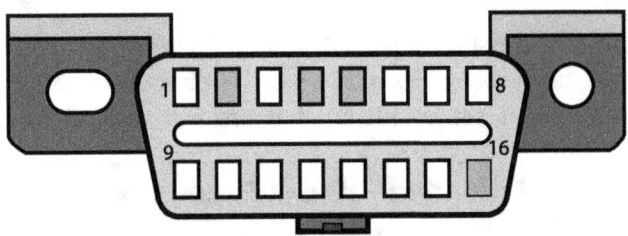

For standalone conversions, the DLC for Gen III PCMs requires only serial data, ground, and 12V battery. OBD-II scan tools use the DLC ground and 12V battery for power.

OBD-II DTC Types

Prefix	System	Example
P	Powertrain (Engine and Transmission) DTCs	P0121 – Throttle Position Sensor
B	Body DTCs	B2947 – Passlock System
C	Chassis DTCs	C0221 – ABS System
U	Network DTCs	U1300 – Class 2 Serial Data Circuit

There are several types of OBD-II DTCs. For clarity, DTCs are prefixed by a character that represents the system reporting a fault. Most standalone engine conversions only experience the powertrain (PXXXX) codes, as other systems are typically not present in a conversion vehicle.

Generic PID Set Examples

Description	Value
Fuel System Status	Open or Closed Loop
Engine RPM	Engine Crankshaft Speed
Throttle Position	Throttle Angle Percentage (or Voltage)
Timing Advance	Degrees of Spark Advance Relative to #1 Cylinder
MAF Sensor	Measured Airflow Through the MAF Sensor

An inexpensive, off-the-shelf OBD-II scan tool retrieves only a small set of PIDs. This "generic" PID set displays useful real-time data for troubleshooting the engine and transmission.

standard, or "generic," set of PIDs contains useful sensor data about engine and transmission operation.

Automobile manufacturers also define their own, non-standard, set of PIDs. These "enhanced" or "extended" set of PIDs are proprietary and greater in number than the standard PID set. Many off-the-shelf OBD-II scan tools do not query on-board ECUs for these PIDs. Scan tool manufacturers must pay a significant fee to obtain information about manufacturer-specific PIDs. Because of the extra costs involved, your basic $35 scan tool does not include the enhanced set of PIDs. Some scan tools offer enhanced PIDs for an extra fee.

Bi-Directional Diagnostic Communication

Advanced OBD-II scan tools have the ability to command control of certain engine and transmission functions. Engine bi-directional controls include, but are not limited to, electric fan operation, A/C compressor clutch operation, manual control of spark advance, commanded idle control, target air/fuel ratio, and injector performance tests. Transmission bi-directional controls include, but are not limited to, torque converter clutch solenoid control and commanded shift solenoids.

Some advanced OBD-II scan tools are capable of performing a crank angle sensor error (CASE) learn procedure (commonly referred to as "crank learn"). The GM service manual explains that due to tolerances in manufacturing, proper misfire detection requires the engine computer to learn the variances in the relationship of the CKP sensor and the crankshaft reluctor wheel.

This crank learn procedure should be performed after installing a new engine computer, engine timing cover, CKP sensor, or crankshaft reluctor wheel. Should the installation of these new parts not set a P1336 DTC, the engine computer relies on the results of the previous, now incorrect, crank learn data.

ECU Programming

The DLC is the connection point for any ECU programming interface. In the 1980s, engine computers stored calibration data in a flash PROM that was programmed outside the vehicle. All GM OBD-II ECUs

---

Extended PID Set Examples

Description	Value
Differential Gear Ratio	Calibrated Rear Differential Gear Ratio
Fan 1 On	Calibrated Engine Coolant Temp to Turn On Fan 1
Fan 1 Off	Calibrated Engine Coolant Temp to Turn Off Fan 1
Speed Limiter	Calibrated Maximum Vehicle Speed

Higher-end scan tools display manufacturer-specific PIDs that reveal a more in-depth look at the operation of the engine and transmission. This "enhanced" PID set is more expensive. This cost is often built into the price or available as an add-on feature.

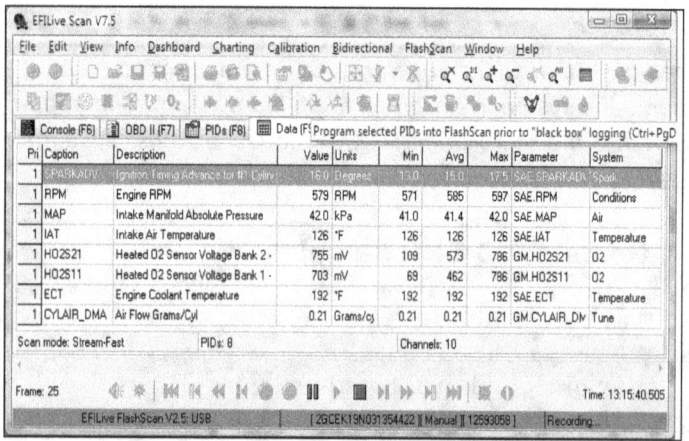

A scan tool package such as EFILive displays generic, enhanced, and user-defined PIDs. EFILive's hardware interface allows for external signal inputs that can be configured within the software to monitor devices such as a wide-band O_2S.

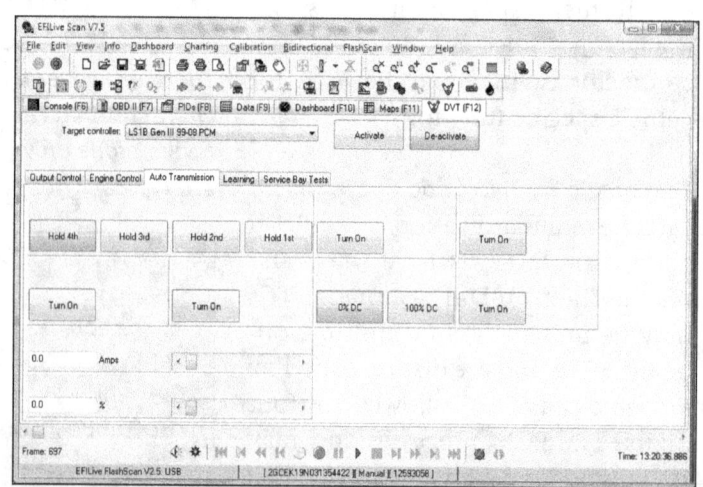

Troubleshooting transmission performance is made easier with EFILive's bi-directional control of the 4L60-E and 4L80-E transmissions. When bi-directional control is active, you can override PCM control of the transmission functions.

have the convenience of reprogramming without removal from the vehicle. Reprogramming is required for ECU replacement, GM service updates, and custom tuning through aftermarket tuning equipment.

Mail-order tuners offer custom programming services to get your vehicle running well enough to be driven or trailered to a local chassis dyno tuning facility. To get programming access to the engine and/or transmission computer, mail-order tuners use an off-board benchtop programming solution such as EFI Connection's Professional Series OBD-II modular benchtop programming equipment. (See Chapter 4 for more information about benchtop programming.)

Troubleshooting Diagnostic Trouble Codes

The OBD-II system's DTC malfunction logging is a fast and convenient way to resolve a problem. With OBD-II being standardized, any off-the-shelf OBD-II scan tool displays a list of DTCs that explain why the MIL is illuminated in the dashboard. Most auto parts stores scan your vehicle for free.

I recall a customer who updated his third-generation Firebird (a TPI car) to the Gen III PCM. He participated in the Hot Rod Power Tour and was well out of reach of his tools and diagnostic equipment.

The MIL illuminated in his dash as the engine began to run poorly. He was able to stop at an auto parts store for a free scan. The scan revealed a misfire-related DTC for a specific cylinder. He chased the spark plug wire from the distributor cap to the spark plug and found that the spark plug was loose. He tightened the spark plug, the auto parts store cleared the DTCs, and he was back on the Power Tour.

Before You Change That Sensor

In some cases the ECU sees several occurrences of a malfunction before setting a DTC. It is important to think through the problem before simply buying new parts.

As an example, let's say a DTC has set indicating prolonged high voltage in the bank 1 O_2 sensor. If you rush to the auto parts store to buy a new O_2 sensor, you may waste your time, as well as about $50.

First look at what the O_2 sensor does. The O_2 voltage ranges from about 0 to 1V. When a lean mixture passes the sensor, the voltage is closer to 0V. When a rich mixture passes the sensor, the voltage is closer to 1V. The target voltage for a healthy running engine is about 0.5V. An O_2 sensor in good working order indicates too much fuel in the air/fuel mixture exhausting from the engine. Such a DTC would not warrant an O_2 sensor replacement, but rather a look at the fuel injectors on bank 1 to inspect for a faulty injector.

Follow the Manufacturer's Procedures

The GM service manual contains step-by-step diagnostic procedures for each DTC. In some cases, the documentation includes wire schematics to help you understand the electronic circuits involved. The diagnostic procedures may call for a visual inspection, voltage test light, or multimeter to check voltage or resistance values. Advanced diagnostics may call for the use of a GM Tech2 scanner. The Tech2 is a necessity for on-board ECUs other than the engine control module and is seldom used with Gen III electronics conversions.

A good scan tool package, such as EFILive, and a GM service manual go a long way in diagnosing just about any DTC that may set.

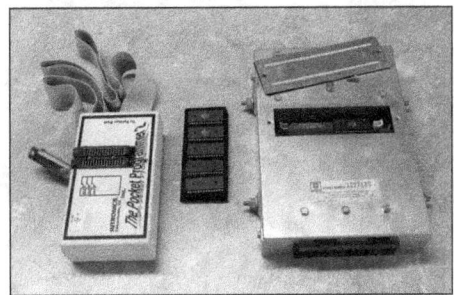

The 1986–1989 TPI ECM (right) contains a PROM carrier (called a MEMCAL) that is installed inside the ECM case. This MEMCAL adapter (beneath the removed ECM cover) bypasses the PROM soldered to its carrier so that a flash PROM can be removed. This equipment requires the removal of the flash PROM for every update made to the engine calibration. The PROM is then inserted into a programming device (left) for erasing and reprogramming. It is a tedious process that many tuners avoid today, making OBD-I tuning a service no longer offered by many engine tuners.

This is an example of an OBD-II bench-top programming solution. The PCM (top left) receives power and data communication through the switch assembly (middle) and can be reprogrammed with a laptop or desktop through a programming interface cable (right).

CHAPTER 15

Gen III LS PCM Conversions

For years now, enthusiasts have been retrofitting early project cars with LS-series engines and Gen III PCM conversions. The available features (cable or electronic throttle, cruise control, forced induction support, and so on) make the Gen III PCMs highly desirable for nearly any conversion.

The following projects are fine examples of Gen III control systems for small-block engines, turbocharged V-8 and V-6 engines, LT1 engines, and big-block engines.

Project 1: 24x Small-Block Chevy in a 1933 Willys

This 1933 Willys was built and owned by Bill Adam. The car originally had a 5.7L TPI engine from a 1987 Camaro Z28 and an ECM from a 1990 Corvette. Bill chose to upgrade the ECM to the GM# 12200411 PCM for greater tune-ability and a future 4L60-E transmission install.

GEN III LS PCM CONVERSIONS

This is Bill Adam's 1933 Willys. I met Bill in 2002 when he and his son, Troy, heard there was a guy down the road (me) playing with TPI engines. Bill is a retired toolmaker and fabricated just about everything in this car. He was one of the first in town to install a fuel-injected V-8 engine in a street rod. When I first met Bill, his Willys had an original 1987 5.7L TPI engine with aftermarket wire harness and an ECM (GM# 1227727) from a 1990 Corvette. The Willys ran great, but after seeing some of the newer technology I was playing with, Bill couldn't leave well enough alone.

GM 4x Vortec Small-Block System

In 2006, Bill and I worked together to upgrade the ECM to a 2002 PCM (GM# 12200411) for single coil and distributor operation using a 1996–2002 ignition system and 2002 Express Van calibration file. In hot rodder fashion, the electronics upgrade turned into a heads-up upgrade, including ported aftermarket heads, LT4 hot cam, and TPIS Mini Ram intake manifold. Ultimately the conversion to the GM truck ignition system with this PCM was a failure due to a persistent corrosion problem within (several different styles of) the Vortec distributor.

EFI Connection 24x Small-Block System

Bill was ready to throw in the towel and go back to the TPI ECM. But by then, the prototyping of an EFI Connection 24x crankshaft reluctor for small-block engines was nearly complete. So, Bill's Willys became the first vehicle to receive a 24x conversion (the second was my S10 *Wildside* pickup).

Bill fabricated his own ignition coil mounts by drilling holes through a set of aftermarket die-cast aluminum valve covers and attaching threaded posts to screws from the back side of each valve cover. These LS1/LS6 ignition coils don't allow much room for oil fill, PCV valve, or breather holes. An alternative choice for better clearance is a set of GM# 12573190 ignition coils.

This was the first engine to receive EFI Connection's 24x conversion. At the time of prototyping, the 1996-newer Vortec V-8 plastic timing cover was the only choice for this application. Due to a slight mismatch of timing cover sealing surfaces between early and late engine blocks, Bill chose to apply JB Weld to the face of the block to extend the seal surface. The TPIS billet-aluminum SBC timing cover now resolves this sealing issue.

Mounting the ignition coils on the valve covers is not for everyone, but this engine bay offers no other room for cleanly mounting the eight coils.

CHAPTER 15

Removing the high voltage from the Vortec distributor, we only needed the camshaft position signal it provides. Moisture or no moisture within the distributor cap, Bill no longer had to worry about ignition problems related to the Vortec distributor. The 4x Vortec small-block crankshaft reluctor was removed and replaced with the first 24x small-block crankshaft reluctor.

Timing Cover

A problem with any crankshaft reluctor installation on an engine that did not originally have a crankshaft reluctor (1995-older) is that General Motors changed the timing cover sealing surface just enough that the 1996-newer plastic Vortec timing covers leak. Although TPIS has since resolved this problem with a machined billet-aluminum timing cover, Bill cleaned the face of this 1987 block to apply JB Weld to the trouble areas, ground the new surfaces flat, and then generously applied red RTV sealant to protect against oil leaks.

For the hassle and oil leak risk involved, you are better off buying the TPIS billet-aluminum timing cover and being done with it. TPIS designed their billet-aluminum small-block timing cover for original crankshaft sensor placement, making this beautiful timing cover a direct bolt on for 1996-newer small-block engines as well.

TPIS designed and manufactures this beautiful billet-aluminum timing cover for small-block chevy engines. This timing cover eliminates the oil leak issues of the 1996-newer Vortec V-8 timing cover when used with a 1995 or older small-block chevy engine.

Speed Density

Bill initially chose the 1990 TPI ECM because it offered speed density operation. The 1990–1992 TPI ECMs use a MAP sensor to determine how much fuel to deliver. With tight clearance ahead of the throttle body, and a mechanical fan, a MAF sensor was not possible in this engine bay. The 1996-newer GM fuel management systems use both a MAF and a MAP but the MAF sensor is often eliminated and the PCM is programmed to rely on the MAP sensor for fuel delivery.

Ignition Coil Selection

Bill chose to use LS1 ignition coils (simply because they were available). Some owners unnecessarily get caught up with ignition coil selection. General Motors has used five types of ignition coils (see Chapter 6). Any set of eight ignition coils can be used interchangeably. In fact, among LS-series engines, all ignition coil wire harnesses match every LS-series engine wire harness.

Be aware that the PCM calibration has dwell settings that may need to be adjusted if you use a different set of eight ignition coils. EFI Connection uses the very common GM# 12573190 ignition coils because they fit best on the small-block/LT1 valve covers to allow clearance for oil fill cap, PCV valve, and breather.

DTCs on Startup

Production GM vehicles contain solenoids, relays, sensors, and on-board modules not used in most conversion projects. Upon initial startup of your Gen III PCM conversion, you may notice DTCs that have set related to something that is not used in your vehicle.

Using a base calibration from a 2002 LS1 Camaro with a 4L60-E transmission, the Willys set more than 30 DTCs immediately following the first engine startup. DTCs related to the 4L60-E transmission, emissions equipment, air conditioning, cooling fans, and alternator (that covers just about all of them) can be disabled because the LS1 PCM is not controlling or monitoring this equipment for this vehicle. The mass airflow DTC (P0102) is actually required for DTC processing for speed density operation, but the calibration is set to never illuminate the MIL. It is "normal" for a conversion and clearly explained in EFILive documentation.

VATS Bypass Modules

Almost daily, enthusiasts throw money away by purchasing VATS bypass modules. I quickly found one of these modules on eBay advertising, "Normally it costs between $150 and $300 to have this feature deleted from the PCM. By using our module you accomplish the same function for less and you won't have to ship your PCM/ECM to have it reprogrammed." A VATS bypass module is often purchased during the parts gathering phase of a project and then not used.

The problem with using a bypass module is that the PCM still requires programming to disable other functions specific to the original car. No matter how well-built these modules are, they do nothing more than allow the engine to run so that you can be greeted with an MIL that indicates you need your PCM reprogrammed.

The PCM calibration requires a few changes beyond disabling VATS. Avoid the VATS bypass module and let your tuner disable VATS in the PCM calibration while making other necessary changes.

700R4 Transmission

Bill and I began with a PCM calibration from a vehicle with a 4L60-E transmission so the idle table values would be appropriate for the 700R4 automatic transmission in the car. The PCM immediately sets DTCs related to the 4L60-E transmission. We disabled these within the PCM calibration using EFILive tuning software. This is an appropriate step as they are disabled in a PCM calibration from a manual transmission vehicle. Had General Motors released an LS-series vehicle with the 700R4 transmission, they too would have disabled these DTCs. Bill and I had the foresight to build the engine wire harness to support a 4L60-E transmission.

Cruise Control

Adding cruise control to the Willys was an afterthought. The installation was completed; start to finish, over the better part of a Saturday. We scored a used 1998 LS1 Camaro cruise control module on eBay for about $50 and pulled a brake switch from a 1996 LT1 brake pedal assembly that was lying around. The addition of cruise control set us back about $75 and several hours of labor. The Willys required a slight variation on the typical cruise control wiring (see Chapter 14).

First, Bill prototyped a throttle body linkage adapter for the TPI throttle body. This was the most difficult part of the installation because the cruise control cable was designed for an LS1 engine throttle bracket and throttle body. This adapter can be reworked for a better, and cleaner, installation.

Bill identified a stealthy location for the cruise control module beneath the driver's seat and on the bottom side of the floor. The F-Body cable is plenty long enough to mount the cruise control module out of sight.

While we could have used just about any GM brake switch from a vehicle with cruise control, we had a 1996 F-Body brake switch that fit nicely within the tight space of the dash. We tapped into the stop lamp circuit and TCC brake signal circuit to satisfy the cruise control module's brake switch signal requirements. Bill used a steering column from an early GM vehicle with cruise control. The multifunction lever (turn signal and cruise control switch lever) only had the set/coast feature, so we wired the cruise ON/OFF to

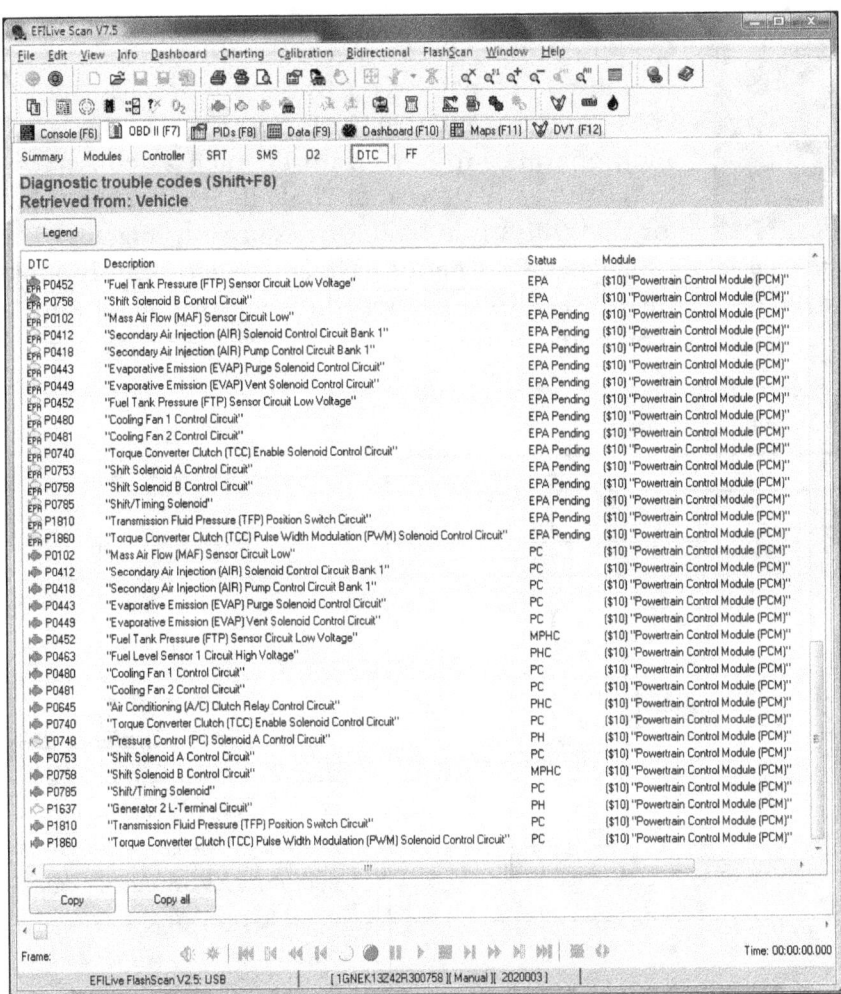

General Motors appropriately enables (and disables) DTCs for production vehicles according to the features specific to each vehicle. A Gen III LS PCM conversion requires certain DTCs to be disabled according to the features being used in the retrofit vehicle. The first engine startup revealed this list of DTCs that were later disabled (turned off). These DTCs are appropriate for the 2002 Camaro LS1/4L60E, but not for a 1933 Willys.

CHAPTER 15

switched 12V ignition, ignoring the resume/accel feature.

The cruise control module requires a 4,000-pulse-per-mile VSS signal, so we looked to the LS1 PCM. The PCM's primary VSS output was already being used for the speedometer (red connector, cavity 50, green/white wire), so we used the PCM's secondary VSS output wire at the red

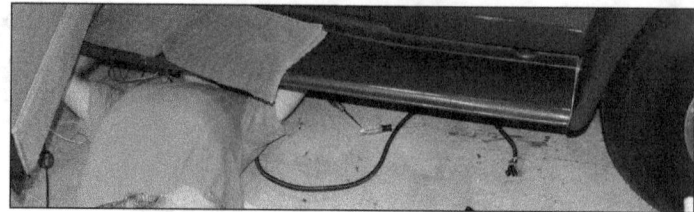

A new wire harness for the cruise control module is shown on the floor next to Bill as he is routing the wires up the pillar in front of the door.

connector, cavity 49. The final step was to change the PCM's secondary VSS output signal to 4,000 pulses per mile using EFILive tuning software.

Conclusion

Bill's 1933 Willys is a fine example of a Gen III PCM bringing modern fuel injection, tuning, and additional nice-to-have features (such as cruise control) to an early street rod. The only improvement left for the Willys is a 4L60-E transmission upgrade. The 700R4 has seen better days and Bill is already looking forward to the drivability improvements after a 4L60-E installation.

Bill had to make a custom throttle cable adapter to receive the 1998 Camaro Z28 cruise control cable. Here a prototype is shown during installation.

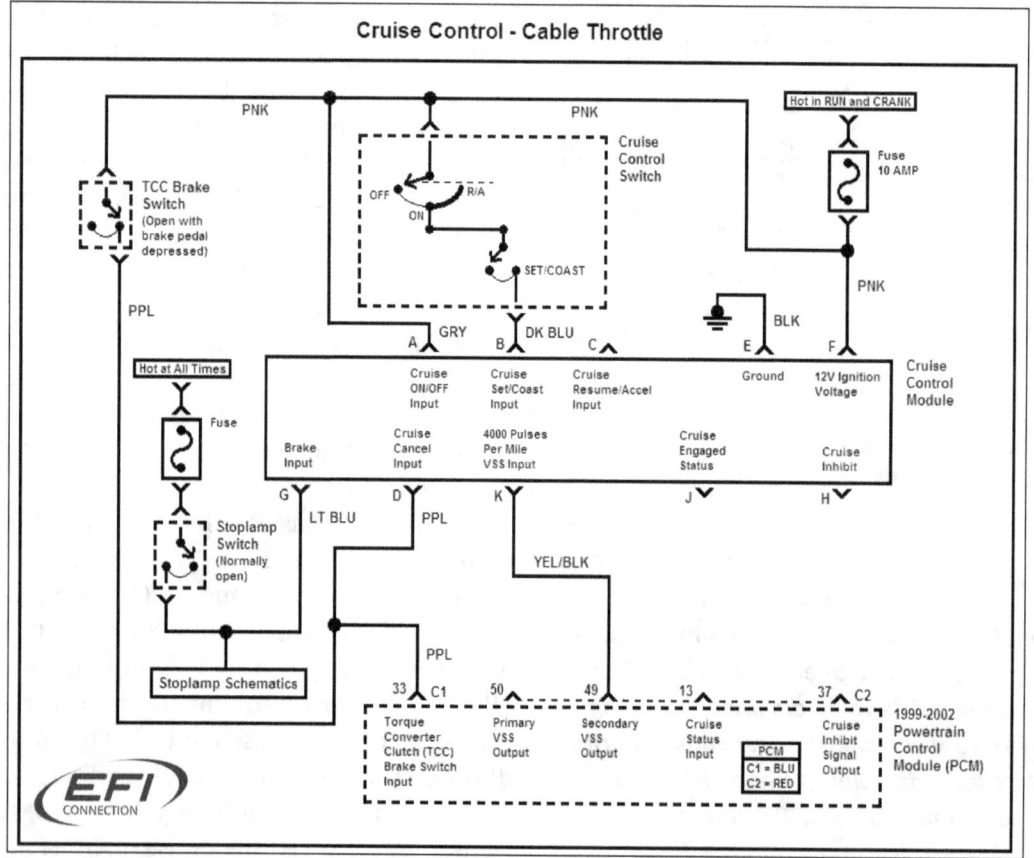

This wire schematic represents the implementation of a 1998 Camaro Z28 cruise control module into the Willys. Notice the PCM's secondary VSS output was used to provide a 4,000-pulse-per-mile signal to the cruise control module as the primary VSS output was already used for the speedometer. The 1998 Camaro Z28 cruise control module does not require the cruise engaged status or cruise inhibit signals.

GEN III LS PCM CONVERSIONS

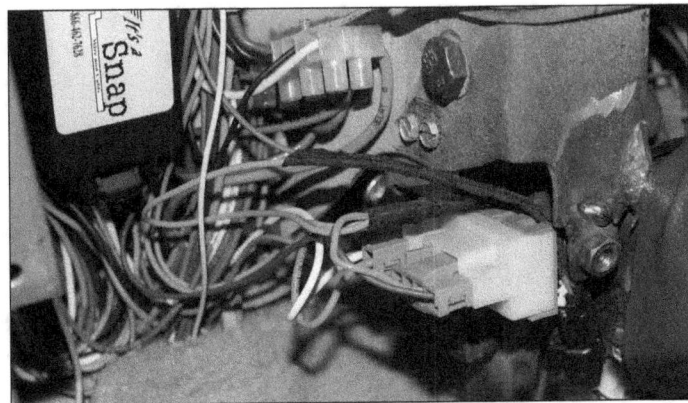

Although a 1996 Camaro/Firebird brake switch was installed for proper cruise control signals, many other GM brake switches provide the same signals.

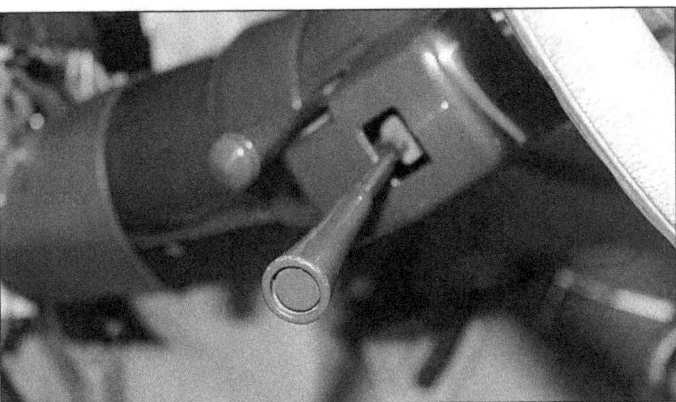

This early GM steering column contained a cruise control set/coast switch only. There was no provision for the accelerate/resume functions.

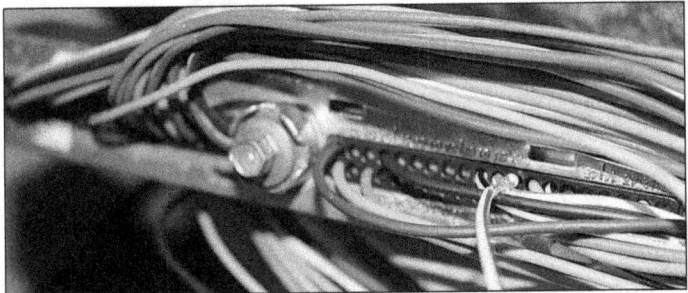

To satisfy the cruise control module's 4,000-pulse-per-mile VSS input requirement, a terminated wire was inserted into cavity 49 of the red PCM connector (PCM secondary VSS output).

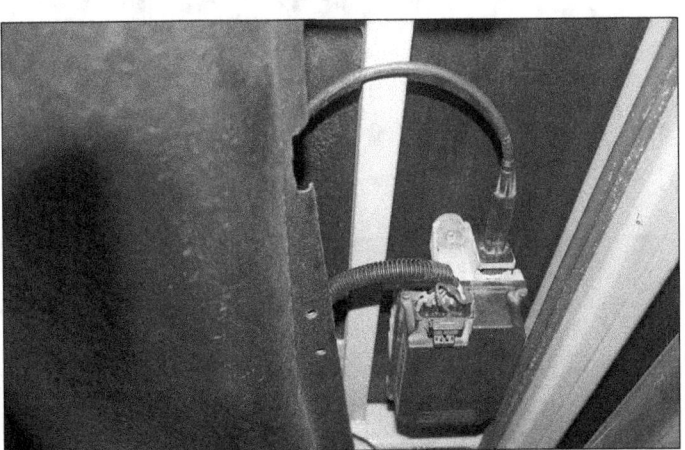

The 1998 Camaro Z28 cruise control module fit comfortably between the frame rails of this Willys. The Camaro/Firebird cruise control cable is much longer than the GM truck cables. This cable length was ideal for hiding the cruise control module under the vehicle.

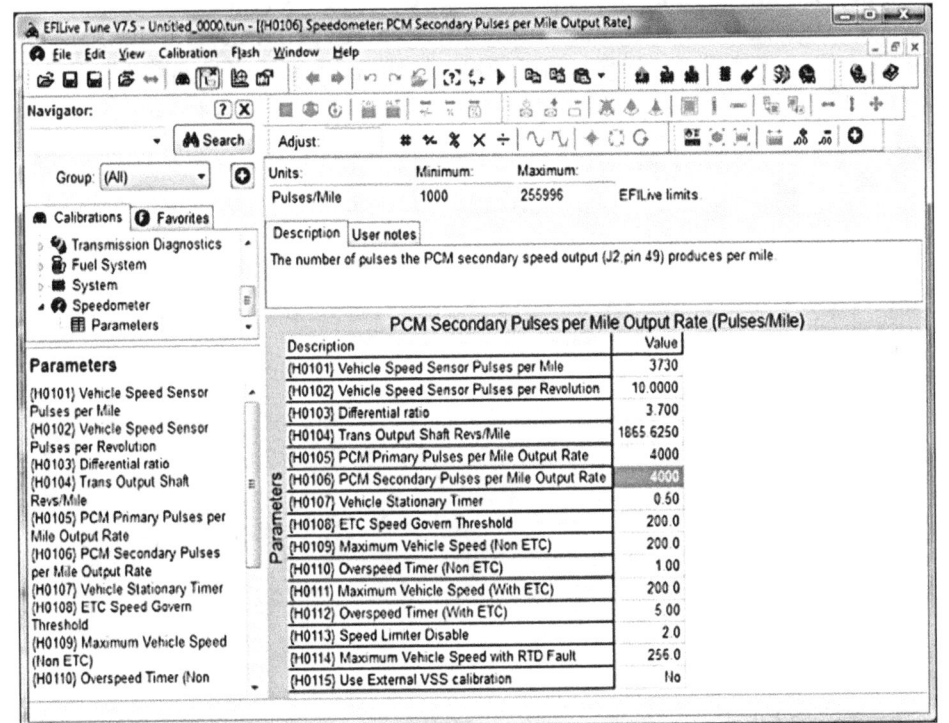

With the PCM's secondary VSS output circuit now attached to the cruise control module's 4,000-pulse-per-mile VSS input, a calibration change was made to set the PCM's pulse count to 4,000.

CHAPTER 15

Jeff Jones' Twin-Turbo 1998 GMC truck. (Photo Courtesy Jeff Jones)

Project 2: Twin-Turbo Small-Block Chevy in a 1998 GMC Truck

Jeff Jones is the owner of a unique 1998 GMC Sierra. Although his professional automotive day job is as a Lexus technician, his automotive hobby includes GM engine performance. Looking for more performance from his 5.0L Vortec engine, he went to the salvage yard to source two turbos for a little added "boost."

The plastic Vortec intake manifold was problematic for several reasons, including the inability to properly size fuel injectors for the additional demands of using two turbos. A Ram Jet 350 intake manifold was a direct fit to the 5.0L Vortec engine and allowed for external fuel injectors, a forward-facing throttle body, and better airflow than the original intake manifold. The next issue was to address the limitations of the 1996–2000 Vortec "black box" PCM that General Motors designed to power the truck.

PCM Considerations

Jeff's twin-turbo build required a better PCM than was in the car. The truck's original black box PCM is not capable of reading boost or MAP sensor values above 105 kpa. He dismissed aftermarket ECUs with a hunch that a newer GM PCM may allow for the rest of his truck (gauges, transmission, air conditioning, etc.) to remain fully functional. Jeff knew that the Vortec 5.0L engine in his GMC was used through 2002 in the Chevy Express Van and that the

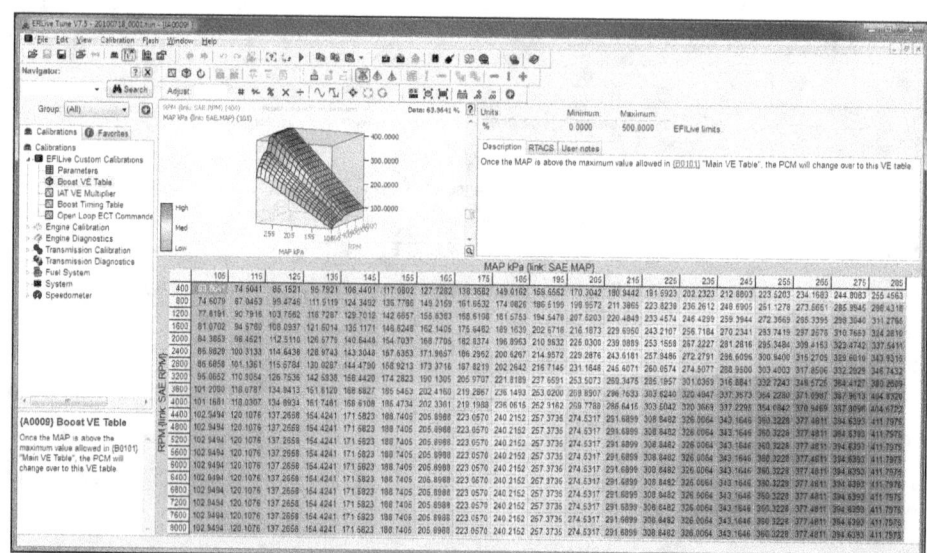

EFILive COS forced-induction table showing MAP above 105 kpa.

GEN III LS PCM CONVERSIONS

LS1 PCM connectors, retainers, dress covers, terminals, and removal tool.

2002 Express Van used the same PCM (GM# 12200411) that is used with 2002 LS-series engines.

With the buzz on Internet message forums discussing LS1 vehicles being tuned for forced induction while using the original GM PCM, he had a promising direction forward. Thanks to EFILive, the GM PCM can be loaded with a custom OS to fully support forced induction.

Repinning the Engine Wire Harness

While wiring in a new PCM may seem like an enormous task, General Motors has made this rather easy by using the same connector terminals for 1996–2000 truck PCMs and the 2001–2002 GM# 12200411 PCM.

The connector family and series are Delphi Micro-Pack 100W. Although the connectors are different, the terminals are interchangeable. All that is required is a terminal removal tool (or your fingernail), wiring diagrams, and a little time.

GM# 12200411 LS1 PCM installed in the truck. (Photo Courtesy Jeff Jones)

Jeff has been helping truck owners repin their black box PCMs for the newer PCM (GM# 12200411) for years through a well-documented repin guide. The Gen III PCMs require two 80-cavity Micro-Pack 100W connectors; each connector uses two colored and indexed retainers. This PCM requires two blue retainers and two red retainers.

The 1996–2000 PCM is located on the driver-side fender in the engine bay. The engine wire harness is easily accessed and serviceable when disconnected from the PCM. The Vortec black box PCM uses four (sometimes five) connectors.

The new PCM fits nicely in the location of the original black box PCM. The engine wire harness is repinned, one wire at a time, with the two 80-cavity LS-series PCM connectors. If you take your time, you can make the harness rework of the new PCM look as if it has always been there.

Instrument cluster removed. (Photo Courtesy Noel Schnell)

Gear Select Switch

In an automatic transmission vehicle, the PCM needs to know when the transmission is in park or neutral (P/N), or in gear. Manual transmission vehicles do not have a gear select switch.

In 1996–2000 GM trucks, the automatic transmissions have a gear select switch mounted on the side of the transmission case. The four-gear select switch wires are routed to the instrument cluster. Jeff chose to splice into these four wires from inside the truck to avoid corrosion and weather-related issues that can occur if the splices are made under the truck.

CHAPTER 15

Because the first use of this PCM (GM# 12200411) in this 1998 GMC truck was with a calibration from a 2002 Express Van (4x crankshaft reluctor), the calibration's gear select switch type was already set to PRNDL (because the 2002 Express Van has a gear select switch on the side of the transmission).

After the 24x conversion, Jeff began with a 2002 LS1 Camaro/Firebird calibration and had to change the gear select switch type from P/N Switch to PRNDL. The LS1 Camaro and Firebird do not use a gear select switch on the side of the transmission since a P/N switch is in the center console that applies a single ground signal to the PCM (blue connector, pin 34) to indicate P/N.

An alternative after a 24x conversion is to begin with a calibration from an LS-series truck because the calibration is already set to the gear select switch type of PRNDL, as LS-series trucks have a gear select switch mounted on the side of the transmission case.

Electric Fans

Dual electric fans from a 2002 LS1 Firebird were installed after the PCM conversion. The Gen III PCMs can control up to two electric fans. The PCM does not supply power and ground for the fans, it supplies the ground trigger to the fan relays. The fan relays supply the power and ground for the fans. A quick trip to the local salvage yard sourced three relays and connectors for the wiring involved. By using the three relays, as is done in the LS1 Camaro/Firebird, the PCM can command low-/high-speed operation of the two electric fans. (See Chapter 9 for more about electric fan operation.)

After the dual electric fan installation, Jeff added the Camaro/Firebird three-wire A/C pressure sensor for proper operation of the electric fans when the A/C was on. Now the cooling fans cycle properly to meet the demands of the A/C system. (See Chapter 11 for more information about A/C operation.)

The LS1 Firebird electric fans are mounted neatly behind the radiator.

4x Crankshaft Signal: Single Coil and Distributor

On a Vortec small-block engine, the CKP sensor signal output is 4x and CMP sensor signal output is 1x. The ignition system for all Vortec small-block engines is single coil and distributor. Although the ignition system remained the same, the new PCM brought the benefits of forced induction support, electric fan operation, engine speed beyond 5,800 rpm, and popular tuning software support. After all, locating a chassis dyno facility that is fluent with the LS-series PCMs is rather easy.

24x Crankshaft Signal: Coil-Per-Cylinder Ignition

Several years after the PCM conversion, this 5.0L Vortec engine received an EFI Connection 24x crankshaft reluctor and new crankshaft sensor. Having already repinned the engine wire harness at the PCM, all that had to be done was add 10 ignition coil control wires and use the 12V switched ignition and ground wires from the original ignition module and coil wiring to power the eight LS ignition coils. Rather than mount the ignition coils on the valve covers, a bracket was made to mount them on the firewall.

Throttle Swap

Jeff has been gathering parts for a swap from cable throttle to electronic throttle. With a 24x crankshaft reluctor in the engine, he may install a 2003-newer Gen III PCM. Electronic throttle equipment is plentiful in 2003-newer LS-series trucks, but he will run into a snag with electric fan operation while the A/C is on because the 2003-newer GM trucks eliminated the 12V A/C request to the PCM.

A workaround is to activate the electric fan relays from the A/C control switch

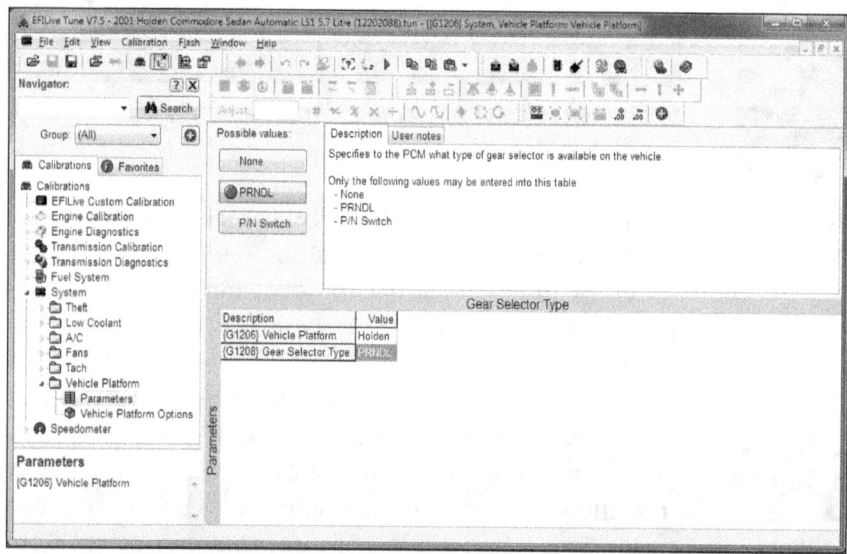

Gear select switch type.

GEN III LS PCM CONVERSIONS

(and disable the resulting electric fan DTCs in the PCM calibration).

To keep PCM-controlled electric fan operation while the A/C is on, either LS1/LS6 Corvette electronic throttle equipment or 1999–2002 GM truck electronic throttle equipment may be used while retaining the PCM (GM# 12200411). (See Chapter 8 for more information about electronic throttle equipment.)

Regardless of his choice, the Ram Jet 350 intake manifold accepts any Gen III throttle body and the cruise control switches in the steering column multifunction lever integrate seamlessly with any Gen III TAC module. With several electronic pedal assembly options, a custom mount and possible alterations to the pedal length may be required to properly locate the accelerator pedal pad.

Final Thoughts

The PCM swap was the foundation for every modification that has been done to Jeff's truck. He considers this project and PCM-related upgrades to be one of the most educational and fun things he has ever done. From Internet message forums, Jeff has learned from people around the world with this same passion, and they shared information and creative ideas. Through this DIY project, he has created unexpected friendships that help to keep this passion alive.

I met Jeff at his home while en route to the 2009 Car Craft Summer Nationals event. Sharing his genuine passion for GM engine management fuels my flame for this exciting hobby. Don't let the Lexus technician title fool you; Jeff represents GM performance through and through!

Engine bay. (Photo Courtesy Jeff Jones)

Engine bay showing electric fans. (Photo Courtesy Jeff Jones)

Ignition coils on firewall. (Photo Courtesy Jeff Jones)

Front of truck with "LEX TEK" plate. (Photo Courtesy Jeff Jones)

CHAPTER 15

Syclone/Typhoon lower intake manifold with six injectors.

Project 3: Turbo 4.3L V-6 3x Conversion

Fuel injection for GM's popular 4.3L V-6 engines was introduced in the 1980s with a TBI unit on the top of the engine's intake manifold. These TBI units use two fuel injectors to distribute fuel in a central location within the intake manifold. Engine vacuum pulls the air/fuel mixture into each cylinder for combustion. These early 4.3L engines are controlled by ECMs designed to be used with the two TBI injectors.

The 1991 GMC Syclone received the first 4.3L V-6 engine to feature multi-port injection; it had six individual fuel injectors for fuel delivery into each cylinder head intake runner. This improved method of fuel delivery required a new ECM with internal drivers capable of operating the six high-impedance fuel injectors. Although six fuel injectors are used, the ECM has only two injector drivers to run a batch fire mode (one bank of three injectors at a time). Sequential fire injection was not available for the GMC Syclone or GMC Typhoon.

The 1991 GMC Syclone and 1992–1993 GMC Typhoon do not share the ECM or ignition system with any other 4.3L V-6 engine application. The unique requirement for forced induction, a turbocharger fitted on these 4.3L V-6 engines, was an ECM and calibration capable of controlling the engine's six fuel injectors and spark advance while under boost (2-bar) conditions. The typical 4.3L V-6 ECM of those days was not designed to be used with this turbocharged engine.

With upgraded engine components (and more boost), 4.3L V-6 owners have gone to the aftermarket to install new (and expensive) fuel management systems for greater tuneability and control of their powerplant. Unfortunately, aftermarket systems may lack support for the vehicle's gauges, cruise control, and transmission torque converter lockup control, thus requiring additional aftermarket solutions that only add to the expense of an upgraded fuel management and ignition system.

Gen III PCM

Here is great news for the 4.3L V-6: General Motors has inexpensive production parts available to use the Gen III PCM with any 4.3L V-6 engine. The 2001–2002 PCM (GM# 12200411) was used with both LS-series V-8 engines and the 4.3L V-6 engines found in S-series trucks and vans. These engines are fitted with the 1996-newer 3x crankshaft reluctor and single coil and distributor Vortec ignition system. The same tuning software, such as EFILive, is used with this PCM, regardless of V-6 or V-8 calibration. Other tuning benefits, such as custom operating systems for 2- and 3-bar MAP support, are conveniently included.

GM's 3x crankshaft reluctor for Vortec V-6 engines is shaped to allow clearance for only a single roller timing chain. Production GM engines use a single roller timing chain, so if upgrading to a double roller timing chain, EFI Connection's 3x billet-steel crankshaft reluctor is

ECM, distributor, and ignition coil.

3x GM reluctor and 3x EFI Connection reluctor.

 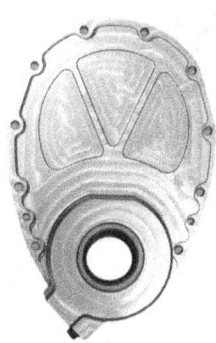
Plastic Vortec timing cover and TPIS billet small-block timing cover.

required for reluctor-to-timing chain clearance.

The 1996 4.3L Vortec V-6 engine was updated with an upper balance shaft. The changes to the face of the engine block required a new, and taller, timing cover. This timing cover made provision for the CKP sensor that is used to receive an engine position signal from the 3x crankshaft reluctor.

Those with an early 4.3L V-6 are not able to use the GM plastic Vortec timing cover because the upper portion of the cover does not seal to the early engine block. Fortunately the early 4.3L V-6 engines share the same timing cover as Gen I small-block engines. For CKP sensor provision for early 4.3L engines, the TPIS billet-aluminum small-block timing cover provides the best fitment while properly sealing to the face of the engine block.

The GM# 12200411 PCM controls the six fuel injectors in sequential fire (not batch fire) mode. This means individual control of the fuel injectors. With the requirement of six fuel injectors, this newer PCM cannot be used with TBI units.

Early 4.3L TBI engines must receive a multi-port injection intake manifold upgrade so that six fuel injectors may be used. This requirement may be filled by sourcing a used Syclone or Typhoon intake manifold, aftermarket or custom manifold, or upgrading to Vortec cylinder heads and a production GM intake manifold. An attractive option for 4.3L engines using Vortec cylinder heads is the 4.3L marine manifold because it features external fuel injectors and a Gen III 3-bolt type throttle body.

The Syclone/Typhoon, Vortec truck, and LS-series throttle body TPS and IAC engines are directly compatible with this PCM. In fact, so are the ECT, IAT, and MAP sensors used with these V-6 and V-8 engines. The only remaining sensors to add are knock sensors, heated O_2 sensors, optional MAF sensor, CMP sensor, and CKP sensor.

Single Coil and Distributor Ignition

The GM# 12200411 PCM was only used with the 4.3L V-6 engines in a single coil and distributor configuration. General Motors wrote the calibration software to expect 3x crankshaft and 1x camshaft signals for engine operation. This PCM uses the 3x crankshaft signal (and other engine sensor inputs) to control the ignition spark advance through the Vortec ignition module and single coil.

It may seem that by providing a higher-resolution crankshaft signal (such as a 24x LS-series crankshaft signal), the PCM controls one coil per cylinder but it simply does not work that way. GM's 24x encoded signal is mapped for V-8 engines only. Had General Motors released a PCM calibration that supported coil-per-cylinder ignition for the V-6, an appropriate crankshaft reluctor with increased tooth count (higher resolution) could be installed to eliminate single coil and distributor ignition. What General Motors has provided, however, is no disappointment.

Tuning software, such as EFILive, delivers the same tuning benefits that sell us on the use of the Gen III PCM for LS-series engines as it does for V-6 engines. Through

CHAPTER 15

Iron marine intake manifold.

Modified Syclone intake manifold installed on Vortec heads.

Vortec ignition module and coil.

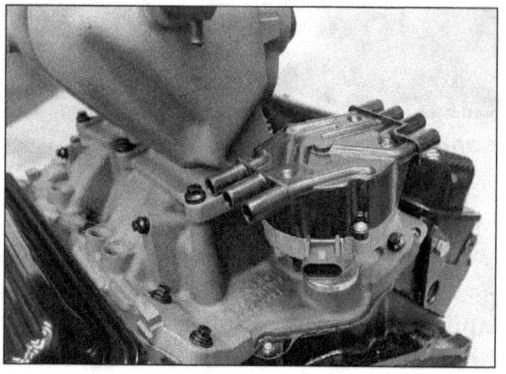

Vortec distributor installed in engine.

the same calibration tables and parameters, the same tuning software and hardware, and the same tuning techniques, this PCM is a fantastic engine controller for any 4.3L V-6 engine.

Intake Manifold

Vortec cylinder heads are plentiful in the boneyards and offer excellent performance gain compared to the early 4.3L cylinder heads. The lower Syclone and Typhoon intake manifold may be modified to accommodate the raised intake runners of the Vortec cylinder heads. Rather than machine the Syclone or Typhoon intake manifold for the Vortec head bolt pattern, the Vortec heads can be drilled for the early 4.3L V-6 bolt pattern to create a better seal and clamping force.

3x Crankshaft Reluctor

The 3x crankshaft reluctor installs on the crankshaft and is firmly held in place between the crankshaft timing sprocket and crankshaft balancer. GM's 3x crankshaft reluctor fully seats against the crankshaft timing sprocket only when using a single roller timing chain. Double roller timing chain installations require EFI Connection's 3x crankshaft reluctor.

Vortec Distributor Assembly

The 1996-newer 4.3L V-6 distributor assembly installs in the traditional distributor location and is used to provide a 1x camshaft signal to the PCM. The PCM uses this camshaft signal to determine intake or exhaust stroke for any given cylinder during engine operation.

EFI Connection's 3x crankshaft reluctor, double roller timing chain, and front Engine.

Going Beyond the Gen III PCM

General Motors improved the 4.3L V-6 ignition system in 2007 with the release of a new 4.3L V-6 engine and wasted spark ignition system. The 2007 Silverado 4.3L engine uses a Gen IV ECM. Labeled as an "E37" ECM, this engine controller's capabilities go beyond the GM# 12200411 PCM's abilities by using increased-resolution 2- and 3-bar MAP sensor lookup tables which are a perfect match for this powerful, turbocharged Syclone 4.3L V-6 engine.

The E37 ECM requires 58x crankshaft and 4x camshaft signals for engine operation. The 58x crankshaft signal can be accomplished with EFI Connection's 58x small-block crankshaft reluctor. This reluctor installs just as the 3x crankshaft reluctor used with the GM# 12200411 PCM. The same crankshaft position sensor and timing cover are used.

The E37 ECM's 4x camshaft signal requirement is accomplished with EFI Connection's press-fit 4x camshaft reluctor that installs onto the upper shaft of any GM Vortec distributor assembly. Installation of the 4x reluctor requires the removal of the 1x reluctor pressed on the top of the Vortec distributor shaft. The 4x camshaft reluctor provides a camshaft position signal to the ECM through the camshaft position sensor already installed on the Vortec distributor.

The ignition coil module assembly contains three coils (one for each pair of cylinders). The elimination of the single coil and distributor means increased ignition accuracy. This ignition module mounts cleanly behind and beneath the Syclone/Typhoon intercooler assembly.

Gen IV controllers feature an integrated TAC system and have no provision for cable throttle body use. This means electronic throttle control only. EFI Connection's electronic throttle body for TPI and LT1 engines is a perfect fit for the Syclone and Typhoon intake manifolds.

Fitted with a 58x crankshaft reluctor and sensor, 4x camshaft signal distributor, wasted spark module, and an electronic throttle body, all that is needed is EFILive tuning software and an experienced tuner.

E37 ECM.

4x Vortec distributor.

Ignition coil module.

58x reluctor.

Assembled 4.3L V-6 engine with 58x equipment.

Electronic throttle body on Sy/Ty intake manifold.

CHAPTER 15

Project 4: 24x LT1 Conversion to Eliminate Optispark in an F-Body

This 1997 Trans Am has been previously modified with a 383-ci LT1 engine and Pacesetter long-tube headers. Here, the car is loaded on the lift to prepare for the 24x LT1 installation.

The 24x LT1 conversion is considered one of the best upgrades for a 1993–1997 F-Body. LT1 owners are finding limited tuning support and must fight ignition system problems due to the front-mount Optispark distributor. EFI Connection's well-designed 24x conversion hardware brings the LS1 PCM to the LT1 car in similar fashion to how General Motors would have done it.

This owner's intent was to get the most power possible out of the engine and eliminate an ignition hiccup experienced in the upper RPM. This 24x conversion accomplished both goals and has forever eliminated woes associated with the LT1 Optispark distributor.

Retrieve LT1 PCM Calibration

1 Because this car has been previously tuned, we pull the calibration file out of the LT1 PCM using the C.A.T.S. OBD-II tuner. The calibration will be used later as a reference while making a starter calibration file for the LS1 PCM using EFILive software.

GEN III LS PCM CONVERSIONS

Inspect Engine Bay Prior to Disassembly

2 Here is the engine bay before disassembly. The LT1 PCM and engine wire harness will be removed and replaced with an LS1 PCM and new 24x LT1 wire harness from EFI Connection.

Drain Coolant

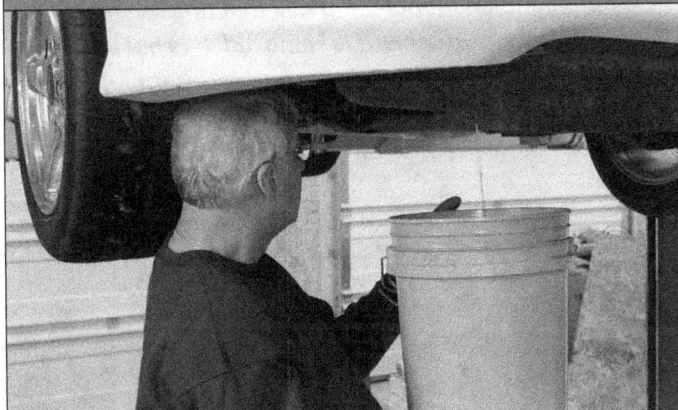

3 The 24x conversion requires that the timing cover be removed from the engine. The water pump must be removed before the timing cover, so the coolant is drained.

Remove Balancer

4 A proper puller, such as this Kent Moore J-39046 tool, is used to remove the balancer from the crankshaft hub. Without this tool, there may be difficulty pulling the balancer due to the tight space between the engine and electric fan assembly.

Note LT1 Hub Configuration

5 The LT1 engine has a separate crankshaft balancer and hub. (Other engines have a one-piece balancer.) The bolt pattern of the Camaro/Firebird hub is not the same as other LT1 engines. The Kent-Moore J-39046 provides alternate through-hole configurations to remove any LT1 crankshaft hub.

GM GEN III LS-SERIES POWERTRAIN CONTROL SYSTEMS

Remove Water Pump

6 The water pump is removed to allow for timing cover removal. This includes removing the hoses, ECT sensor harness connector, and six attaching bolts. The water pump is held in place by two locating pins in the engine block near the top of the front timing cover. The water pump housing is gently pried from the two locating pins to remove the water pump.

Remove Ignition Module and Coil

7 The ignition module and coil mounted on front of bank 1 cylinder head is removed. It is not used after the 24x conversion. This car also had its aftermarket ignition controller removed. An aftermarket ignition module is not needed for any 24x conversion.

Remove Optispark Attaching Bolts

8 The three Optispark attaching bolts are removed. Two are easily reached from above and one is easily reached from below. The Optispark is then removed from the timing cover.

Remove Optispark

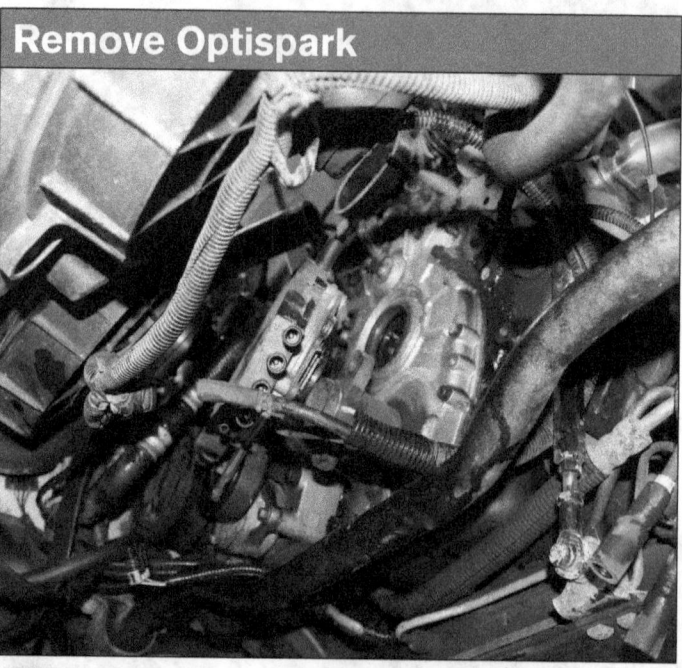

9 With the removal of nine spark plug wires and vacuum/vent hose the Optispark distributor is removed from the front of the engine. The Optispark timing cover seal and three attaching bolts will be used with the installation of the CMP sensor housing.

Use Hub Removal Tool and Bar

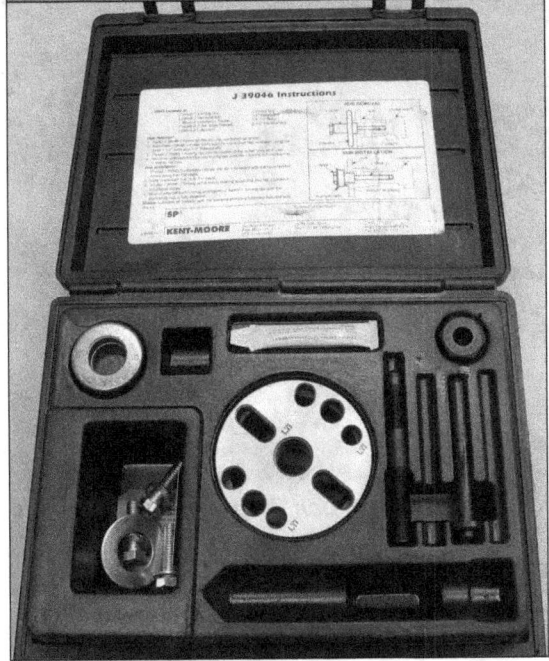

10 GM service shops use the Kent Moore J-39046 hub removal and installation tool to service the variety of LT1 crankshaft hubs. This tool makes removal and installation of an LT1 hub safe and easy. (Although the tool is expensive, you can do yourself a big favor by buying and reselling it on ebay.)

11 A hub removal bar is inserted into the front of the crankshaft. The removal bar bottoms out in the crankshaft bolt hole and will be used with the removal tool to pull the crankshaft hub from the snout of the crankshaft.

12 The hub removal tool flange is installed on the hub with three attaching bolts. The flange has alternate through-hole patterns for the removal of other LT1 crankshaft hubs (such as Corvette and Caprice/Impala). The front nut is first lubricated with antiseize compound to prevent galling of the threads. With the nut threaded into the removal tool flange, it is tightened to apply pressure against the hub removal bar. As the nut is turned, the crankshaft hub is pulled away and removed from the snout of the crankshaft.

CHAPTER 15

Loosen Oil Pan

Remove Timing Cover

13 Before the timing cover can be removed, the front of the oil pan must drop. All but the rear two oil pan fasteners are removed. As the rear two oil pan nuts are loosened, the front of the oil pan drops to allow the timing cover to be removed.

14 With the front of the oil pan dropped, the timing cover is carefully pried from the engine. The 1996–1997 4x crankshaft reluctor was used by the PCM for misfire detection. It will be removed and replaced with EFI Connection's 24x crankshaft reluctor.

Test Fit 1x Camshaft Reluctor

Attach 1x Camshaft Reluctor Bolts

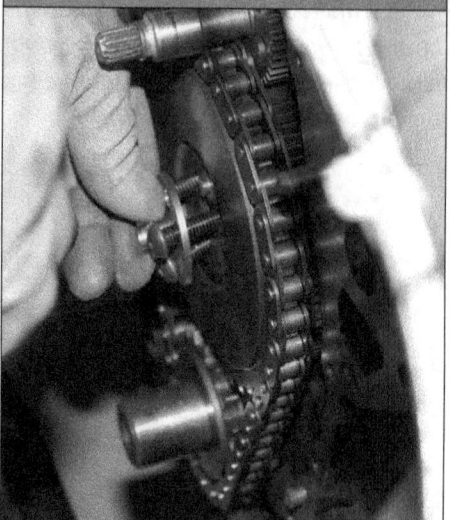

15 The Gen III PCM requires a 1x camshaft signal so that the stroke (intake or exhaust) is known for any given cylinder during engine operation. This 1x camshaft reluctor is installed in front of the camshaft timing sprocket using three new button-head bolts.

The 1995–1997 LT1 engines have a long dowel pin in the front of the camshaft that is used to drive the Optispark distributor. For 1995–1997 camshafts only, the pin must be replaced (if possible), tapped in (if possible), or cut near-flush with the surface of the 1x camshaft reluctor.

No other camshaft requires modification to the camshaft pin. Some aftermarket camshafts use a slightly oversized pin that requires very light reaming or drilling of the 1x camshaft reluctor dowel pin hole.

A test fit of the camshaft reluctor should allow it to fully seat against the face of the camshaft timing sprocket and the camshaft dowel pin near-flush with the reluctor flange.

16 The 1x camshaft reluctor is installed using the three new button-head bolts, which have received removable liquid thread locker. Assembly requires each bolt to be turned the distance of several threads at a time in a clockwise or counter-clockwise order to avoid binding the camshaft reluctor with the attaching bolts.

Install 1x Camshaft Reluctor

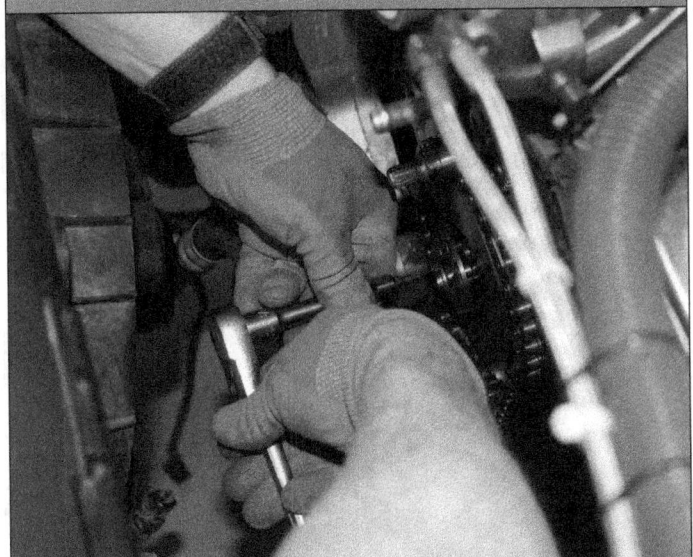

17 With the attaching bolts finger tight, they are then torqued to GM's recommended 18 ft-lbs. If the bolts need to be removed for future timing set or camshaft service, they should be removed several turns at a time in a clockwise or counter-clockwise order. Removal with an impact gun pushes the head of the bolts through the top of the camshaft reluctor, causing permanent damage to the reluctor.

Install 24x Crankshaft Reluctor

18 EFI Connection's 24x crankshaft reluctor is installed. Notice the crankshaft woodruff key is flush with the face of the 24x crankshaft reluctor. LT1 hubs do not have a keyway, so the key must be flush with the reluctor. The 1992–1995 LT1 engines require the removal of the crankshaft timing sprocket, removal of the woodruff key, and installation of the 1996–1997 LT1 crankshaft key. The OBD-I LT1 engines do not have a crankshaft reluctor, so the early woodruff key does not engage with the 24x crankshaft reluctor.

Install Timing Cover

19 The timing cover is installed. An aluminum water pump seal tool was used to prevent damage to the water pump drive seal. This was a $25 tool from eBay.

Install Crankshaft Hub

20 The crankshaft hub is ready for installation. The 1992–1995 (OBD-I) LT1 engines do not have a 4x crankshaft reluctor. These early hubs are longer than the 1996–1997 (OBD-II) LT1 hubs used with engines that do have a 4x crankshaft reluctor. For this reason, when installing the 24x crankshaft reluctor in a 1992–1995 LT1 engine, the hub must either be shortened by the thickness of the 24x crankshaft reluctor or a 1996–1997 hub must be used.

Use Installation Tool

21 The Kent Moore J-39046 installation tool is used to install the crankshaft hub. The installation screw is first threaded into the crankshaft, then loosely set onto the snout of the crankshaft. An installation thrust bearing and forcing nut are then installed onto the installation screw.

Push Hub onto Crankshaft

22 Using a wrench, the installation forcing nut is tightened against the installation thrust bearing. As the forcing nut is tightened, the hub is pulled onto the crankshaft. The crankshaft hub bolt is torqued to GM's recommended 75 ft-lbs.

Fully Seat Crankshaft Hub

23 Proper installation of the crankshaft hub is very important. If the crankshaft hub is not fully seated, the crankshaft reluctor wheel is loose and the engine runs very poorly while intermittently stalling as the CKP sensor loses signal from a wobbly crankshaft reluctor wheel.

Install Camshaft Sensor Housing

24 EFI Connection's camshaft sensor housing is installed in the location where the Optispark distributor used to be, using the same three Optispark attaching bolts through the timing cover. A Gen IV CKP sensor is used to get the 50-percent duty-cycle signal from the 1x camshaft reluctor installed on the front of the camshaft timing sprocket.

GEN III LS PCM CONVERSIONS

Remove Kick Panel Trim

25 Prior to removing the engine wire harness from the engine bay, four connections must be disconnected in the passenger-side kick-panel area. The kick panel trim is carefully lifted up and out of the car after removing the Phillips-head attaching screws.

Disconnect Dash Harness Connectors

26 Four dash harness connectors must be disconnected. The 10-cavity white (connector C220), 10-cavity blue (connector C230), 4-cavity black (connector C210), and A/C evaporator housing temperature sensor connectors are disconnected. The LS1 PCM does not use the A/C evaporator housing temperature sensor for A/C operation. The LS1 PCM properly, and seamlessly, controls the A/C system in the LT1 car.

Remove Engine Wire Harness

27 The LT1 engine wire harness is removed. Removal is a bit tedious and needs some patience and care. The front of the car must be elevated to remove harness connections near the bottom of the engine and at the transmission.

Disconnect HVAC Vacuum Line

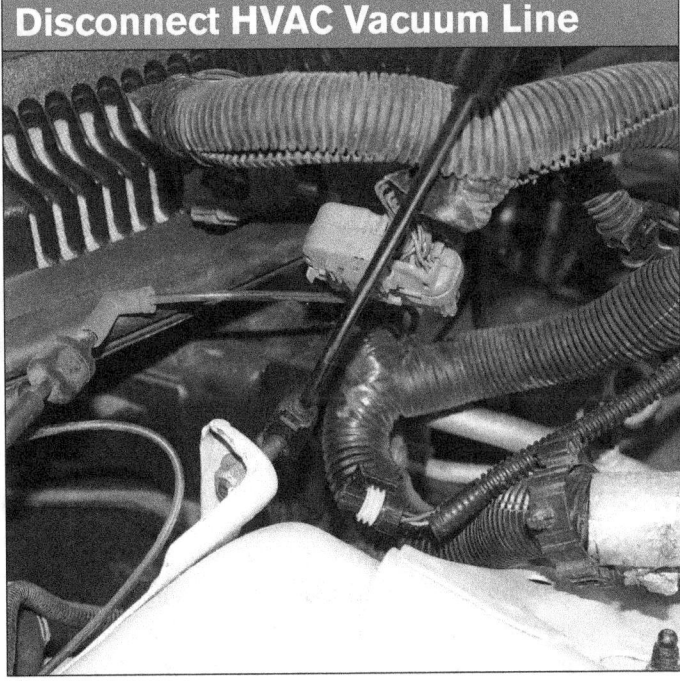

28 The HVAC temperature control vacuum hose must be disconnected. This hose is taped within the LT1 engine wire harness to supply engine vacuum to the HVAC controls inside the vehicle.

CHAPTER 15

Prep Ignition Coil Bracket for Installation

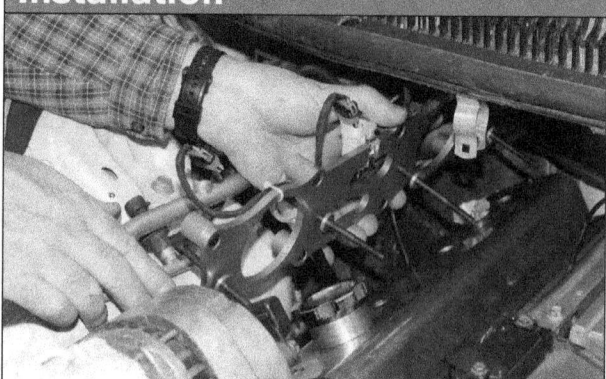

29 The ignition coil bracket assemblies are installed on each valve cover by removing the four center bolts. The bolts are replaced with new, longer bolts and spacers between the ignition coil bracket and valve cover. The coil bracket is carefully fitted to the valve cover so that the aluminum spacers do not slide off the attaching bolts.

Install Ignition Coil Bracket

30 After tightening the four coil bracket bolts, the ignition coils are installed onto the coil bracket assembly. The ignition coil harness is then connected to each of the four coils on each bracket. The center, seven-cavity connector is the same as found with any GM LS-series ignition coil harness; allowing compatibility with any new or reworked LS-type engine harness.

Inspect Engine Wire Harness

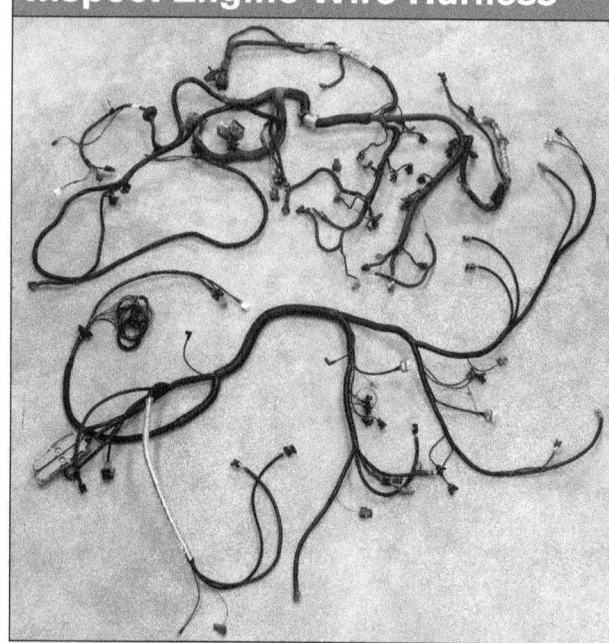

31 The original LT1 engine wire harness (top) will no longer be used. The new EFI plug-and-play engine wire harness (bottom) is ready for installation. It contains several extra wires bundled beyond the firewall grommet that are unique to this car's installation. These wires are for nitrous installation and conversion from a 4L60-E automatic transmission to a T56 manual transmission.

Inspect 24x Conversion

32 After installing the water pump and refilling the coolant, this 1997 Trans Am is now fully equipped for LS1 PCM use. EFI Connection's 24x hardware and new plug-and-play wire harness provide a factory-look installation. Many who see the vehicle at local car show events do not notice the LS1 PCM upgrade.

Transport to Dyno

33 This 1997 Trans Am was trailered to Smokey's Dyno & Performance in Akron, Ohio, for final tuning. Since this photo was taken, Smokey's Dyno & Performance has been relocated to a new, and larger, facility in the same area.

Calibrate PCM

34 The previous LT1 PCM calibration is used only as a reference while a starter calibration file is creatd for the LS1 PCM using EFILive tuning software. This starter calibration file allows the engine to run well enough to begin the custom tuning process while the car is run on the dyno.

Dyno Tune

35 The car is properly strapped to the chassis dyno. An ideal location for the wide-band O_2 sensor is in the exhaust and close to the engine. When a third O_2 sensor bung is not available in the exhaust, the wide-band sensor is often installed in the tailpipe (as here). By using the wide-band sensor's air/fuel mixture readings, adjustments are made to the PCM calibration.

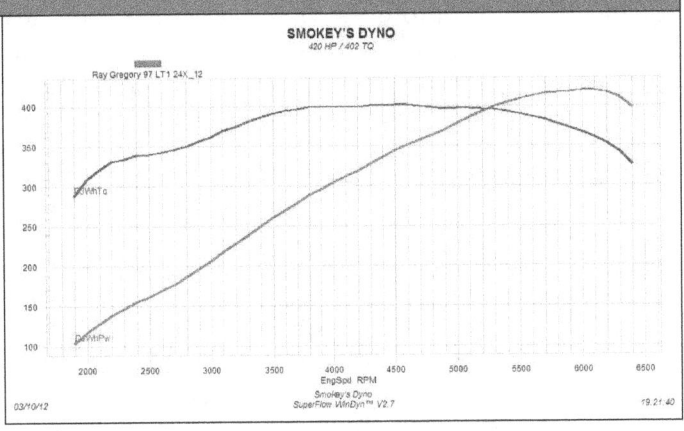

36 This car was tuned previously with the same engine configuration. The 24x conversion yielded an increase of roughly 10 hp and 10 lb-fts of torque. The final results are an impressive 420 hp and 402 lb-fts of torque.

CHAPTER 15

Project 5: Big-Block Ram Jet 502 24x Conversion

This is GM's Ram Jet 502 engine assembly. It has the early (1987 TPI-type) distributor, ignition module, and ignition coil. The engine is controlled with the MEFI ECM, and has the traditional sensor inputs such as ECT, IAT, KS, TPS, IAC, and MAP.

Without question, GM's Ram Jet 502 crate engine is designed to impress. This engine is big, beautiful, and boasts an impressive 502 hp and 565 lb-fts of torque! What it lacks is modern features including OBD-II diagnostics, distributor-less ignition, electronic automatic transmission support, cruise control, electric fan control, and popular tuning support from a tuning package such as EFILive.

The Ram Jet 502 shortcomings can be summed up in one word: MEFI. The marine electronic fuel injection (MEFI) ECM bundled with this engine had marine use in mind and not the comforts of on-road use.

Let's take a look at what is required to use the Gen III PCM with the Ram Jet 502.

Remove Valve Cover

1 A 24x conversion on this engine requires eight ignition coils. For convenience, LS1 ignition coils can be mounted on top of the valve covers using two valve covers (GM# 12554353). Although the Gen VII 8.1L valve cover looks similar, the bolt pattern and height is incorrect for Gen VI big-block engines.

Remove Distributor and Valve Covers

2 The small-cap HEI distributor, plug wires, valve covers, and valve cover gaskets are not used.

Install Valve Covers and Ignition Coils

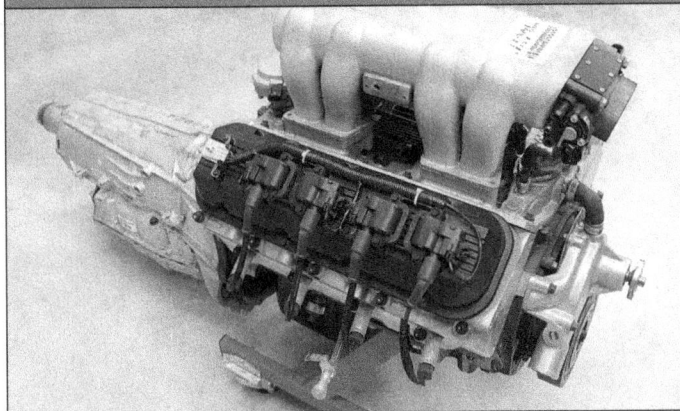

3 These valve covers require LS1/LS6 ignition coils (GM# 12558948). Any other ignition coil does not fit the mounting holes.

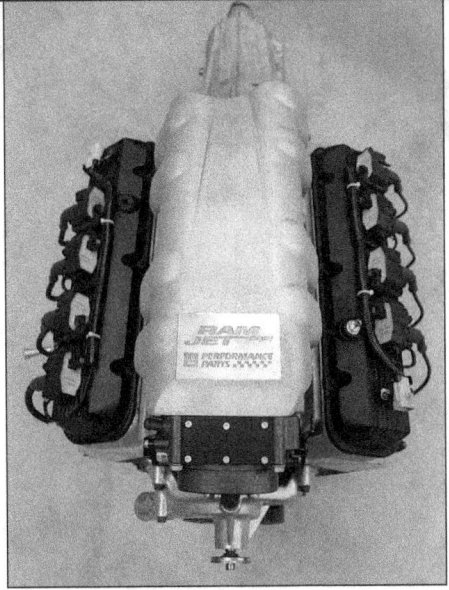

4 Notice how the layout of ignition coils matches the angle of the spark plug configuration. Bank 1 ignition coils are toward the rear of the engine; bank 2 ignition coils are toward the front of the engine. This is the best layout for the angled spark plugs.

Remove Old Distributor

5 The early small-cap HEI distributor is replaced with a 1996–2002 Vortec distributor assembly. Hold on to the distributor clamp because it is required with the new distributor.

Install Distributor

Choose New Distributor

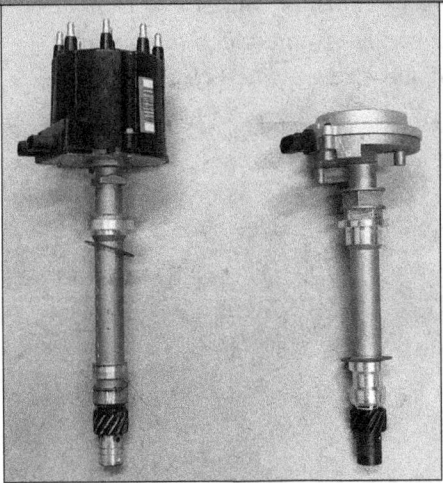

6 The small-cap HEI distributor (left) bundled with the Ram Jet 502 crate engine is for use with 1985–1992 TPI-type ECMs and MEFI-series ECMs. This distributor is replaced with a 1996–2002 Vortec distributor (right) for the purpose of driving the oil pump and providing a camshaft signal to the Gen III PCM. This Vortec distributor is offered through the aftermarket. It has an improved design as it is made of cast aluminum rather than the plastic GM equivalent. The Vortec distributor cap is replaced with EFI Connection's cast-aluminum cap to eliminate spark plug wire provision.

7 The Vortec distributor uses a CMP sensor to output a 1x signal (50-percent duty cycle) to the PCM for the purpose of indicating the stroke for each cylinder while the engine is running. In fact, this is the only electronic purpose of this distributor.

CHAPTER 15

Install Aluminum Distributor Cap

8 Any 1996-newer Vortec 4.3, 5.0, 5.7, or 7.4L distributor assembly may be used to accomplish the Gen III PCM requirement of a 1x camshaft signal. EFI Connection's cast-aluminum cap is then installed to eliminate spark plug wire provision and provide a clean look.

Remove Balancer

9 The balancer must be removed to remove the timing cover. A quality removal tool is inexpensive, and preferred to avoid damage to the crank snout and/or balancer.

Remove Oil Pan Bolts

10 With the balancer removed, the front of the oil pan must drop before the timing cover can be removed. All but the rear two oil pan bolts are removed. The rear two oil pan bolts are loosened to allow the front of the oil pan to drop.

Remove Timing Cover

11 With the balancer and timing cover removed, the crank is nearly ready to receive the 24x crankshaft reluctor.

GEN III LS PCM CONVERSIONS

Inspect Timing Set

12 For any big-block 24x conversion, this is the point of the installation that becomes critical. Not all GM big-block timing sets are the same. More specifically, not all Gen VI big-block engine timing sets are the same. With varying crankshaft timing sprocket thicknesses, the 24x crankshaft reluctor may be located too far forward of the CKP sensor, causing a no-start condition and wear on the timing cover as the crankshaft reluctor binds with the timing cover during engine rotation.

Remove Crankshaft Timing Sprocket

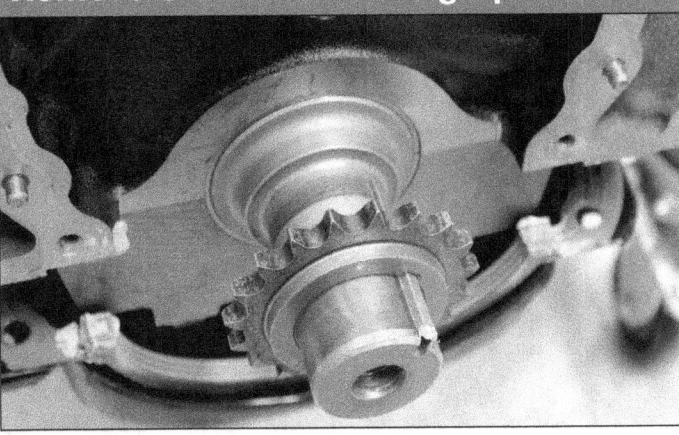

13 This Gen VI timing cover is production equipment from a 1996-newer Gen VI 7.4L engine. That engine has a 4x crankshaft reluctor. The placement of that 4x crankshaft reluctor is determined by the thickness of the crankshaft timing sprocket used with the engine. The timing cover sensor hole is located in a position where the CKP sensor gets a signal from the crankshaft reluctor.

Because we are using a Gen VI 7.4L timing cover with the Ram Jet 502, we must consider the difference in crankshaft timing sprocket thickness between the 7.4L crankshaft timing sprocket and Ram Jet 502 timing sprocket. For this reason, the crankshaft timing sprocket is removed.

Mill Timing Sprocket to Fit

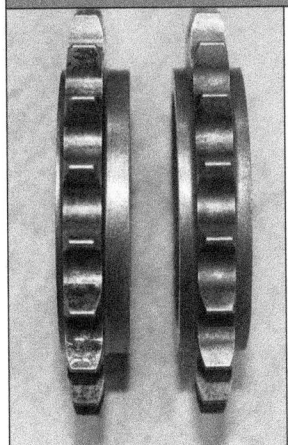

14 The Ram Jet 502 crankshaft timing sprocket (left) is noticeably different than the Gen VI 7.4L crankshaft timing sprocket (right). It appears that the Ram Jet 502 sprocket seats closer to the engine. In reality, the sprocket is seated quite differently on the 502 crankshaft.

Measurements of the 7.4L and Ram Jet 502 camshaft timing sprockets confirm that the location of the sprocket teeth is the same on the two engines. What varies is the distance from the front of the sprocket teeth to the seating surface of the crankshaft reluctor. The 7.4L sprocket measures .143 inch from the sprocket teeth to the front of the sprocket. The Ram Jet 502 sprocket measures .203 inch from the sprocket teeth to the front of the sprocket. The .060-inch difference is milled from the front of the Ram Jet 502 crankshaft sprocket before installation so that the crankshaft reluctor is within the CKP sensor range and does not bind against the timing cover.

Install Crankshaft Reluctor

15 With the crankshaft timing sprocket and timing chain reinstalled, the 24x crankshaft reluctor simply slides on the front of the crank snout and is seated against the crankshaft timing sprocket.

CHAPTER 15

Choose Timing Cover

16 The MEFI system does not use a CKP sensor, so the timing cover is cast without the sensor hole.

17 The 502 engine's timing cover (right) was replaced by a factory 7.4L (left) timing cover with a provision for the CKP sensor, which is easier than modifying the 502 cover from the crate engine.

Install Timing Cover

18 The Gen VI 7.4L timing cover is installed and the oil pan is ready for reassembly.

Install Balancer

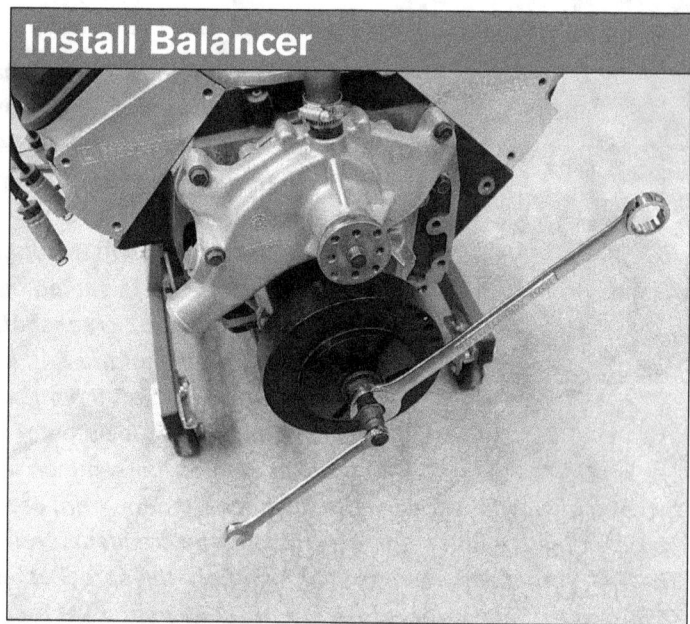

Modify Balancer

19 For proper crankshaft pulley alignment (so that the belt rides in-line with the rest of the front engine accessories), the snout of the balancer must be machined. For this installation, the 24x crankshaft reluctor that was installed measures .190-inch in thickness, so .130 inch is removed from the snout of the balancer before installation.

20 The balancer is installed using a proper installation tool. A mallet should never be used to force the balancer onto the crankshaft. A proper installation tool is inexpensive and avoids damage to the engine and balancer.

GEN III LS PCM CONVERSIONS

Reassemble Front of Engine

21 This Ram Jet 502 is now equipped with the 24x crankshaft signal requirement of the Gen III PCM. There is no need for an external crankshaft reluctor and sensor solution when an internal solution is available.

Remove Throttle Body

22 With the throttle body removed, the two bores in the front of the intake plenum can be seen. A throttle body upgrade requires modification to the front of the plenum for throttle blade clearance.

Remove Throttle Body (continued)

23 EFI Connection's electronic mono blade throttle body (top) is designed for the bolt pattern of the Ram Jet 502 (and TPI/LT1) intake plenum. The mono-blade throttle body flows nearly 1,250 cfm of air, making the most of the 502's breathing ability.

The original twin 48-mm throttle body (bottom) flowing approximately 670 cfm has plenty of room for additional horsepower and torque with a throttle body upgrade. TPIS offers a cable-driven, mono-blade throttle body for the Ram Jet 502.

Inspect Complete Conversion

24 This Ram Jet 502 is now ready for Gen III PCM control. This particular configuration, with an electronic mono-blade throttle body, supports cruise control through an LS1 Corvette TAC module. This engine can just as easily be configured for use with a cable throttle body and an external, cable-driven, cruise control module (see Chapter 12).

GM GEN III LS-SERIES POWERTRAIN CONTROL SYSTEMS

GLOSSARY

A/F Ratio: The ratio of air to fuel in the exhaust—after the combustion process. The PCM calculates the A/F ratio through voltage signals received from oxygen sensors. An example of a rich ratio is 10:1, or 10 parts air to 1 part fuel. An example of a lean ratio is 18:1, or 18 parts air to 1 part fuel. The stoichiometric ratio for an engine running typical pump gasoline is approximately 14.7:1.

APP: Accelerator pedal position. The APP sensor (or up to three sensors) is mounted on or integrated within a throttle pedal assembly. It indicates the angle of the accelerator pedal.

B-Body: The 1994–1996 Chevrolet Caprice and Impala SS, 1994–1996 Buick Roadmaster, and 1995–1996 Cadillac Fleetwood.

Bank 1: Row of cylinders beginning with cylinder 1. Bank 1 for a V-8 engine includes cylinders 1-3-5-7.

Bank 2: Row of cylinders beginning with cylinder 2. Bank 2 for a V-8 engine includes cylinders 2-4-6-8.

BCM: Body control module. An onboard module responsible for controlling body functions such as lights, horn, and (for Gen IV ECMs) cruise control messaging.

Black Box Logging: A data-logging feature of some laptop-to-vehicle interface cables that allows for data acquisition without a laptop.

CAN: Controller area network. A network of messaging that is used by on-board ECUs (such as ECM, TCM, and BCM). LS-series ECMs supporting CAN communication were not implemented with Gen III engines. See *Class 2* for Gen III PCM communication.

CASE: Crankshaft angle sensor error. A service procedure required by the PCM to learn variances in the relationship of the crankshaft sensor to the crankshaft reluctor wheel.

CL: Closed loop. A fueling mode where the PCM applies fuel trims to each bank of cylinders based on readings from the O_2 sensors.

CKP: Crankshaft position. The CKP sensor is used by the PCM to determine the position of the crankshaft for spark and fuel events.

Class 2: OBD-II communication protocol used with all Gen III PCMs.

CMP: Camshaft Position. The CMP sensor is used by the PCM to determine the stroke (intake or exhaust) for any given cylinder.

ECM: Engine control module. An electronic module that serves the purpose of controlling an engine.

ECT: Engine coolant temperature. A GM early ECT sensor was referred to as a coolant temperature sensor (CTS) until SAE standardization.

ECU: Electronic control unit. Generally refers to any on-board module in a vehicle. Modern vehicles contain ECUs such as an engine control module (ECM), transmission control module (TCM), body control module (BCM), and often many more.

EFILive Limited: A New Zealand–based company that sells data logging and ECU reprogramming hardware and software.

EFILive FlashScan: A tuning software and hardware package that serves the purpose of monitoring real-time data and ECU recalibration functions.

F-Body: The Chevrolet Camaro and Pontiac Firebird.

Flash: When a control module's flash memory is programmed or reprogrammed.

Gen III: Third-generation LS-series small-block Chevy engine. This engine design was a significant overhaul of the previous generations of small-block engines. All Gen III engines are fitted with a 24x crankshaft reluctor.

Gen IV: Fourth-generation LS-series small-block Chevy engine. This engine design shares many similarities with the Gen III engine. With the exception of the early LS2 engine, all Gen IV engines are fitted with a 58x crankshaft reluctor. The early LS2 engines use an E40 ECM and can be found in the 2005 Corvette and 2005–2006 GTO, SSR, and Trailblazer SS.

HO_2S: Heated oxygen sensor.

IAC: Idle air control. A motorized valve that moves in a two-way linear direction to allow air to bypass the throttle blade(s). By allowing air to travel through a passage around the throttle blade(s), the PCM can allow the engine to idle smoothly.

IAC: Idle air control. For electronic throttle systems, the IAC function is handled through the TAC system to add and remove throttle angle to allow the engine to idle smoothly.

GLOSSARY

IAT: Intake air temperature. The IAT sensor is installed in the airstream ahead of the throttle body and returns an electronic signal to the PCM to determine the temperature of incoming air.

LTFT: Long-term fuel trim. The PCM's long-term adjustment to fuel injector pulse width when the engine is in closed-loop (CL) mode. LTFTs react based on long-term monitoring of short term fuel trims (STFTs). If STFTs' values remain at, say, a value above +5 percent, after a predetermined length of time, LTFTs adjust injector pulse width by, say, +3 percent. The PCM monitors STFTs to see if adjustment percent falls. If both STFTs and LTFTs reach their maximum calibrated limits, the PCM sets a DTC and go into open-loop (OL) operation.

LS-Series: A redesigned small-block engine introduced in 1997. The LS-series engines feature many improvements over the classic small-block engine. Available sizes include 4.8, 5.3, 5.7, 6.0, 6.2, and 7.0L. LS engines are available in many 1999-newer GM cars and trucks.

LS1: GM RPO code for a 5.7L Gen III engine. Variations among LS1 engines include throttle type (cable or electronic), EGR valve equipped, camshaft, cylinder heads, and front accessory drive components.

LT1: GM RPO code for a 5.7L Gen II engine, which was used in production vehicles beginning with the 1992 Corvette and ending with the 1997 Camaro/Firebird. As used in B-Body vehicles, the LT1 engine was fitted with cast-iron cylinders.

MAF: Mass airflow. The amount of incoming air is measured by the PCM through a MAF sensor.

MAT: Manifold air temperature. TPI engine computers measure the temperature of incoming air through a MAT sensor mounted in the bottom of the upper intake manifold. Through SAE standardization, MAT has been renamed intake air temperature (IAT). To avoid heat soak from the hot aluminum intake manifold, the MAT is often relocated to the airstream ahead of the throttle body.

MEFI: Marine electronic fuel injection. GM acronym referring to an ECM that was designed for marine use.

O_2 Sensor: Oxygen sensor.

OBD: On-board diagnostics. The process by which the PCM uses sensor data to report errors. Specifically, OBD-I and OBD-II.

OL: Open loop. A fueling mode where the PCM does not apply fuel trims to each bank of cylinders. Readings from O_2 sensors are not used to adjust fuel delivery.

OS: Operating system. Refers to a software layer of the PCM on which all other calibration segments reside. Think of the OS as Microsoft Windows on your PC and the individual calibration segments as applications installed on Windows for your PC to perform certain functions.

PCM: Powertrain control module. An onboard module that serves the purpose of controlling not just the engine, but also other powertrain functions, such as transmission control.

PE: Power enrichment. During WOT conditions, and when certain engine operating conditions are met, the PCM applies fuel delivery specific to the PE mode, delivering additional fuel.

PID: Parameter ID. A (lookup) code that represents a vehicle's sensor data. As an example, a representative name for the crankshaft rotational speed PID is "engine speed."

PRNDL: Park reverse neutral drive low. Refers to a gear select switch that is mounted to the side of the 4L60-E and 4L80-E transmission case.

RPM: Revolutions per minute. Engine crankshaft rotational speed.

SAE: Society of Automotive Engineers. The organization responsible for the standardization of automobile engineering. SAE develops technical standards that impact manufacturers and consumers.

STFT: Short-term fuel trim. The PCM's active adjustment to fuel delivery when the engine is in closed-loop (CL) mode. STFTs are more active than long-term fuel trims (LTFTs).

TAC: Throttle actuator control. An onboard module that has the sole purpose of controlling the electronic throttle body motor. The TAC module opens and closes the throttle blade based on sensor inputs and cruise control commands. The GM TAC module features diagnostic reporting and fail-safe operation of the electronic throttle system.

TAC: Throttle actuator control. Gen IV ECMs integrate the TAC within the ECM. The TAC opens and closes the throttle blade based on sensor inputs and cruise control commands. The TAC system features diagnostic reporting and fail-safe operation of the electronic throttle system.

TBI: Throttle body injection. Essentially an engine with carburetor-like throttle body that delivers fuel through ECM-controlled fuel injectors. Used in many production GM vehicles. With V-8 TBI engines having only two fuel injectors, modern PCMs cannot control these engines without a complete swap of intake manifold to multi-port fuel injection.

TCM: Transmission control module. An on-board module that serves the purpose of controlling a transmission. TCMs are not standalone as they require CAN communications with an ECM for operation.

TIS2Web: GM's Internet subscription-based service programming system. It is used by repair technicians to reprogram control modules for use with their intended vehicles.

TPI: Tuned Port Injection. A 5.0 or 5.7L engine with multi-port fuel injection used with the 1985–1992 F-Body and 1985–1991 Y-Body vehicles. TPI engines feature a long intake manifold runner design that generates excellent low-RPM torque and weak high-RPM power.

TPS: Throttle position sensor. A sensor that is typically mounted to the throttle body assembly and used to return a voltage signal (or signals) to the PCM that represents the throttle blade angle.

VSS: Vehicle speed sensor. A sensor typically mounted in the tail housing of a transmission. It sends an electronic signal to the PCM that is used to calculate vehicle wheel speed.

Y-Body: The Chevrolet Corvette.

WOT: Wide open throttle. The throttle angle range (near maximum throttle blade angle) where the PCM determines that maximum engine effort is requested. During WOT, the PCM targets a richer A/F ratio while advancing spark timing.

Source Guide

B&M Racing & Performance
   Products
100 Stony Point Rd., Suite 125
Santa Rosa, CA 95401
707-544-4761
www.bmracing.com

Chevrolet Performance
www.chevroletperformance.com

Computer Automotive Tuning
   Systems, LLC
14327 Dogwood Ln.
Belle Haven, VA 23306
www.tunercat.com

Drew Technologies
3915 Research Park Dr., Suite A10
Ann Arbor, MI 48108
734-222-5228
www.drewtech.com

EFI Connection, LLC
6586 Station Rd.
Erie, PA 16510
814-566-0946
www.eficonnection.com

EFILive Limited
New Zealand
+64 (9) 534 1188
www.efilive.com

HP Tuners, LLC
725 Hastings Ln.
Buffalo Grove, IL 60089
www.hptuners.com

Innovate Motorsports
15312 Connector Ln.
Huntington Beach, CA 92649
714-372-5910
www.innovatemotorsports.com

Moates.net
225-341-3547
www.moates.net

Rostra Precision Controls, Inc.
2519 Dana Dr.
Laurinburg, NC 28352
800-782-3379
www.rostra.com

Smokey's Dyno & Performance
3435 Fortuna Dr., Suite A
Akron, Ohio 44312
330-644-0021
www.smokeysdyno.com

Tuned Port Induction Specialties
4255 Creek Rd.
Chaska, MN 55318
952-448-6021
www.tpis.com

www.ingramcontent.com/pod-product-compliance
Lightning Source LLC
Chambersburg PA
CBHW081451070526
44586CB00019B/2309